D0496067

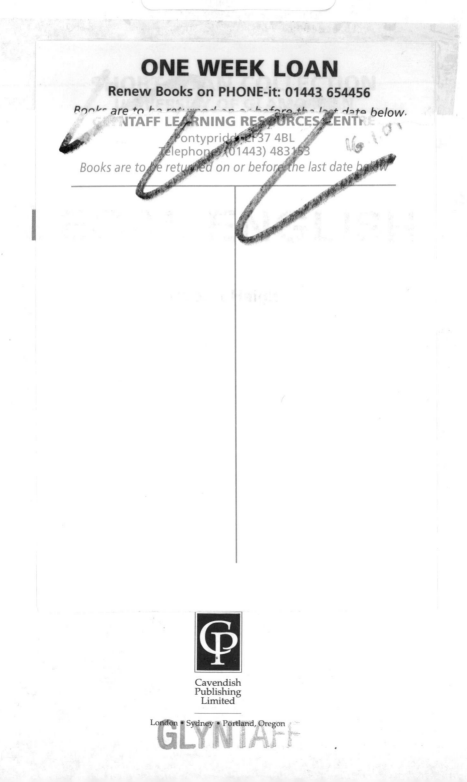

Cavendish
Publishing
Limited

London • Sydney • Portland, Oregon

GLYNTAFF

First published in Great Britain 2004 by
Cavendish Publishing Limited, The Glass House,
Wharton Street, London WC1X 9PX, United Kingdom
Telephone: + 44 (0)20 7278 8000   Facsimile: + 44 (0)20 7278 8080
Email: info@cavendishpublishing.com
Website: www.cavendishpublishing.com

Published in the United States by Cavendish Publishing
c/o International Specialized Book Services,
5824 NE Hassalo Street, Portland,
Oregon 97213-3644, USA

Published in Australia by Cavendish Publishing (Australia) Pty Ltd
45 Beach Street, Coogee, NSW 2034, Australia
Telephone: + 61 (2)9664 0909   Facsimile: + 61 (2)9664 5420
Email: info@cavendishpublishing.com.au
Website: www.cavendishpublishing.com.au

British Library Cataloguing in Publication Data
Haigh, Rupert
Legal English
1 Law – Terminology   2 Law – Language
3 English language – Usage   4 English language – Business English
I Title
340.1'4

Library of Congress Cataloguing in Publication Data
Data available

ISBN 1-85941-950-X
ISBN 978-185941-950-2

1 3 5 7 9 10 8 6 4 2

Printed and bound in Great Britain

CONTENTS

CONTRACTUAL LEGAL ENGLISH

GLOSSARIES

PREFACE

This book is intended for legal and business professionals whose first language is not English but who sometimes have to communicate in English and read legal documents written in English in the course of their work. It aims to be a practical reference resource which will help you both understand English legal language and to use clear, accurate English in everyday legal and business contexts.

The book commences with an introduction to the English language which provides insights into the development of legal English, the difficulties of the language and the key differences between British and American usage. It is then split into three substantive sections: *Writing Legal English, Speaking Legal English,* and *Contractual Legal English*. The first section, *Writing Legal English,* is designed to help you maximise the effectiveness of your English and write clear and accurate letters and legal documents in English. These aspects are covered:

Grammar & punctuation

Style

Creating legal documents

Writing legal letters, emails and internal communications

Applying for legal jobs

The second section, *Speaking Legal English,* is designed to help you communicate effectively in English in work situations. The section begins with an analysis of the features of spoken English as compared to written English. The roles played by body language, tone of voice and emphasis are discussed. The chapters that follow focus on the key situations in which legal and business professionals need to use the spoken word. These are:

Interviewing and advising

Negotiation

Chairing a meeting

Making a presentation

Telephoning

Concise notes are given on each of these situations. These notes are designed to maximise your effectiveness in preparing for and conducting the proceedings. Extensive language suggestions are given as to the actual words you should use in particular situations. Where appropriate, checklists are provided. These can be used to structure your approach to a negotiation, interview or presentation, as the case may be.

The third section, *Contractual Legal English*, aims to help you understand how business contracts are put together and seeks to demystify the language they contain. It focuses on the difficult words and phrases used in contracts and clearly explains what they mean, what they are designed to achieve, and analyses the contexts in which they are used. This section contains chapters which deal with the following:

The basic concepts of Anglo-American contract law

Contractual language

Structure of a contract

Content of a contract

An analysis of the language used in 30 common contract clauses

A specimen contract

The book concludes with a series of helpful glossaries which explain the meaning of different kinds of words and phrases often found in legal and business English.

Comments and questions about this book are most welcome, and these may be emailed to rupert.haigh@forum-legal.com.

INTRODUCTION

1   The development of modern English

The English language contains elements from many different European languages and has also borrowed words from a wide variety of other languages. It is impossible to grasp how these influences affect the language without understanding a little about the history of the British Isles.

Prior to the Roman invasion in 55 BC, the inhabitants of Britain spoke a Celtic dialect. Latin made little impression until St Augustine arrived in 597 AD to spread Christianity. Latin words are regularly used in English, particularly in professional language. In the legal profession, Latin phrases like *inter alia* (amongst others) and *per se* (in itself) remain in current use.

Subsequently, the Angles, Saxons and Jutes invaded the British Isles from mainland northern Europe. The language they brought with them forms the basis of what is known as Old English. This gives us the 100 most commonly used words in the English language (words like *God, man, woman, child, love, live, go, at, to*).

The Vikings began to raid the north east of England from Scandinavia from the 8th century onwards. At a later date, a significant number of Vikings settled in this area, bringing with them their own linguistic contribution (which can be seen for example in the numerous place names in the north-east of England (and Scotland) ending in *-by* or *-thorpe, -wick, -ham* and in words such as *egg, husband, law, take, knife*).

In 1066 the Normans invaded from northern France and conquered England. Words such as *court, parliament, justice, sovereign* and *marriage* come from this period.

Later, the English helped themselves initially to further words from French, such as *chauffeur, bourgeois, elite*. As the British Empire expanded, further opportunities to borrow words arose – words such as *taboo* and *pukka* came into the English language from that period.

The result of this multiplicity of linguistic influences is a rich and diverse language with a complex grammar and many synonyms. For example, a coming together of two or more people could be a *meeting* or *gathering* (Old English), *assignation* or *encounter* (Old French), a *rendezvous, rally* or *reunion* (French), a *caucus* (Algonquin), *pow-wow* (Narragansett) or a *tryst* (Old French).

2   Sources of legal English

Legal English reflects the mixture of languages which has produced the English language generally. However, modern legal English owes a particular debt to French and Latin. Following the Norman invasion of England in 1066, French became the official language of England, although most ordinary people still spoke English. For a period of nearly 300 years, French was the language of legal proceedings, with the result that many words in current legal use have their roots in this period. These include *property, estate, chattel, lease, executor* and *tenant*.

During this period, Latin remained the language of formal records and statutes. However, since only the learned were fluent in Latin, it never became the language of legal pleading or debate.

Therefore, for several centuries following the Norman invasion, three languages were used in England. English remained the spoken language of the majority of the population, but almost all writing was done in French or Latin. English was not used in legal matters.

In 1356, the Statute of Pleading was enacted (in French). It stated that all legal proceedings should be in English, but recorded in Latin. Nonetheless, the use of French in legal pleadings continued into the 17th century in some areas of the law. In this later period, new branches of, in particular, commercial law began to develop entirely in English and remain relatively free of French-based terminology.

As the printed word became more commonplace, some writers made a deliberate effort to adopt words derived from Latin, with the aim of making their text appear more sophisticated. Some legal words taken from Latin in this way are *adjacent, frustrate, inferior, legal, quiet* and *subscribe*. Some writers also started to use a Latin word order. This led to an ornate style, deliberately used to impress rather than inform. Even today, Latin grammar is responsible for some of the ornateness and unusual word order of legal documents. It also lies behind the frequent use of *shall* constructions in legal documents.

English was adopted for different kinds of legal documents at different times. Wills began to be written in English in about 1400. Statutes were written in Latin until about 1300, in French until 1485, in English and French for a few years, and in English alone from 1489.

Different registers of English

Different registers of English (ie, whether the language used sounds down-to-earth or sophisticated) are primarily dictated by whether the words used are mostly Old English or Old Norse in origin, or whether they come from Latin or French. As noted above, Latin and French have particular relevance to legal and professional language, while Old English and Old Norse are more relevant to daily speech. To demonstrate the truth of this, look at the following sentences:

Example 1

> The merchandise contained in the consignment is of inferior quality to that anticipated by the purchaser.

The – Old English

Merchandise – from Old French

Contained – from Latin

In – from Latin

The – Old English

Consignment – from Latin

Is – Old English

Of – Old English

Inferior – from Latin

Quality – from Latin

To – Old English

That – Old English

Anticipated – from Latin

By – Old English

The – Old English

Purchaser – from Old French

16 words: 8 Old English, 6 from Latin, 2 from Old French

Now consider the same idea expressed in a different way:

> The standard of the goods contained in the delivery is worse than the buyer expected.

The – Old English

Standard – from Old French

Of – Old English

The – Old English

Goods – Old English

Contained – from Latin

In – from Latin

The – Old English

Delivery – from Old French

Is – Old English

Worse – Old English

Than – Old English

The – Old English

Buyer – Old English

Expected – from Latin

15 words: 10 Old English, 3 from Latin, 2 from Old French

We notice the following:

- The first sentence seems more sophisticated than the second, and more appropriate to legal English.
- The first sentence consists of 50% Latin or French-derived words, whereas in the second only 33% of the words are Latin or French-derived.
- In both cases, the basic words (eg, the prepositions and articles) mainly come from Old English, while the conceptual words mainly come from Latin or French.

Example 2

The difference is even more marked when we speak of everyday things:

I went to the nearest shop with the dog, and met my wife on the way.

I – Old English

Went – Old English

To – Old English

The – Old English

Nearest – Old Norse

Shop – Old French

With – Old English

The – Old English

Dog – Old English

And – Old English

Met – Old English

My – Old English

Wife – Old English

On – Old English

The – Old English

Way – Old English

16 words: 14 Old English, 1 Old Norse, 1 Old French

We could also express the same thing as follows:

I proceeded to the closest emporium accompanied by the dog and encountered my spouse along the route.

I – Old English

Proceeded – from Latin

To – Old English

The – Old English

Closest – from Old French

Emporium – from Greek

Accompanied – from Old French

By – Old English

The – Old English

Dog – Old English

And – Old English

Encountered – from Old French

My – Old English

Spouse – from Latin

Along – Old English

The – Old English

Route – from Old French

17 words: 10 Old English, 2 from Latin, 4 from Old French, 1 from Greek

We notice the following:

- The second sentence seems more sophisticated than the first, but it is unnecessarily sophisticated and formal for the ideas it describes. It runs the risk of sounding pretentious. The first sentence appears more straightforward.

- The first sentence is predominantly Old English. The second sentence is 41% Latin, Old French and Greek-derived. The apparent formality and sophistication of the sentence comes from the use of these alternative words.

Example 3

The sentence taken below follows the wording of a typical *force majeure* clause. Looking at the linguistic breakdown, we note clearly that the words which describe legal concepts (*party, liable, failure, delay, performance, obligations*) come from French or Latin, while the basic and concrete words mainly come from Old English.

> Neither party shall be liable to the other for failure to perform or delay in the performance of its obligations caused by any circumstances beyond its reasonable control.

Neither – Old English

Party – Old French

Shall – Old English

Be – Old English

Liable – probably from French

To – Old English

The – Old English

Other – Old English

For – Old English

Failure – Latin

To – Old English

Perform – Old French

Or – Old English

Delay – Old French

In – Old English

The – Old English

Performance – Old French

Of – Old English

Its – Old English

Obligations – Latin

Caused – Latin

By – Old English

Any – Old English

Circumstances – Latin

Beyond – Old English

Its – Old English

Reasonable – Old French

Control – Old French

28 words: 17 Old English, 7 Old French, 4 Latin

3 What makes English difficult?

It is said of chess that the game takes a day to learn, and a lifetime to master. In a similar vein, English is reputed to be an easy beginner's language in which it is nevertheless very hard to achieve native-level fluency. Why is this?

There are probably five main factors that make English difficult to master. These are as follows:

1 Lack of clear rules of grammar. We have seen how English is a product of various different linguistic traditions. One of the results of this is a comparative lack of consistent grammatical rules. Prepositions are a clear example of this.

2 Extensive vocabulary. There are many different ways of saying the same thing in English. This is again due to the fact that English draws upon different linguistic traditions. For example, if you wanted to say that something was legally permissible, you could use the Old Norse (Scandinavian)-derived word, *lawful*. Alternatively, you could use the Latin-derived word, *legitimate*. Or, if you wanted a more emotive word, you could use the Old English word, *right*. To take another example, when talking about employment, do you say *calling*, *career*, *profession*, *employment*, *job*, *work*, *occupation* or *vocation*?

3 The use of phrasal verbs in English (and legal English). For example, you *put down* a deposit, and you *enter into* a contract. These combinations must be learned individually because they involve using a verb with a preposition or adverb or both; and, as noted above, prepositions do not follow clear grammatical rules. Some of the phrasal verbs most commonly used in legal English are set out in a glossary at the back of this book.

4 The use in legal English of words which mean something different in ordinary English. For example, one hears of the *construction* of a contract, or about the parties seeking *relief*.

5 The use of idioms. Idioms are groups of words whose combined meaning is different from the meanings of the individual words. For example, the expression *over the moon* means 'happy'. Idioms are frequent in ordinary English – they are a distinctive element of the way native English speakers use the language. They are found less often in legal English, but exist in some legal jargon. For example, the expression *on all fours* is used to refer to the facts of a case which correspond exactly to the facts of a previous case.

4   What makes legal language difficult?

One of the main reasons why legal language is sometimes difficult to understand is that it is often very different from ordinary English. This comprises two issues:

1   The writing conventions are different: sentences often have apparently peculiar structures, punctuation is used insufficiently, foreign phrases are sometimes used instead of English phrases (eg, *inter alia* instead of *amongst others*), unusual pronouns are employed (*the same*, *the aforesaid*, etc) and unusual set phrases are to be found (*null and void*, *all and sundry*).

2   A large number of difficult words and phrases are used. These fall into four categories, brief details of which are given below.

Legal terms of art

Legal terms of art are technical words and phrases which have precise and fixed legal meanings and which cannot usually be replaced by other words. Some of these will be familiar to the layperson (eg, *patent*, *share*, *royalty*). Others are generally only known to lawyers (eg, *bailment*, *abatement*).

A number of frequently encountered terms of art are defined in the Glossary of Legal Terminology at the back of this book.

Legal jargon

Terms of art should be differentiated from legal jargon. Legal jargon comprises words used by lawyers which are difficult for non-lawyers to understand. Jargon words range from near-slang to almost technically precise words. Well-known examples of jargon include *boilerplate clause* and *corporate veil*.

Jargon includes a number of archaic words no longer used in ordinary English. These include *annul* (to declare that something, such as a contract or marriage, is no longer legally valid) and *bequest* (to hand down as an inheritance property other than land).

It also includes certain obscure words which have highly specialised meanings and are therefore not often encountered except in legal documents. Examples include *emoluments* (a person's earnings, including salaries, fees, wages, profits and benefits in kind) and *provenance* (the origin or early history of something).

Jargon words should be replaced by plain language equivalents wherever possible.

Legal meaning may differ from the general meaning

There is also a small group of words which have one meaning as a legal term of art and another meaning in ordinary English. One example is the word *distress*, which as a legal term of art refers to the seizure of goods as security for the performance of an obligation. In ordinary English it means anxiety, pain or exhaustion. Here are some further examples:

Consideration in legal English means an act, forbearance or promise by one party to a contract that constitutes the price for which the promise of the other party is bought. Consideration is essential to the validity of any contract other than one made by deed.

Consideration in ordinary English means: (1) careful thought, (2) a fact taken into account when making a decision, (3) thoughtfulness towards others.

Construction in legal English means interpretation. 'To construe' is the infinitive verb form of the term.

Construction in ordinary English means: (1) the action of constructing (eg, a building), (2) a building or other structure, (3) the industry of erecting buildings.

Redemption in legal English means the return or repossession of property offered as security on payment of a mortgage debt or charge.

Redemption in ordinary English usually means Christian salvation.

Tender in legal English means an offer to supply goods or services. Normally a tender must be accepted to create a contract.

Tender in ordinary English means: (1) gentle and kind, (2) (of food) easy to cut or chew, (3) (of a part of the body) painful to the touch, (4) young and vulnerable, (5) easily damaged.

Further examples may be found in the Glossary of Obscure Words Used in Business Contracts at the back of this book.

Words may be used in apparently peculiar contexts

A number of words and phrases which are used in ordinary English are also used in legal English but in unusual contexts. Examples include *furnish, prefer, hold*. For details of the meanings of these and other words and phrases, refer to the glossaries dealing with obscure words and phrases at the back of this book.

5   British and American English usage

It is often said, with humorous intent, that Britain and America are two countries divided by a common language. In fact, despite the different branches of English having developed separately on each side of the Atlantic (also known as 'the pond') for over 200 years, language differences remain comparatively minor. However, the underlying cultural differences between the British and the Americans, as well as between other English-speaking countries, are more significant.

This chapter deals solely with language usage differences. General cultural differences are dealt with in the *Speaking* section of the book.

British and American English can be differentiated in three ways:

1   Differences in language use conventions: meaning and spelling of words, grammar and punctuation differences.

2   Vocabulary: there are a number of important differences, particularly in business terminology.

3   Differences in the ways of using English dictated by the different cultural values of the two countries.

It is necessary to choose between British or American English and then apply the conventions of the version you choose consistently. If you muddle up British and American standards, it implies that you do not understand that they are different.

Differences in language use conventions

Here are some of the key differences in language use conventions:

1   Dates. In British English, the standard way of writing dates is to put the day of the month as a figure, then the month (either as a figure or spelled out) and then the year: for example, 19 September 1973 or 19/09/73. The standard way of writing dates in American English is to put the month first (either as a figure or spelled out), then the day of the month, then the year: for example, September 19th 1973 or 9/19/73. Commas are also frequently inserted after the day of the month in the USA: for example, September 19, 1973.

2   o and *ou*. In British English, the standard way of writing words which might include either the letter *o* or the letters *ou* is to use the *ou* form: for example, *colour, humour, honour, behaviour*. The standard way of writing such words in American English is to use only *o*: for example, *color, humor, honor, behavior*.

3   *Through*. In American English, the word *through* (or *thru*) can be used to mean *until*: for example, 'September 19th thru October 1st' would be in British English '19 September until 1 October'.

4   Hyphens. Hyphens are often used in British English to connect prefixes with the main word: for example, *pre-emption, pre-trial, co-operation*. They are less common in American English; for example, *preemption, pretrial, cooperation*.

5   z or s? In British English, *s* is generally used in such words as *recognise, authorise*. The letter *z* is used in American English in such words as *recognize* or *authorize*. However, it is not wrong to use *z* in such words when using British English as standard.

Note, however, that some words must always end in *-ise* whether you are using British or American English standards. These include:

advertise	advise
arise	comprise
compromise	demise
despise	devise
disguise	enfranchise

excise	exercise
franchise	improvise
incise	merchandise
premise	revise
supervise	surmise
surprise	televise

6   *l* or *ll*? In American English, a single *l* is used in such words as *traveled* or *counseled*. In British English, *ll* is used (eg, *travelled*, *counselled*).

Note, however, that in British English, some words which end in a double *ll* lose one *l* when a suffix is added: *skill* becomes *skilfully*, *will* becomes *wilfully*. In American English, the double *ll* is retained: *skill* becomes *skillfully*, *will* becomes *willfully*.

7   *-re* or *-er*? In American English, the *-er* ending is used in words like *theater*, *center*, *meter* and *fiber*. In British English, these words are spelt *theatre*, *centre*, *metre* and *fibre*.

8   *oe* and *ae*. Some scientific terms retain the use of the classical composite vowels *oe* and *ae* in British English. These include *diarrhoea*, *anaesthetic*, *gynaecology*, and *homoeopathy*. In American English, a single *e* replaces the composite vowel: *diarrhea*, *anesthetic*, *gynecology*, *homeopathy*.

9   *-e* or *-ue*? In British English, the final silent *-e* or *-ue* is retained in such words as *analogue*, *axe* and *catalogue*. In American English, it is omitted: *analog*, *ax* and *catalog*.

10 *-eable* or *-able*? The silent *e*, produced when forming some adjectives with a suffix is generally used in British English in such words as *likeable*, *unshakeable* and *ageing*. In American English, it is generally left out: *likable*, *unshakable* and *aging*. The e is however sometimes used in American English where it affects the sound of the preceding consonant: *traceable* or *manageable*.

11 *-ce* or *-se*? In British English, the verb that relates to a noun ending in *-ce* is sometimes given the ending *-se*. For example, *advice* (noun)/*advise* (verb), *device*/*devise*, *licence*/*license*, *practice*/*practise*. American English uses *-se* for both the noun and verb forms of these words. It also uses *-se* for other nouns which in British English are spelt *-ce*, including *defense*, *offense*, *pretense*.

12 Prepositions. In American English, it is acceptable to omit prepositions in certain situations. In British English, this habit is less common: for example, an American lawyer might find a certain clause in a contract to be 'likely enforceable'. A British colleague would be more likely to say that it was 'likely to be enforceable'. An American civil rights activist might 'protest discrimination', while his British colleagues would 'protest against discrimination'.

13 *Have* and *got*. In American English, it is quite acceptable to use the word *got* without *have* in sentences like 'I got two tickets for the show tonight'. In British English, it is more usual to say 'I've got two tickets for the show tonight'.

14 *Gotten*. *Gotten* is a proper word in American English, but is only used as an Americanism in British English, except in certain phrases such as 'ill-gotten gains'.

15 *While* or *whilst*? Both *while* and *whilst* are used in British English. In American English, *while* is the right word to use, and *whilst* is regarded as a pretentious affectation.

Vocabulary

Here are some key vocabulary differences.

Ordinary words and phrases

British	American
aerial (TV)	antenna
aluminium	aluminum
anti-clockwise	counterclockwise
at weekends	on weekends
aubergine	eggplant
autumn	fall
banknote	bill
bill (in a café or restaurant)	check
biscuit	cookie
braces	suspenders
building society	savings and loan association
calibre	caliber
camp bed	cot
car bonnet	hood
car park	parking lot
car windscreen	windshield
caravan	trailer
centre	center
cheque (bank)	check
chips	french fries (or, recently, 'freedom fries')
cinema	movie theatre
clerk (bank)	teller

clever	smart
cling film	plastic wrap
conscription (in the sense of compulsory military service)	draft
cooker	stove
co-operation	cooperation
cosy	cozy
courgette	zucchini
crisps	potato chips
crossroads/junction	intersection
curriculum vitae	resumé
dialled	dialed
dived	dove
draught	draft
dressing gown	bathrobe/housecoat/robe
dual carriageway	four-lane highway
endeavour	endeavor
estate agent	realtor/real estate agent
film	movie
flat	apartment
flyover	overpass
frying pan	skillet
fuelled	fueled
fulfil	fulfill
full stop (punctuation)	period
give way	yield
grey	gray
ground floor	first floor
haggle	dicker
high street	main street
holiday	vacation
humour	humor
increase (of money)	hike

in the event of/in the event that	in the event that
lent	loaned
lift	elevator
lorry	truck
maize/sweetcorn	corn
manoeuvre	maneuver
meet	meet with
metre	meter
motorway	highway/freeway/expressway/throughway
mum	mom
muslin	cheesecloth
nappy	diaper
oblige	obligate
ordinary	regular, normal
pack of cards	deck of cards
pants	underpants
pavement	sidewalk
petrol	gasoline/gas
plough	plow
post	mail
power point	electrical outlet
programme	program
property (land)	real estate
quarters (three-quarters)	fourths (three-fourths)
queue	line/line-up
railway	railroad
rationalisation (personnel)	downsizing
riding (horses)	horseback riding
ring road	beltway
rivalled	rivaled
rowing boat	rowboat
sceptical	skeptical

seven-thirty OR half-past seven OR half seven (of time)	seven-thirty
sizeable	sizable
skilful	skillfull
solicitor	attorney/lawyer
sombre	somber
stand (for election)	run
starter	appetizer
storey (of building)	story/floor
stupid	dumb
sweet shop	candy store
tap	faucet
tartan	plaid
terraced house	row house
till	checkout
to protest against discrimination	to protest discrimination
towards	toward
transport	transportation
trainers	sneakers
travelled	traveled
trousers	pants/slacks
tyre	tire
underground/tube train	subway
until/to (as in '4 January until/ to 6 January')	through/thru (as in 'January 4th through January 6th')
upmarket	upscale
vest	undershirt
waistcoat	vest
while or whilst	while
work out (problem)	figure out
Yours faithfully	Respectfully yours OR Yours truly
Yours sincerely	Sincerely yours
25/12/03 (for 25 December 2003)	12/25/03 (for December 25th, 2003)

Differences in legal and business terminology

British	American
action for misrepresentation	tort of negligent misrepresentation
articles of association	bylaws
balance sheet	statement of financial position
barrister	counselor
bills	notes
bonus or scrip issue	stock dividend or stock split
burgle	burglarize
called to the bar	admitted to the bar
company	corporation
company law	corporate law
competition law	antitrust law
conditions and warranties	warranties
creditors	payables
Dear Sirs	Dear Sir or Madam
debtors	receivables
defence	defense
depreciation	amortization
employment law	labor law
exceptional items	unusual items
flotation	Initial Public Offering (IPO)
indecent assault	sexual assault
indemnify	hold harmless and indemnify
land and buildings	real estate
maintenance	alimony
Mr (or Mrs) Justice Smith (or other depending on judge's rank)	Judge Smith
nominal value	par value
non-performance	nonperformance
offence	offense
ordinary shares	common stock
postal rule	mailbox rule

pre-emption	preemption
preference shares	preferred stock
pre-trial	pretrial
profit and loss	account income statement
provisions	allowances
receivership	Chapter 11 bankruptcy
solicitor	attorney
share premium	additional paid-in capital
shareholders' funds	stockholders' equity
stocks	inventories
theft	larceny
turnover	revenues
undistributable reserves	restricted surplus

Differences related to cultural values

British and American English have a number of differences which relate to the different cultural values of the two countries. For example, British English contains a number of frequently used metaphors relating to football ('scoring an own goal') and cricket ('a sticky wicket'), while American English uses metaphors relating to baseball ('in the ball park').

The two versions of the language also have certain tendencies which are worth bearing in mind. These are not absolute, since individual writers have their own styles which may incorporate aspects of both British and American tendencies. However, in general:

- British English tends to react more slowly to new words and phrases than American English. American English enthusiastically adopts new usages, some of which later pass into general use (eg, *corporate citizen*, *social performance*), and some die out after a short period in fashion (eg, *synergy*).

- British English has a slight tendency to vagueness and ponderous diction. American English (at its best) tends to be more direct and vivid.

- American English tends to be more slangy than British English.

- Both American and British English are keen on euphemisms. In British English, these are often used for humorous purposes (eg, 'to be economical with the truth') or to smooth over something unpleasant. In American English, they may be used for prudish reasons (thus *lavatory* or *WC* becomes *restroom* or *bathroom*), to make something mundane sound important (thus *ratcatcher* becomes *rodent operative*), or to cover up the truth of something unpleasant (thus *civilian deaths* in war become *collateral damage*).

- American English has a tendency to lengthen existing words unnecessarily in an effort to make them sound more important (thus *transport* becomes *transportation*).

WRITING LEGAL ENGLISH

1 GRAMMAR & PUNCTUATION FOR LEGAL WRITING

The aim of this chapter is not to cover all the aspects of English grammar, but to deal with those areas which cause the most problems in legal writing.

1.1 Parts of speech

Articles

Articles in English include *the*, *a* and *an*.

A few simple rules clarify the way in which these articles should be used.

A is used when mentioning something for the first time ('a client walked into the office'). *An* is used in the same circumstances but only where the following word begins with a vowel ('an attorney walked into the office').

The is used when referring to something already mentioned before ('the client then sat down'), or when referring to something that is the only one of its kind ('the sun') or when referring to something in a general rather than specific way ('the internet has changed our way of life').

In some circumstances, articles should be omitted. For example, when a sentence links two parallel adjectival phrases, the article should be omitted from the second phrase. Here is an example:

> The judge ruled that Cloakus Ltd was a validly registered and ~~an~~ existing company.

In addition, when using certain abstract nouns in a general, conceptual sense, it is not necessary to use an article to precede the noun. For example:

> In the event of conflict between the definitions given in appendix I and the definitions given in the contract, the contract shall prevail.

There is no need here to precede *conflict* with *a*, since *conflict* is used in a general conceptual sense. However, when referring to a specific conflict, articles should be used, as in *the opposing factions took part in the conflict*.

Prepositions

Prepositions are words used with a noun or pronoun which show place, position, time or method.

Prepositions such as *to, in, from, between, after, before*, etc, normally come before a noun or pronoun and give information about how, when or where something has happened ('she arrived before lunch', 'I travelled to London').

The preposition *between* should be followed by an object pronoun like *me, him* or *us* instead of a subject pronoun such as *I, she* and *we*. It is therefore correct to say 'this matter is between you and me' and wrong to say 'this matter is between you and I'.

The main problem for the non-native speaker is remembering which preposition to use. There are no clear rules to follow in this respect, but some examples of common usages are set out below:

The parties **to** this agreement ...

The goods must be delivered **to** the purchaser.

The commencement/termination **of** this agreement ...

The price list set out **in** Schedule 1 ...

Royalties will be paid **in** accordance **with** this agreement **for** a period of five years.

The goods must be delivered **within** 14 days.

The Company agrees **to** provide training **for** service personnel.

The agreement may be terminated **by** notice.

An arrangement **between** the Seller and the Buyer ...

It is agreed that the goods will be collected **from** the Seller's warehouse **at** 21 Redwoods Road.

Interest will be charged **on** any unpaid instalments **after** the expiration of a period of 28 days **from** the date hereof.

He was charged **with** murder.

The property **at** 2 Parker Street is sold **with** vacant possession.

It is important to note that in certain circumstances it may be possible to use more than one preposition, and that there may be small but important differences in meaning between them. For example, the sentence:

The goods must be delivered within 7 days.

---

is subtly different from:

> The goods must be delivered in 7 days.

The use of the word *within* makes it clear that the goods may be delivered at any time up to the seventh day, while the word *in* might imply that the goods should only be delivered on the seventh day. This minor linguistic difference could be critically important in a contract for the sale of goods.

Pronouns

A pronoun is a word used instead of a noun to indicate someone or something already mentioned or known: for example, *I, you, this, that*.

Pronouns are used to avoid repeated use of a noun. They are usually used to refer back to the last used noun.

Legal drafters have traditionally avoided using personal pronouns such as *he, she, we, they*, instead replacing them with formulations such as *the said, the aforesaid* or *the same*. The reason for this is a fear of ambiguity in cases where it is unclear to which noun the pronoun might refer if a number of parties are mentioned in the document. Here is an example of a sentence made ambiguous by unclear use of personal pronouns:

> He arrived with James and John. John then continued his journey by car. James stayed at the depot, and he followed John later.

The modern trend, however, is to use pronouns where possible, as their use makes documentation less formal and intimidating. For example, 'you must pay the sum of £100 per month to me' is easier for a layperson to understand than 'the Tenant must pay the sum of £100 per month to the Landlord'.

However, their use is inappropriate where the aim of the drafter is to impress the reader with the seriousness of the obligations being undertaken, as pronouns often lead to a chattier and lighter style than is found in traditional legal documentation.

One aspect of pronoun use which is now highly relevant lies in the desire to avoid sexist language in legal and business English. This subject is discussed further in Chapter 5.1. A list of common gender-neutral pronouns and adjectives which can be used to avoid using sexist language is set out below:

any

anybody

anyone

each

every

everybody

nobody

no one

some

somebody

someone

Adjectives

An adjective is a word used to describe a noun or make its meaning clearer (eg, *excellent*, as in 'an excellent horse'). Some words in the English language have the ability to change parts of speech. For example, the word *principal*, often used in legal English, can be used as an adjective ('the principal sum') or as a noun ('the principal instructs the agent').

Some adjectives are described as uncomparable adjectives, meaning that they describe something which can only be absolute. Such adjectives cannot be qualified by words like *most, more, less, very, quite* or *largely*. For example, if a provision in a contract is void, it cannot be 'largely void' or 'more void' – it is simply void.

A short list of uncomparable adjectives is set out below:

absolute

certain

complete

definite

devoid

entire

essential

false

final

first

impossible

inevitable

irrevocable

manifest

only

perfect

principal

stationary

true

uniform

unique

void

whole

Adverbs

An adverb is a word which modifies or qualifies a verb (eg, *walk slowly*), an adjective (eg, *really small*) or another adverb (eg, *very quietly*).

Most adverbs consist of an adjective + the ending *-ly*. There are a number of words which act both as adjectives and as adverbs, to which the suffix *-ly* cannot be added. These include:

alone

early

enough

far

fast

further

little

long

low

much

still

straight

Collective nouns

A collective noun is one that refers to a group of people or things (*jury, government*). Such nouns can be used with either a singular verb ('the jury was made up of people from many different backgrounds') or a plural verb ('the jury are all in the court now').

It should be remembered that if the verb is singular, any following pronouns (words such as *he, she* or *they*) must also be singular, eg, 'the firm is prepared to act, but not until it knows the outcome of the negotiations' (not '... until they know the outcome').

In general it is better to use the singular when referring to collective nouns. The exception to this is where the plural is used to indicate that one is referring not primarily to the group but to all the individual members of the group (eg, 'the staff were unhappy with the changes that had been proposed').

Here is a short list of collective nouns found in legal English:

board (eg, of directors)

the Cabinet

class

club

committee

company

government

group

jury

majority

nation

parliament

party (a body of persons)

the public

staff

team

union

Past tenses

One of the main difficulties experienced by non-native speakers in using tenses concerns which form of past tense to use in different situations. The subject is more complex than the guidance given below might indicate, but these notes cover the most common areas of difficulty.

Past-perfect or pluperfect tense: This tense refers to a past action which is completed before a more recent time in the past, and is formed using *had*. For example:

> In 1998 I lived in New York. In 1997 I had decided to move to the United States the following year.

Simple past: This tense refers to completed actions which occurred in the past, and is formed with the ending *-ed*. For example:

> I lived in New York.

Past continuous: This tense refers to an action which occurred in the past and is not described as having been completed. For example:

> In 1998 I was living in New York.

A common mistake made by non-native speakers is to use the past continuous when the simple past or past-perfect tense should be used. In legal contexts this can easily lead to ambiguity. For example, to say 'In 1998 I was working as a commercial lawyer' leaves it unclear as to whether you still work as a commercial lawyer.

Verb forms

The conditional form: This form is used to express a condition or, to put it another way, to express that something is dependent on something else. For example:

> I would go if I felt better (I would in fact go if I felt better).
>
> I could go if I felt better (I would be able to go if I felt better).
>
> I should go if I felt better (I would in fact go if I felt better).
>
> I should go if I feel better (I ought to go if I feel better in the future).

When used for the conditional, *should* goes with *I* and *we*, and *would* goes with *you, he, she, it* and *they*. However, this rule is often disregarded even by well-educated English native speakers. Consequently, using the wrong word is not a very serious error.

A mistake often made by non-native speakers is to use the conditional instead of the subjunctive in a sentence in which both forms should be used. Consequently, the sentence, 'I wouldn't try it if I were you' is often wrongly expressed as 'I wouldn't try it if I would be you'.

The subjunctive form: This form of a verb is in the following circumstances:

- to express what is imagined ('Let's imagine that he were here today');
- to express what is wished ('I wish that he were here today');
- to express what is possible ('if only that were possible!').

It is usually the same as the ordinary form of the verb except in the third person singular (*he, she, it*), where the normal -*s* ending is omitted: for example, you should say *face* rather than *faces* in the sentence 'the report recommends that he face the tribunal'.

The situation is slightly different when using the verb *to be*. The subjunctive for *to be* when using the present tense is *be*, whereas the ordinary present tense is *am, are* or *is*. For example, 'the report recommends that he be dismissed'.

When using the past subjunctive form of *to be*, you should use *were* instead of *was*. For example, 'I wouldn't try it if I were you'.

Phrasal verbs

Phrasal verbs are phrases which consist of a verb used together with an adverb (eg, *break down*) or a preposition (eg, *call for*) or both (eg, *put up with*). They are often found in legal English: for example, *account for, enter into, serve upon, put down*.

Phrasal verbs can cause particular problems for non-native speakers of English where the verbs used have ordinary meanings when used without an adverb or preposition, but form an idiom when used with an adverb or preposition. In such cases the literal meaning of the words differs from the real meaning. For example, the phrasal verb *to brush up on* means to practise or study something in order to get back the skill or knowledge you had in the past but have not used for some time: for example, 'I must brush up on my French before visiting Paris'.

Here are the main adverbs and prepositions which may be used with a verb to form a phrasal verb:

aback	ahead
about	ahead of
above	along
across	among
after	apart
against	around
as	off
aside	on
at	onto
away	out
back	out of

before	over
behind	past
between	round
by	through
down	to
for	together
forth	towards
forward	under
from	up
in	upon
into	with
of	without

See also the Glossary of Phrasal Verbs Used in Legal English at the back of this book.

Negatives

Negatives are formed in English by using prefixes. The most common of these are *un-, in-, il-, im-, ir-, non-* and *anti-*.

Here are some common negative forms often used in legal English:

unlawful

unfamiliar

impractical

illegal

unfair

invalid

independence

injustice

impartiality

inequitable

unwritten

impracticable

unconstitutional

illicit

The prefix *dis-* is often used in a slightly different way to the prefixes listed above. It is not usually a direct negation but generally indicates dissent: for example, 'we disagree'.

Note also that there are some words in English which look like negatives but are in fact synonyms. For example, *flammable* and *inflammable* both mean easily set on fire.

1.2   Punctuating legal writing

Punctuation

One of the most unusual aspects of old-fashioned contract drafting was the belief among lawyers and judges that punctuation was unimportant. The prevailing view in common law jurisdictions was that the meaning of legal documents should be ascertained from the words of the document and their context rather than from punctuation. Accordingly, old-fashioned legal drafting tends to involve little or no punctuation. This makes it extremely hard to read and potentially highly ambiguous. For example, consider these unpunctuated sentences:

This man said the judge is a fool.

Woman without her man would be a savage.

Now consider the same sentences with punctuation:

This man, said the judge, is a fool.

Woman – without her, man would be a savage.

Fortunately, modern legal drafters have begun to use punctuation in the same way that ordinary writers use punctuation – to give guidance about meaning. A list of all the most important punctuation marks follows.

Full stops/periods (.)

Full stop is the British English term for this punctuation mark, and *period* is the American English term for it. Full stops should be used in the following situations:

- At the end of all sentences which are not questions or exclamations. The next word should normally begin with a capital letter.
- After abbreviations. For example, 'Sun. 10 June'.
- When a sentence ends with a quotation which itself ends with a full stop, question mark or exclamation mark, no further full stop is required. However,

if the quotation is short, and the sentence introducing it is more important, the full stop is put outside the quotation marks. For example:

> On the door were written the words 'no entry'.

- A sequence of three full stops indicates an omission from the text. A fourth full stop should be added if this comes at the end of a sentence. For example: 'this handbook … is exceptionally useful …. I refer to it every day.'

Commas (,)

Commas are used to show a short pause within a sentence. They should be used with care as a misplaced comma can alter the intended meaning of the sentence. For example:

> James hit Ian and Edward, then ran away.
>
> James hit Ian, and Edward then ran away.

At the same time, commas should be used where necessary to clarify meaning. Simply omitting the commas often leads to ambiguity or an unintended meaning. For example:

> This lawyer, said the judge, is a fool.
>
> This lawyer said the judge is a fool.

The principal circumstances in which commas should be used are as follows:

- To separate items in a list of more than two items. For example, 'cars, trucks, vans, and tractors'. In this sentence, it may be crucial to put the comma after *vans* to ensure that it is clear that *tractors* does not form part of the same category of items.
- To separate co-ordinated main clauses. For example, 'cars should park here, and trucks should continue straight on'.
- To mark the beginning and end of a sub-clause in a sentence. For example, 'James, who is a corporate lawyer, led the seminar'.
- After certain kinds of introductory clause. For example, 'Having finished my work, I left the office'.
- To separate a phrase or sub-clause from the main clause in order to avoid misunderstanding. For example, 'I did not go to work yesterday, because I was unwell'.

- Following words which introduce direct speech. For example, 'He said, "my lawyer is a genius!"'.
- Between adjectives which each qualify a noun in the same way. For example, 'a small, dark room'. However, where the adjectives qualify the noun in different ways, or when one adjective qualifies another, no comma is used. For example, 'a distinguished international lawyer' or 'a shiny blue suit'.

The importance of using commas correctly cannot be overstated. In one Australian case, the court had to look at a worker's insurance policy which described the employer's business as 'Fuel Carrying and Repairing'. The question the court had to decide was whether the policy covered an employee who was injured when driving the employer's vehicle carrying bricks. The court interpreted the policy as if it read either 'Fuel, Carrying, and Repairing' or 'Fuel Carrying, and Repairing'. Litigation could have been avoided if a comma had been inserted in the first place.[1]

Commas are softer in effect than full stops and semicolons, and are therefore unsuitable for long lists. They should not be used simply as an alternative to using short sentences or if there is any risk of ambiguity.

Colons (:)

The colon is usually used to point to information which follows it. It may also be used to link two clauses. Here are some examples of usage:

- To precede a list (eg, 'The following items are included:').
- To introduce a step from an introduction to a main theme or from a general statement to a particular situation (eg, 'The remedy is simple: introduce new rules.').
- To show cause and effect (eg, 'An energetic new director has been appointed: this accounts for the rise in share prices.').
- To precede an explanation (eg, 'The argument used by the defence was as follows:').

Colons should not be followed by a dash (–). The dash serves no useful purpose in this context.

Semicolons (;)

The semicolon is used to separate parts of a sentence when a more distinct break is needed than can be provided by a comma but the parts of the sentence are too closely connected for separate sentences to be used. For example, 'To err is human; to forgive, divine'.

In legal writing, semicolons are used to punctuate the end of any sub-clause or paragraph which forms part of a longer sentence. However, if the sub-clause or paragraph constitutes the last part of the sentence, a full stop may be more appropriate.

---

1   *Manufacturers' Mutual Insurance Ltd v Withers* (1988) 5 ANZ 60–853.

Parentheses ( )

These are used to enclose words, phrases or whole sentences. If a whole sentence is in parentheses, the end punctuation stays inside it. For example:

> (Stanning plc is hereinafter referred to as 'the Company'.)

Where only the end part of the sentence is in parentheses, the end punctuation goes outside the parentheses. For example:

> Stanning plc (hereinafter referred to as 'the Company').

The main circumstances in which parentheses are used are as follows:

- To enclose remarks made by the writer of the text himself or herself. For example, 'Mr X (as I shall call him) then stood up to speak'.
- To enclose mention of an authority, definition, explanation, reference or translation.
- In the report of a speech, to enclose interruptions by the audience.
- To enclose reference letters or figures. For example, '(1)(a)'.

Avoid parentheses within parentheses – use commas or dashes instead. Dashes are a useful way of separating concepts within sentences.

Square brackets [ ]

These enclose comments, corrections, explanations or notes not in the original text but added at a later stage by new authors or editors.

Square brackets are used in legal writing to adjust the format of quoted material. For example, they may be used to indicate that a letter now in lowercase was in capitals in the original text ('The court ruled that "[e]xistence of the subject matter of the contract precluded a finding of *force majeure*".').

Dashes (– and —)

Dashes can be used in two circumstances. They can be used to enclose a subclause in a sentence. For example:

> Very few – in fact almost none – of the lawyers working in this city have additional expertise in accountancy.

This can be a handy way to clarify sentences which might otherwise be filled with confusing commas.

A long dash can also be used as a substitute for the word *to*. For example:

The proposed route is Helsinki—London—New York—Helsinki.

Hyphens (-)

Hyphens are used in two circumstances. They are used, particularly in British English, to join together two words in respect of which the first word is a prefix of the second: for example, *pre-trial*, *non-statutory*. These words are usually run together in American English: *pretrial*, *nonstatutory*.

Hyphens are also used to make phrasal adjectives, which are adjectives made up of more than one word: for example, *health-care provider* or *real-estate purchase*.

Apostrophes (')

The apostrophe is often used incorrectly both by native and by non-native English speakers. However, mistakes can be avoided by following a few simple rules.

There are two uses for the apostrophe. Firstly, it is used to show that a word has been shortened or that two words have been combined. For example:

I'll be there, so don't say that I won't.

This use of the apostrophe to shorten a word is not usually seen in legal writing as it is considered too informal for most situations.

Secondly, the apostrophe is used to show that something belongs to somebody or something else. For example:

The client's payment was late.

When more than one person or thing owns something, put the apostrophe after the *s*. For example:

The clients' payments were late.

You could put this another way by saying 'the payments of the clients were late'. However, this looks very clumsy and laborious by the standards of modern English.

Take care when using *its*. It only takes an apostrophe when it is short for *it is* or *it has*. For example:

> It's a straightforward case.

When using *its* in a possessive sense, the apostrophe should be omitted. For example:

> This agreement has its advantages.

Quotation marks (' ' & " ")

In British English, single quotation marks (") should be used for a first quotation. For example:

> He wrote, 'that is the most important question'.

Double quotation marks should be used for any quotation within a quotation. For example:

> He wrote, 'she said "that is the most important question"'.

Single quotation marks should be used again for any quotation inside a quotation inside a quotation. For example:

> He wrote, 'she said "that is the most important question he asked during his 'manor house' speech"'.

The closing quotation mark should come before all punctuation marks unless these form part of the quotation itself. For example:

> Did the judge really say, 'that lawyer is a fool'?

but:

> The judge asked: 'is that lawyer a fool?'

Question marks (?)

The circumstances in which question marks are used are as follows:

- To follow every question which requires a direct answer. For example, 'what does that mean?'. However, note that a question mark is not required after indirect questions. For example, 'he asked me what that meant'.

- A question mark may also be placed before a word or phrase the accuracy of which is doubted. For example, 'Joe (?) Zanuderghosh'.

Exclamation mark (!)

The exclamation mark is used after an exclamatory word, phrase or sentence. It usually forms the concluding full stop but need not do so. It may also be used within square brackets after quoted text to indicate the writer's feelings of, for example, amusement, surprise or disagreement. For example, 'The court then heard the defendant mutter, "this judge is a fool"[!]'.

Capital letters

Capital letters should only be used in the following situations:

- At the beginning of a sentence (eg, 'Thank you for your letter.').
- When writing proper names (eg, London, George W Bush).
- When writing names which derive from proper names (eg, Christianity, Marxism).
- For certain abbreviations (eg, USA, NATO, WTO).
- For a defined term in a legal document where the definition uses a capital letter (eg, 'Roggins plc, hereinafter referred to as "the Company"').

In lower case sub-headings, use a capital letter only at the beginning of the first word (and for defined terms).

When inserting information in tables or lists, only use a capital letter if a separate sentence is being started (lists often occur within a sentence, in which case the only capital should be at the start of the sentence).

When writing headings or titles, capitalise the first letter of every important word (eg, nouns, pronouns, verbs, adjectives and adverbs). Capitalise the first letter of the first and last word in the heading. Put articles, prepositions and conjunctions (*and, or*) in lower case.

1.3   So-called rules

There are a number of conventions of written English which are sometimes regarded as rules of grammar. Many of these so-called rules owe their existence to long use rather than to any particular merit. Applying such rules in all circumstances often leads (1) to clumsy phrasing, or (2) to introducing a shade of meaning into the phrase that the writer may not have intended.

The point to remember about so-called rules is that one should be prepared to break any of them rather than write clumsily.

Ending sentences with prepositions

The old rule that one should not end a sentence with a preposition derives from Latin grammar. As discussed in section 2 in the Introduction, lawyers were for a long period of time greatly attached to Latin forms as a result of Latin being used as the language of record in the early years of the history of English law.

In fact, sentences very frequently end with prepositions in ordinary English due to the role played by idiomatic phrasal verbs – such as *put up with* – in the language. Winston Churchill wittily drew attention to this point by describing the rule about ending sentences with prepositions as 'the type of arrant pedantry up with which I shall not put'.

As Churchill's comment graphically illustrates, the problem with adhering strictly to this rule is that it can lead to very clumsy and artificial-sounding sentences. This often involves using stilted constructions such as *of which*, *on which* and *for which*. For example, a sentence like 'the document of which I spoke' is technically correct but would be more naturally expressed as 'the document I spoke about'.

Splitting infinitives

A split infinitive occurs when the basic verb form (eg, 'to write', 'to go', 'to run') is divided by the insertion of another word between the parts of the verb. The most famous example of this is the phrase from Star Trek, *to boldly go*. This phrase should correctly have been 'to go boldly' or 'boldly to go' depending on whether one wished to emphasise going or boldness as the most important aspect of the phrase. However, the phrase 'to boldly go' emphasises boldness and going equally and therefore captures a shade of meaning which the correct alternatives do not. Therefore, the splitting of the infinitive was justifiable.

The main circumstance in which splitting an infinitive should be avoided is when the split is so wide that the sentence starts to become unclear. For example, 'the main aim of this project is to more effectively, quickly and cheaply transact business' would be better rewritten 'the main aim of this project is to transact business more effectively, quickly and cheaply'.

Beginning sentences with 'and', 'but' or 'because'

Generations of English teachers have taught their pupils that it is incorrect to begin sentences with *and*, *but* or *because*. There is, however, no grammatical or stylistic reason why sentences should not commence with these words.

The only possible reason for avoiding the use of because is to avoid fragmented sentences; for example: 'Then we went home. Because we were tired.' These sentences should be joined together to read: 'Then we went home because we were tired.'

Writing one-sentence paragraphs

One-sentence paragraphs should be used sparingly but can be very useful in the following situations:

- When you wish to emphasise a particular point.
- When you wish to indicate an important transition point from one stage of your argument to the next.
- When you wish to break up the text to make it easier for the reader to understand.

Using the personal pronouns 'I', 'me' and 'you'

The question of whether or not to use personal pronouns is linked to the question of whether to use the active or passive voice (see 'Active and passive voice' in Chapter 4). Although there are situations in which personal pronouns should be avoided in order to preserve a formal tone, in most cases using personal pronouns ensures that your writing retains a connection with the reader.

1.4 Problem words

Certain words cause problems, either because they have a number of meanings or because it is unclear to writers when one word should be used instead of another. The notes set out below cover some of the worst offenders.

Only

Only, when used as an adverb, has four meanings:

1 It can be used to mean 'nothing or no one else but' ('only qualified lawyers are able to draft these documents').

2 It can also be used to mean 'with the negative result that' ('he turned, only to find his path was blocked').

3 A further meaning is 'no longer ago than' ('it was only on Thursday that the document arrived').

4 Lastly, it can mean 'not until' ('we can finalise the contract only when the document arrives').

The positioning of this word in a sentence is of critical importance. The meaning of the whole sentence can change profoundly according to where it is placed. Generally, it should go immediately in front of the word or phrase which it is qualifying: for example, 'the only cows are seen on the northern plain' has a different meaning to 'the cows are only seen on the northern plain' which in turn has a different meaning to 'the cows are seen on only the northern plain'.

Who or whom?

The correct use of *who* and *whom* is a matter which many non-native and native speakers of English alike have difficulty with. The distinction between them is that *who* acts as the subject of a verb, while *whom* acts as the object of a verb or preposition. This distinction is not particularly important in informal speech but should be observed in legal writing.

For example, *whom* should be used in the sentence, 'I advised Peter, John and Mary, all of whom are contemplating claims against RemCo Ltd'.

Who should be used in the sentence, 'I saw Peter, who is contemplating a claim against RemCo Ltd'.

When *who* is used, it should directly follow the name it refers to. If it does not, the meaning of the sentence may become unclear. For example, 'I saw Peter, who was one of my clients, and James' instead of 'I saw Peter and James, who was one of my clients'.

Which or that?

Which or *that* can frequently be used interchangeably. However, there are two rules to bear in mind:

1   When introducing clauses that define or identify something, it is acceptable to use *that* or *which*. For example, 'a book which deals with current issues in international trade law' or 'a book that deals with current issues in international trade law'.

2   Use *which*, but never *that*, to introduce a clause giving additional information about something. For example, 'the book, which costs £30, has sold over five thousand copies' and not 'the book, that costs £30, has sold over five thousand copies'.

Who, whom, which or that?

Who or *whom* should not be used when referring to things which are not human. *Which* or *that* should be used instead. For example, 'the company which sold the shares' is correct. 'The company that sold the shares' is also correct. 'The company who sold the shares' is incorrect.

That should be used when referring to things that are not human, and may be used when referring to a person. However, it is usually thought *that* is more impersonal than *who/whom* when used in this way. As a result it is better to say 'the client who I saw yesterday' than 'the client that I saw yesterday'.

Fewer or less?

Fewer should be used with plural nouns, as in 'eat fewer cakes' or 'there are fewer people here today'.

Less should be used with nouns referring to things that cannot be counted, as in 'there is less blossom on this tree'. It is wrong to use less with a plural noun ('less people', 'less cakes').

Can or may?

Can is mainly used to mean 'to be able to', as in the sentence 'Can he move?', which means, is he physically able to move?

May is used when asking to be allowed to do something as in 'May we leave now?', as *can* is thought to be less correct or less polite in such cases.

Imply or infer?

Do not confuse the words *imply* and *infer*. They can describe the same situation, but from different points of view.

If a speaker or writer *implies* something, as in 'he implied that the manager was a fool', it means that the person is suggesting something though not saying it directly.

If you *infer* something from what has been said, as in 'we inferred from his words that the manager is a fool', this means that you come to the conclusion that this is what they really mean.

Non- or un-?

The prefixes *non-* and *un-* both mean 'not', but they tend to be used in slightly different ways. *Non-* is more neutral in meaning, while *un-* often suggests a particular bias or standpoint. For example, *unnatural* means that something is not natural in a bad way, whereas *non-natural* simply means 'not natural'.

If or whether?

Although *if* can mean 'whether', it is better to use the word *whether* rather than if in writing ('I'll see whether he left an address' rather than 'I'll see if he left an address').

Specially or especially?

Although *especially* and *specially* can both mean 'particularly', they are not exactly the same. *Especially* also means 'in particular, chiefly', as in 'he distrusted them all, especially Karen', while *specially* also means 'for a special purpose' as in 'the machine was specially built for this job'.

Save

Save usually means to rescue from harm or danger. However, it can also be used to mean 'except'. It is frequently used in this sense in legal documents. For example:

No warranties are given save as to those set out in Schedule 3.

Grow

Grow is very often used incorrectly. Growing is an organic process that happens by itself. It is not something that can be forced to happen. Therefore, it is acceptable to write, 'last year our profits grew 20%'. However, it is wrong to write, 'we are keen to grow the company next year'. Use *expand* instead.

Client or customer?

Generally speaking, businesses that provide professional services (eg, lawyers, accountants) have clients, while businesses that sell products (eg, retailers) have customers.

2 LEGAL WRITING STYLE

Style is a matter of personal preference or company policy. The only unbreakable rules of style in legal documents and letters are that your writing should be as easy to understand as possible and that it should avoid offensive terms.

However, all legal writing should aim at achieving three goals – clarity, consistency and effectiveness. The notes set out below show how these goals can be achieved in practice.

2.1 Clarity

When we speak of good style, what do we mean? Primarily we mean clarity. Writing of all kinds should be as easy to understand as possible. Clarity of writing is achieved by various means:

- Clear thinking. Clarity of writing usually follows clarity of thought.
- Saying what you want to say as simply as possible.
- Saying it in such a way that the people you are writing for will understand it – consider the needs of the reader.
- Keep it short.

The next question is, how do we achieve this in practice?

Sentences

Keep sentences as short as possible. This does not necessarily mean that all sentences should be short (which might create a displeasing staccato effect) but that all unnecessary words should be removed.

Try to have only one main idea per sentence. Where you want to add more than one piece of additional information about a subject introduced in a sentence, consider starting a new sentence. Always start with the most important piece of information, then deal with lesser matters. For example, the sentence:

> The company, the headquarters of which are in Oxford, specialises in pharmaceutical products and made a record profit last year.

would be better split up as follows:

> The company specialises in pharmaceutical products. Its headquarters are in Oxford, and it made a record profit last year.

If you can cut words out without affecting the meaning of the sentence, do it. It will make your writing much more vigorous. In particular, pay attention to phrases which introduce new pieces of information or argument. These can often be reduced to single words. Here are some examples:

Commonly used phrase	Single word equivalent
be a significant factor in	affect, influence
be inclined to the view that	think (that)
by dint of	because
give rise to	cause
have a detrimental effect upon	harm
have a tendency to	tend
have an effect upon	affect
have the effect of	(in most contexts) cause
having regard to	concerning
impact upon	affect
in spite of the fact that	despite, although
in the interests of (eg, saving time)	to (eg, save time)
in view of	because
it is arguable that	perhaps
make contact with	contact
meet with	meet
notwithstanding the fact that	despite, although
the fact that	delete phrase – replacement word usually unnecessary
with regard to the question of	concerning, regarding

Paragraphs

Paragraphs should not be defined by length. They are best treated as a unit of thought. In other words, each paragraph should deal with a single thought or topic. Change paragraphs when shifting to a new thought or topic.

Paragraphs should start with the main idea, and then deal with subordinate matters. The writing should move logically from one idea to the next. It should not dance about randomly between different ideas.

One-sentence paragraphs should not be used too often, but can be useful in certain circumstances.

Pay attention to the way the paragraphs look on the page. Text evenly divided into manageably sized paragraphs, with occasional shorter ones, looks inviting to the reader. Huge, unbroken sections of text are very off-putting to the reader and should be avoided. So too should untidy sequences of very short paragraphs.

Negatives and positives

Avoid negative structures where possible. There is a tendency in much business and legal writing to try to soften the impact of what is being said by using *not un-* (or not *im-*, *il-*, *in-*, etc) formations such as:

- not unreasonable
- not impossible
- not unjustifiable
- not unthinkable
- not negligible

Such structures make what you are saying less clear and definite. They also represent an improper use of English. No one would use the *not un-* construction when writing about concrete things, as this sentence demonstrates:

> A not unblack dog was chasing a not unsmall rabbit across a not ungreen field.[2]

Precision

Use precise language and terminology. This means two things: choosing your words carefully and avoiding ambiguity. See 'What to avoid in legal writing' in Chapter 5 for notes on avoiding ambiguity.

Differentiate between legal jargon and terms of art (see Introduction, section 4). A *boilerplate clause* can be replaced by other words; *patent*, *waiver* and *rescission* cannot.

Use the words that convey your meaning, and nothing more. Never use words simply because they look impressive and you want to try them out, or because you like the sound of them. There is a tendency in legal writing to use unnecessary obscure words rather than their ordinary equivalents, perhaps out of a feeling that the obscure words are somehow more impressive. Here are some examples:

---

2   This example was used by George Orwell in his essay, 'Politics and the English Language'.

Obscure word	Ordinary equivalent
annex	attach
append	attach
cease	stop
conceal	hide
demise	death
desist	stop, leave off
detain	hold, delay
determine	end OR decide (according to context)
donate	give
effectuate	carry out
employ (when not used in connection with labour relations)	use
endeavour	try
evince	show
expedite	hasten
expend	spend
expiration, expiry	end
extend	give
forthwith	immediately, soon
inaugurate	begin
indicate	state, show, say
initiate	begin
institute	begin
necessitate	require
occasion (as verb)	cause
peruse	read
possess	have
present (as verb)	give
prior	earlier
proceed	go (ahead)
retain	keep
suborn	bribe (eg, a juror or witness)
terminate	end
utilise	use

Vigour

As a general rule, the fewer the words you can use to convey your meaning, the more vigorous your writing will be. Every time you write something, look back at it and think how many words you can cut out. Then do it. You will be surprised at what a difference it makes to the vigour and clarity of your writing.

Certain other issues are relevant when trying to write vigorously. Here are some of them:

(1) Use active verbs where possible

Use active verbs rather than nominalisations where possible (see 'What to avoid in legal writing', Chapter 5). Nominalisations should usually be avoided because they make writing longer and less dynamic. For example:

> We are in agreement that our firm will give consideration to the documents.

This sentence would be better expressed as follows:

> We agree that our firm will consider the documents.

However, there are certain occasions in legal writing when we need to use nominalisations. For example, lawyers don't agree to arbitrate but to go to arbitration: arbitration is a defined legal process and should be referred to in its nominalised form.

(2) Use short words where possible

Never use a long word where a short one can be used. For example, avoid words like *notwithstanding* where simple words like *despite*, *still* or *even if* can be used instead.

Never use a phrase where you can use one short word. There is a creeping tendency to include unnecessary phrases like with *regard to*, *with respect to*, *in reference to* and so on (see above).

However, this rule is modified by the need to use (1) terms of art, and (2) defined terms properly – and a number of them are long.

(3) Use ordinary English words where possible

Do not use a foreign phrase or jargon if you can think of an ordinary English word which means the same thing. For example, do not write *modus operandi* when you can write *method*, nor *soi-disant* when you can write *so-called*. In legal English, this is more difficult to achieve in practice than it is in ordinary English, because much of the terminology used (*inter alia, ab initio, force majeure, mutatis mutandis*) comes from French and Latin. These often act as shorthand for a longer English phrase. For example, *inter alia* comes out in English as 'including but not limited to'. Your choice of vocabulary – between English or French and Latin – will be influenced by who you are writing for.

Clarity summary

These considerations will help you to focus your mind on writing well:

- When starting to write a letter or document, ask yourself three questions:

  (1) What am I trying to say?

  (2) What words will express it?

  (3) Could I make it shorter?

- Keep sentences as short as possible. If you can cut words out without affecting the meaning of the sentence, do it. For example, do not write 'in spite of the fact that ...'. Write 'although' instead.

- Try to have only one main idea per sentence.

- Paragraphs should start with the main idea, then deal with subordinate matters.

- The writing should move logically from one idea to the next.

- Avoid negative structures. For example, 'not unreasonable' should be simply 'reasonable'.

- Use precise language and terminology. Avoid ambiguity.

- Use active verbs rather than nominalisations. For example, do not write 'we are in opposition to that idea'. Write 'we oppose that idea' instead.

- Never use a long word where a short one can be used. For example, avoid words like *notwithstanding* where simple words like *despite, still* or *even if* can be used instead.

- Do not use a foreign phrase or jargon if you can think of an ordinary English word which means the same thing. For example, do not write *modus operandi* when you can write *method*, nor *soi-disant* when you can write *so-called*.

- Use terms of art with care. Differentiate between terms of art and jargon. A *corporate veil* can be replaced with other words, but *bailment* and *patent* cannot.

- Try to produce text which looks as if it has been written by a normal human being. Break any of the rules above sooner than write like a robot.

2.2 Consistency

English is full of synonyms. It is therefore easy to start writing about something using certain words, and then later on in the document start using other words to describe it. This can lead to lack of clarity or ambiguity. It is crucial to be consistent in your use of terminology. For example, if you start off with *buyer* and *seller*, do not start using *vendor* and *purchaser* later in the document. Never mix parts of different pairs: eg, *landlord* and *lessee, vendor* and *buyer*.

This issue can be dealt with in part by using defined terms in your contract drafting. However, defining too many terms can be counter-productive. See 'What to avoid in legal writing', Chapter 5.

Commonly used synonyms

Here are some examples of commonly used synonyms for legal concepts used in contracts. The key is to choose one word per concept and stick to it:

assign, transfer

breach, violation

buyer, purchaser

clause, provision, paragraph, article

contract, agreement

default, failure

lessee, tenant

lessor, landlord

obligation, liability

promise, assurance, undertaking

seller, vendor

unenforceable, ineffective

void, invalid, ineffective

2.3 Effectiveness

When drafting legal documents, clarity and consistency are worth nothing if the document is not actually legally effective. The following checklist will help focus your mind on how to achieve legal effectiveness:

1   Does the language you use correctly state an obligation, authorisation, condition or discretion? (eg, *shall*, *may* etc). See 'Peculiarities of contractual language' (in Chapter 2 of *Contractual Legal English*) for more details on the language needed to state obligations, authorisations, conditions or discretions.

2   Does it state it in such a way that it is clear to whom or what it relates? A key point here is to avoid the passive – ie, do not write *'a meeting must be called if …'*, but *'James Thorpe (or the Managing Director) must call a meeting if …'*.

3   Does it state it in such a way that it is enforceable (1) under the terms of the document itself, and (2) according to the law that governs the document?

4   Have you set clear time limits for the performance of any obligation?

5   Does it conflict with any other terms of the document?

6   Does the document clearly state what will happen in the case of breach of any obligation? It is important to define the nature of the innocent party's rights and the nature of the penalty that will be imposed on the breaching party.

7   Are the obligations, authorisations, conditions and discretions actually capable of being exercised in practice? A key point here is to be careful with

precedent legal documents – if used, they must be adapted rigorously to the deal in hand.

8 Is it precise enough? In particular, set clear time-frames rather than using words like *forthwith*; specify precise standards rather than use formulations like *to a reasonable standard*; state enforceable obligations rather than use formulations like *use their best endeavours to*, etc.

3 STANDARDS IN LEGAL WRITING

Numbers

The general rule is that all numbers ten and below should be spelt and numbers 11 and above should be put in numerals. However, there are certain exceptions to this:

- If numbers recur through the text or are being used for calculations, then numerals should be used.
- If the number is approximate (eg, 'around six hundred years ago') it should be spelled out.
- Very large numbers should generally be expressed without using rows of zeros where possible. For example, $3.5 million instead of $3,500,000.
- Percentages may be spelled out (twenty percent) or written as numbers (20 percent or 20%).
- Numbers that begin sentences should be spelled out.

In English writing, the decimal point in a number is represented by a dot (.). For example, the number 1.5 means one and five-tenths. Commas (,) are used to break up long numbers. For example, 10,000,000 is 10 million. Commas cannot be used to indicate a decimal point.

When referring to sums of money, the following rules apply:

- When writing numerical sums, the currency sign goes before the sum, eg, £100.
- When spelling out numbers, the name of the currency is normally placed after the number, eg, 'one hundred pounds sterling'. Certain abbreviations for common currencies may also be used, including USD for US dollars and EUR for Euros.

Note also that in America, one billion means one thousand million (= 1,000,000,000). In Britain, it means one million millions (= 1,000,000,000,000). However, the American definition is now becoming more widely used. For this reason, where billions are mentioned without numerals being used, it is prudent to check which definition is being followed.

Dates

Dates should be written 1 February 1999, 3 March 2000 – not 1st February or 3rd day of March.

Note, however, that dates are written differently in American English, since the month is placed before the day (see Introduction, section 5).

Abbreviations

There are two kinds of abbreviations. The first kind is the acronym. An acronym is made from the initial letters or parts of a phrase or compound terms. It is usually referred to as a single word. For example, *radar* = radio detection and ranging.

The second kind is an initialism, which is made from the initial letters or parts of a phrase or compound term. These are usually referred to, and pronounced, letter by letter rather than as a single word, eg, *USA* = United States of America.

In general, those abbreviations which refer to an entity, such as *UK, USA, NATO,* should be capitalised without dots between the letters.

Those abbreviations which are used as grammatical shorthand such as *eg,* and *ie,* are usually written in lowercase letters, and it is acceptable to either include or leave out dots between the letters.

There are also certain terms which are referred to in speech as a single word but which are capitalised in writing. For example, *NATO* = North Atlantic Treaty Organisation.

Here is a list of some common abbreviations and their usages:

AGM = Annual General Meeting

aka = also known as ('John Smith aka King of Style')

am = ante meridiem ('before noon')

AOB = any other business (often used in meeting agendas)

cc = carbon copy (used to show that a copy of a letter has also been sent to another person or persons)

CEO = chief executive officer

cf = compare(d) with

cif = cost, insurance, freight contract

cod = cash on delivery

EC = European Communities

eg = *exempli gratia*

enc = enclosed

etc = *et cetera*

EU = European Union

FBI = Federal Bureau of Investigation

fob = free on board contract

GATT = General Agreement on Trade and Tariffs

GBH = grievous bodily harm

GM = genetically modified

GmbH = German business vehicle equivalent to the common law limited company (Ltd)

GMT = Greenwich mean time

GNP = gross national product

HR = Human Resources

Ibid = *ibidem* ('in the same source')

ID = identification

ie = *id est* ('that is to say')

Inc = incorporated (USA)

IOU = I owe you

IPO (USA) = Initial Public Offering (of shares of a company)

IT = Information Technology

Ltd = limited company (UK)

MD = managing director

MEP = Member of the European Parliament

NAFTA = North American Free Trade Agreement

NATO = North Atlantic Treaty Organisation

NB = *nota bene* ('note well')

pa = per annum

PA = personal assistant

PC = (1) personal computer; (2) politically correct; (3) police constable

pc = per cent

plc = public limited company (UK)

pm = post meridiem ('afternoon')

pp = *per procurationem* (used when signing a letter on someone else's behalf)

PO = post office

PPS = post postscript

PR = public relations

PS = postscript

PTO = please turn over

QC = Queen's Counsel

QED = *quod erat demonstrandum* ('thus I prove')

TLC = tender loving care

UK = United Kingdom

UN = United Nations

USA = United States of America

VAT = value added tax

viz = *videlicet* ('namely', 'in other words')

vs = versus, against

The following abbreviations are often found in emails and other informal communications:

ASAP = as soon as possible

BR = best regards

BTW = by the way

c/w = comes with

FYI = for your information

POV = point of view

TBA = can mean 'to be advised', or 'to be announced', or 'to be agreed'.

TOC = table of contents

w/e = weekend

See also the Glossary of Business Abbreviations at the back of the book.

Referring to statutes and cases

These notes explain the common practices to observe when referring to statutes, treaties and cases in a legal document.

Statutes should be written without a comma between the name of the statute and the year it was enacted. For example, the 'Treaty of Amsterdam 1999'.

The word 'the' should not form part of the name of a statute. Therefore, one should write 'the Single European Act 1986' and not 'The Single European Act 1986'.

When referring to a section of a statute write 'section' in full using a lowercase 's' (unless starting a sentence). For example, 'section 2 of the Law of Property (Miscellaneous Provisions) Act 1989'.

When referring to a particular sub-section of a statute do not use the word 'sub-section'. Use the word 'section' followed by the relevant number and letter, for example, 'section 722(1) of the Companies Act 1985'.

The names of cases should be written in italics and the word 'versus' should appear as 'v'. For example, *'Donoghue v Stevenson'*.

Clauses and sub-clauses

Each clause in a document should deal with a separate issue. If it contains a number of sentences which deal with different areas of the main topic of the clause, these should be split into separate sub-clauses. Where the clause is long and complex, such sub-division is essential.

Sub-clauses should be arranged in a clear and logical way. For example, a sub-clause can include:

- definitions of terms used only in the clause;
- the basic proposition;
- exceptions to the basic proposition; and
- any restrictions on the scope of the exceptions.

Detailed provisions such as timetables or formulae can be placed in a separate clause or in a schedule to the document and then cross-referenced.

4 LEGAL WRITING CONSIDERATIONS

Active and passive voice

Voice refers to the relationship between a clause's subject and its verb. The phrase 'the lawyer considered the documents' is active because the verb 'considered' performs the action of the subject. The phrase 'the documents were considered by the lawyer' is passive because the verb is acted upon.

The passive voice has the effect of deadening the impact of the action by burying it in the subsidiary part of the sentence. The active form highlights the action in the first part of the sentence.

Legal drafters have a tendency to use passive forms ('a meeting is to be called') rather than active forms ('John Smith will call a meeting'). The reason for this is that the passive permits an indirect and formal tone with which lawyers instinctively feel comfortable.

However, over-use of the passive can lead to lack of clarity. The example given above leaves it unclear as to who is going to call the meeting. It also leads to less effective and less forceful communication with the reader.

Sentences using the active voice are shorter and more direct. In most cases the active voice is preferable. However, there may be cases in which the writer's intention is to divert attention from the real subject. For example, 'the contract was signed' (passive) as opposed to 'I signed the contract' (active).

Alternatively, the writer may use the passive voice to focus attention on the object in a case where that is more important than the subject. For example, 'the meeting will be held' (passive) as opposed to 'the company will hold a meeting' (active).

In these last two cases, the passive should be used. In other cases it should be avoided.

Positives and negatives

A positive phrase is usually better than a negative one. For example, 'Clause 2 shall apply only if ...' is clearer than 'Clause 2 shall not apply unless ...'.

However, restrictions are often difficult to express in the positive rather than the negative without either:

- changing the meaning ('A shall not sell goods except those made by B' is a restriction whereas 'A shall sell goods made by B' is a positive obligation and therefore fundamentally different); or

- using indirect language ('A may build anything except a house' is less direct than saying 'A may not build a house').

In these cases, therefore, the negative forms should be used. In other cases, they should be avoided.

Euphemisms

Euphemisms are supposedly soft or unobjectionable terms substituted in place of harsh or objectionable ones. The purpose of their use is to soften the impact of what is being said. For example, one might speak of a person being *intoxicated* rather than *drunk* or having *passed away* rather than *died*.

Used sensibly, euphemisms allow the speaker or writer to deal with difficult issues in tactful and diplomatic language.

However, the over-use of euphemisms can lead, sometimes deliberately, to lack of clarity (*revenue enhancement* rather than *tax increase*) or absurdity (*rodent operative* rather than *ratcatcher*).

In other cases, the attempt to soften the impact of what is being expressed simply appears dishonest: for example, when NATO uses the term *collateral damage* to indicate that civilians have been killed in a bombing raid.

Use euphemisms sparingly: over-use can lead to lack of clarity or unintentionally humorous results.

Here are some further examples of euphemisms in current use in legal and business English (from which you will gather that euphemisms can also be used with intentionally humorous or critical intent):

Bandwagon: a chance to make profits which attracts opportunists.

Bean counter: accountant.

Economically disadvantaged: poor.

Headhunter: recruiting agent.

Kickback: a secret illegal payment.

Let go: fired, dismissed.

Lunchtime engineering: bribery.

Negative equity: owing more on an asset than it is worth.

Negative growth: decline.

Negatively impacted: loss-making.

Permanent layoff: fired, dismissed.

Rainmaker: a person working in a business who is valued for his or her contacts.

Metaphors

A metaphor is a figure of speech in which a word or phrase is used to refer to or represent something else. The expression *food for thought* is a typical example.

Metaphors should be used very carefully in legal writing. As British judge, Lord Keith, has noted 'A graphic phrase, or expression, has its uses even in a law report and can give force to a legal principle, but it must be related to the circumstances in which it used'.

The use of mixed metaphors, in particular, is to be discouraged. Mixed metaphors are a combination of metaphors that do not make sense when combined. This extract from a speech of Boyle Roche in the Irish Parliament delivered in about 1790 provides a classic example:

> Mr Speaker, I smell a rat. I see him floating in the air. But mark me, sir, I will nip him in the bud.

A number of metaphors are engrained in English legal language. For example, plaintiffs may have *clean* or *unclean hands* and statutes of limitation are said to *run*.

Oxymorons

Oxymorons are immediate contradictions in terms (eg, *bittersweet, a deafening silence*). A number of oxymorons exist in English legal terminology, such as *involuntary bailee, innocent fraud, intentional negligence*.

Relative clauses

A relative clause is a clause introduced by a relative pronoun and used to qualify a preceding noun or pronoun (eg, 'the parcel which I was expecting').

Relative pronouns include the following:

- who ('the lawyer who acted in that case')
- whom ('the client about whom I told you')
- whose ('the man whose wife works for our company')
- which ('the company which you are suing')
- that ('the problem that we are facing')

Note that *what* is only used as a relative pronoun in nominal relative clauses (eg, 'much of what he said was nonsense').

The main use of relative clauses is to achieve economy of style. For example, the sentence:

> I have faith in my lawyer. She told me about a new procedure we can use to claim back our money.

can be expressed:

> I have faith in my lawyer who told me about a new procedure we can use to claim back our money.

5 WHAT TO AVOID IN LEGAL WRITING

5.1 Sexist language

Personal pronouns

It is inappropriate to use the personal pronouns *he* or *his* in a document to refer to a person whose sex might be male or female. English has a number of gender-neutral words such as *person*, as well as a number of gender-neutral pronouns such as *anyone*, *everyone* and *no one*. However, it does not have gender-neutral singular personal pronouns.

A good workaround is to use the plural possessive form, *their*. The Oxford English Dictionary 2001 sanctions the use of this form to refer to 'belonging or associated with a person whose sex is not specified'. In this way, the drafter can avoid using sexist language in documentation.

Other methods can also be employed to avoid using *he* or *his*. These include:

- deleting the pronoun reference altogether if possible. For example, 'the lawyer read the documents as soon as they were delivered to him': delete *to him*;

- changing the pronoun to an article like *a* or *the*. For example, 'the lawyer advised the client on his case' can be changed to 'the lawyer advised the client on the case';

- using *who*, especially when *he* follows *if*. For example, 'if he does not prepare cases thoroughly a lawyer cannot be an effective court advocate' should read 'a lawyer who does not prepare cases thoroughly cannot be an effective court advocate';

- repeating the noun instead of using a pronoun. For example: 'When considering the conduct of litigation, the lawyer should retain an objective view. In particular, he [read *the lawyer*] should ...'

Terminology

In addition to paying attention to the use of personal pronouns, it is also important to ensure as far as possible that the terminology used is not gender-specific. This applies particularly to words ending in *-man*. For example, you should consider using *chair* instead of *chairman*, *firefighter* instead of *fireman*, and *drafter* instead of *draftsman*.

It should be remembered, however, that there is a limit to the extent to which the English language can reasonably be manipulated to remove all possible traces of gender discrimination. There is a balance to be struck between avoiding the use of gender-specific language and making your English sound like normal language. A particular problem arises in respect of words for which the only gender-neutral equivalent involves the use of *-person* or *person-*. Words such as *personpower*, *warehouseperson* and *foreperson* (instead of *foreman*) should be avoided where possible.

Equally, avoiding gender-specific language in English writing is not simply a matter of avoiding certain specific words and phrases. The underlying attitudes of the writer are more important.

Some examples of old-fashioned terms and suggested non-sexist alternatives are set out below:

Old-fashioned term	Non-sexist equivalent
air hostess/stewardess	flight attendant
anchorman	anchor
businessman	business executive/manager/entrepreneur
cameraman	camera operator/photographer
chairman	chair
craftsman	artisan
deliveryman	courier/messenger/delivery driver
draftsman	drafter
fireman	firefighter
foreman (in the workplace)	supervisor
foreman (of a jury)	presiding juror
freshman	fresher/first-year student
headmaster	head/principal
juryman	juror
mankind	humankind/humanity
man-made	synthetic/manufactured
manpower	workforce/personnel
ombudsman	ombuds
policeman/policewoman	police officer
postman/mailman	postal worker/mail carrier

salesman	sales representative
spokesman	representative
statesman	political leader
statesmanship	diplomacy
the common man	the average person
warehouseman	warehouser
workman	worker

5.2 Ambiguity

The meaning of English sentences can in many cases be changed completely by altering the order of words or the punctuation. Look at the following sentences:

> My client has discussed your proposal to fill the drainage ditch with his partners.
>
> The judge, said the accused, was the most heinous villain he had ever met.

Most of the problems caused in this respect are due to the separation of different parts of the verb phrase. In the first sentence, the verb phrase is 'discussed with'. By reuniting the parts of the phrase, the real meaning of the sentence becomes clear:

> My client has discussed with his partners your proposal to fill the drainage ditch.

In the second sentence, the verb phrase is 'the judge said'. The use of commas creates a subordinate clause of the words 'said the accused'. This has the effect of severing the verb phrase and linking 'the judge' with 'was'. Removing the punctuation reveals the more likely meaning of the sentence:

> The judge said the accused was the most heinous villain he had ever met.

5.3 Constantly litigated words

Two words and phrases commonly used in English legal drafting have produced constant litigation: *best endeavours* and *forthwith*.

Best endeavours is often used in contracts to indicate that parties have promised to attempt to do something. The use of the phrase usually suggests a compromise in which neither party is prepared to accept a clear statement of their obligations.

The problem with the phrase is that there are no objective criteria by which best endeavours can be judged. It is easy to conclude that someone has used 'best endeavours' to ensure that something is done if the result is that the thing is done. It is very hard to make the same judgment if, despite certain efforts having been made, the thing is not done.

The phrase poses particular problems in professional undertakings (such as 'X promises to use its best endeavours to obtain the title deeds') due to the vagueness it introduces into the obligation undertaken. For this reason, the Law Society of England and Wales (the national association of solicitors) has warned solicitors against giving a 'best endeavours' undertaking.

Forthwith causes problems because it is too open-ended to introduce any certainty into the contract. According to the context, 'forthwith' could mean a matter of hours or a matter of weeks.

Everything depends on the context. For example, in one English case 'forthwith' was held to be within 14 days. In another, it was held that notice entered on a Friday and given the following Monday was not given 'forthwith'. In yet another, the duty to submit a claim 'forthwith' was held not to arise until a particular state department had the basic information to allow the claim to be determined.

For these reasons, it is preferable to specify a precise time and date by which something must be done if time is of the essence in an agreement.

5.4   Nominalisations ('buried verbs')

Nominalisation is where noun phrases are used instead of verbs. This frequently occurs in legal documents. For example, parties to legal documents don't 'decide' to do something; they 'make a decision'. They don't 'agree', but 'reach an agreement'. They don't agree to 'arbitrate' but to 'submit to arbitration'.

These verbs are effectively buried in a longer noun. These usually end with one of the following: *-tion, -sion, -ment, -ence, -ance, -ity*.

Nominalisations should usually be avoided because they make the legal text longer and less dynamic. The obligations referred to in the text will also be made to seem abstract, indirect and lacking in force.

Some examples of nominalisations commonly found in legal writing, and their active verb equivalents, are set out below.

Nominalisation	Active verb equivalent
arbitration	arbitrate
arrangement	arrange
compulsion	compel
conformity	conform
contravention	contravene
enablement	enable

enforcement	enforce
identity	identify
implementation	implement
incorporation	incorporate
indemnification	indemnify
indication	indicate
knowledge	know
litigation	litigate
mediation	mediate
meeting	meet
negotiation	negotiate
obligation	obligate, oblige
opposition	oppose
ownership	own
perpetration	perpetrate
perpetuation	perpetuate
possession	possess
reduction	reduce
violation	violate

Over-defining

Lawyers often think it necessary to define every term used in a document, even if they are only used once or twice. Often the result is a long list of definitions to which people reading the document have to refer constantly.

A definition is only needed if the meaning of the word or phrase is unclear and cannot be ascertained from the context. The dangers of putting in too many definitions can be summarised as follows:

- The document becomes more difficult to read and use.
- Creating the document becomes difficult and the author is more likely to make mistakes.
- Over-rigid definition of the meaning of certain words may lead to absurd or unintended conclusions.
- Over-defining can be self-defeating – often the attempt to define everything leads to leaving out something which should have been included. A court might then take the view that the omission must have been deliberate (in the light of the fact that everything else in the document is rigidly defined). As a result, the use of definitions can actually lead to loopholes in the document.

6 CREATING LEGAL DOCUMENTS

6.1 Getting started

Before starting to write a document or letter, you need to be sure that you have a clear idea of what the document is supposed to achieve and whether there are any problems that need to be overcome to allow it to be achieved. Ask yourself the following questions:

- Have you taken your client's full instructions?
- Do you have all the relevant background information?
- What is your client's main goal or concern?
- What are the main facts which provide the backbone of the document?
- What is the applicable law and how does it affect the drafting?
- Are there any useful *precedents* (generic legal documents on which specific legal documents can be based) which could be used for the draft?

You should also ask yourself whether there are any good alternatives for the client. Would it be more effective or cheaper to approach the client's goal in a different way? For example, if it seems that drafting the necessary documentation in English will be too difficult, consider the following options:

- draft the document in your native language and have it translated and verified;
- engage the services of a native English-speaking lawyer as a consultant in respect of the case; or
- draft the document as best as you can in English and have a legally-qualified English native speaker check and correct the documents.

6.2 Typical document structure

The exact structure of a document will vary according to the kind of document it is. However, in all cases it should be laid out in a logical way which makes the document as easy as possible to use and understand. The most important clauses should come before the less important clauses.

Here is an example of typical document structure:

- Heading
- Date

- Parties
- Definitions
- The focal point of the deal
- Things to do with the focal point of the deal
- General clauses, dealing for example with duration, assignment, dissolution
- What happens if things go wrong, eg, insolvency, rescission for breach, dispute resolution
- Standard 'boilerplate' clauses such as *force majeure*, service of notices, governing law
- Signature

6.3 Layout and design

The use of clear, readable English and a logical document structure should be complemented by user-friendly document design. The aim of document design should be to help readers find their way around the document. In this way, the document will be simpler to understand.

Here are a few suggestions as to how to improve the layout and design of your documents:

- Use a readable serif font in an appropriate size (generally between 9 and 12 points).
- Use between 45 and 70 characters per line.
- Use plenty of white space – break up slabs of text, use wide margins around the text, double space all text and use generous spacing between clauses.
- Use headings. Give each main clause a bold heading. If possible give subsidiary clauses headings in italics.
- Use italics rather than underlining to emphasise text.
- Use properly indented lists where appropriate.
- Put citations in footnotes rather than having them interrupt the flow of the main text.
- Don't justify the right margin.
- Use a cover sheet for any document over five or six pages long.
- Avoid excessive capitalisation.

6.4 Checklist

This checklist can be used when drafting or evaluating business contracts and other documents.

Before drafting the document

- Have you got all the information you need?
- What is the main aim of the document?
- What are the main facts which form the basis of the document?
- What is the applicable law and how will it affect the drafting?
- Are there any useful *precedents* (generic legal documents on which specific legal documents can be based) which could be used for the draft?

Content

- Do the terms of the document reflect the intentions of the client or – if a contract – the bargain struck between the parties?
- If the document is a contract, does it contain fair mutual obligations?
- Does the document foresee what might go wrong in the future?
- Does the drafting of the document provide protection if something does go wrong?
- If the document is a contract, does it provide a dispute-resolution mechanism in case something goes wrong?

Language

- Is the language used in the document clear and coherent?
- Are there any ambiguities?
- Is terminology used in a consistent way?
- Are the spelling and punctuation correct?
- Will the reader understand the contract?
- Have the following been removed:
  - irrelevant language;
  - jargon;
  - excessive use of capitals;
  - unnecessary definitions; and
  - unnecessary use of foreign terms?

Law

- Is the document legally effective?
- Does it fulfil all formal requirements (if applicable)?
- Are any clauses in the document illegal?
- How will the governing law interpret its terms in the event of breach?

Accuracy

Is all factual matter contained in the document accurate, in particular:

- dates;
- time-limits;
- names and addresses;
- prices;
- identification numbers;
- references to other sections or schedules; and
- list information contained in schedules?

Structure

- Does the document have a logical structure?
- Does each paragraph contain just one main idea?
- Does the order of sentences and paragraphs make sense?
- Are there links between one paragraph and the next?
- Are there links between sentences in each paragraph?

Presentation and layout

- Is the font size big enough (between 9 and 12 points)?
- Are the lines the right length (45–70 characters per line)?
- Is there enough white space in the document?
- Have headings been used for main clauses?
- Have properly indented lists been used where appropriate?

7 WRITING LEGAL LETTERS AND EMAILS

7.1 Letter-writing conventions

When writing a letter, certain conventions used in English legal letter-writing should be remembered. These are, arguably, excessively formal, but are still in current use.

Starting your letter (salutation)

- Use 'Dear Sirs' as the salutation for a letter in which the addressees are a company or institution of which the members are either (i) all male or (ii) made up of both men and women.[3]

- Use 'Dear Mesdames' as the salutation for a letter in which the addressees are a company or institution of which the members are all female.

- Use 'Dear Sir or Madam' when writing to a person of whom you know neither the name nor the sex.

- When writing formally to a particular person whose name you know, use their name and title (eg, 'Dear Mr Thorpe').

Ending your letter

Note that there is no need when writing either to American or British recipients to use old-fashioned flourishes such as 'I remain, Sir, your obedient servant'. This kind of thing is regarded as quaint or ridiculous in today's business environment. The following rules will cover most situations:

- Use 'Yours sincerely' to end a letter in which the salutation is addressed to a particular person (eg, 'Dear Mr Thorpe') if you are using British English as standard. Use 'Sincerely yours' if you are using American English as standard.

- Use 'Yours faithfully' to end a letter in which the salutation is formal (eg, 'Dear Sirs') if you are using British English as standard. Use 'Respectfully

---

3   Note that whilst 'Dear Sirs' is the standard formal salutation in British legal letters to companies or institutions, it is considered discriminating in North America. When writing to American or Canadian firms it should be replaced with 'Dear Sir or Madam'.

yours' (very formal) or 'Yours truly' (less formal) if you are using American English as standard.

When writing to a personal friend, informal endings can be used. These include:

- With best wishes
- Best wishes
- With best regards
- Best regards
- Kindest personal regards
- Best

It is often thought that emails are a less formal medium than letters. This is true up to a point, but may be a dangerous belief for lawyers. Do not allow the informality of writing emails to lead you to forget the importance and possible sensitivity of the information you may be communicating.

Remember that an email is just as permanent as a letter and may be printed out and referred to in the future. Remember also that the exchange of emails leaves an easily traceable trail in both correspondents' inboxes. For these reasons, the same high standards of professionalism should be adhered to when writing emails as one would follow when writing letters.

7.2 Writing an effective letter or email – structure

The most important thing to remember when writing a letter or email is to consider the reader. The content and style of your letter or email will be affected by the following considerations:

- Who is going to be reading it?
- How much do they understand about the subject-matter of the letter?
- What do they need to know?
- How much background information do they need?
- Do you need any information from them?
- What sort of tone should you adopt?

Whoever you're writing to, you should ensure that your letter or email is:

- as short as possible but not shorter;
- clearly written;
- clearly set out; and
- appropriate in tone.

The following hints and tips should lead to you writing effective emails:

- State clearly in the subject line what the communication is about.
- Don't be afraid to use the reader's first name (provided you know them well enough).

- If you have received an earlier communication from the person you are writing to, thank them.
- Be precise when confirming dates, times, advice given, etc.
- Keep it short and simple. Use short sentences with one idea per sentence.
- Check your spelling and grammar.
- Always be polite.
- Write a friendly closing.

When writing a letter of advice to a client, the following points should be remembered:

- Summarise the facts of the case as you recall them ('During our meeting you told me that ...'). In this way, if there are any inaccuracies in your information, the client has the opportunity to correct them.
- Set out clearly, using sub-headings if appropriate, your advice to the client in respect of each matter that he or she raised with you.
- Confirm what action it was agreed would be taken (a) by you and (b) by the client, and indicate whether you require any further information from the client.
- Inform the client as to whom he or she should contact at the firm in case of difficulties.
- Confirm any agreement made with regard to the payment of your fees.

7.3 Letter layout

When setting out your letter, remember the following points:

- Place your own address in the top right corner of the letter.
- Place the date of the letter below your own address, separated by a space and justified to the edge of the line of the address. Do not write the date in figures or abbreviate the name of the month. Instead, write the month and the date in full (eg, 6 May 2004).
- Place the name and address of the person or organisation you are writing to on the left side of the letter and below the level of your own address. If you do not know the name of the person to whom you are writing, it is useful to include his or her title or position in the company if this is known. Here is a short list of some titles commonly used in law firms and firms with legal departments:

Associate/Associate Lawyer

Attorney

Chief Legal Counsel

Director

Director of Legal Affairs

Human Resources Manager

Legal Adviser

Legal Counsel

Legal Officer

Managing Director

Managing Partner

Partner

Personnel Manager

Secretary

Senior Attorney

Senior Partner

- The references of both your organisation and the organisation to which you are writing should be placed below the address of the recipient separated by a space and justified to the left. If references are not used, an underlined 'attention line' may be inserted. For example:

> For the attention of the Director of Legal Affairs

- The salutation (eg, 'Dear Sirs') goes below the references or attention line separated by a space and justified to the left.
- The body of the letter should go below the salutation. The text should be justified to the left and a line space should be left between paragraphs in the body of the letter.
- The letter should close with a complimentary clause (eg, 'Yours faithfully'), followed by your signature above the typed signature and your title or position in the organisation. A letter written to a particular person in an organisation should end with a personal signature (eg, 'James Thorpe'). A letter written generally to an organisation (commencing with 'Dear Sirs') may end with a signature on behalf of the organisation which is sending the letter (eg, 'Roggins Ltd').
- A number of abbreviations may be used at the foot of a letter for certain purposes. Here are some examples:

  Enc/Encl indicates that documents are enclosed with the letter. If there are a number of these, it is usual to list them.

  pp means *per procurationem* (literally *for and on behalf of*). It is used if someone other than the writer has signed the letter.

  cc means carbon copy (although carbon copies are little used nowadays). This abbreviation is used to indicate that copies are sent to persons other than the named recipient. Frequently the letter will specify the persons to whom the copies have been sent.

bcc means blind carbon copies. This abbreviation is used when other persons have been sent copies but you do not want the recipient to know this. The abbreviation is written on the copies only and not on the original version that is sent to the recipient.

7.4   Writing an effective letter or email – language

The list below covers some of the major language functions you, as a legal professional, are likely to perform when writing a letter or email. For each function, language suggestions are given.

The first line (saying 'hello')

> Dear Mr Jones/Dear Sirs
>
> OR
>
> [Informal email only] Hello/Hi David

Confirming client's instructions

> During our meeting you told me that ...
>
> OR
>
> You instructed me as follows ...

Referring to the previous email/letter

> Thank you for your email/letter of 9 January about/concerning ...

Acknowledging letter and promising to write later

> I/we acknowledge receipt of your letter of 9 January to which I/we will provide a substantive response shortly.

Referring to theme of a message received

> You informed me/us that ...
>
> OR
>
> [Informal] It was interesting to hear about ...

Explaining why you are writing

> I/we am/are writing to ...

Referring to something

> With regard/respect to ...

Giving advice

> My/our advice on this matter is as follows.

Refuting an allegation

> Your client's allegation that ... is entirely denied by our client.

Disagreeing on a point of law or fact

> [Strongly] I/we entirely disagree with your analysis/statement to the effect that ...
>
> [Tentatively] I/we are unable to agree entirely with your analysis/statement to the effect that ...

Prefacing a statement of legal opinion

> [Strongly] It is clear that the correct analysis of the facts/applicable law is ...
>
> [Tentatively] It seems to me/us that the correct analysis of the facts/applicable law is ...

Stating a position

> It is our [client's] position that ...

Making an offer

> Our client has instructed us to put forward the following offer: [list]
>
> OR
>
> Our client is prepared to settle this matter on the following terms: [list]

Setting deadlines

> This offer will remain open until 29 April 2002.

Making a threat to take certain action by a specified date

> [Strongly] We have our client's instructions that unless full payment is received by 14 January, we should issue legal proceedings ...
>
> [Tentatively] If payment is not made by 14 January, our client will have to consider instructing us to issue legal proceedings ...

Issuing a rebuke to the other party's lawyers

> [Sarcastically] With the greatest of respect, your statement that ... is not credible ...
>
> [Politely] We feel it our duty to point out that your statement ...

Giving good news

> I/we am/are pleased to be able to ...

Giving bad news

> Unfortunately, I/we have to tell you ...

Asking somebody to do something for you

> I/we would appreciate it if you would/could/might ...

Showing willingness to do something for somebody

I/we would be glad to …

Asking for an immediate response

I/we would greatly appreciate you giving this matter your immediate attention.

OR

[Where a deadline is necessary] This matter is urgent. We should be grateful to hear from you no later than 4 pm on 22 May 2002.

Clarifying what action is to be taken

I/we will now take the following steps:

[list]

Requesting further information

I/we should be grateful if you could provide us with the following information/ documentation:

[list]

Confirming an agreement

As discussed on the telephone on 9 January, it is agreed that …

OR

We confirm that we have reached agreement [concerning the question of …] between us on the following terms:

[list]

Offering further help

If I/we can be of any further assistance, please don't hesitate to contact me/us.

Promising to get back with further help

I/we will be in touch again shortly.

Thanking for help

I/we would like to take this opportunity to thank you for your assistance.

Closing remarks

Please do not hesitate to contact me if you have any queries or require further information.

Ending

Yours faithfully/Yours sincerely/Best regards

7.5 Specimen letter

Roggins Ltd   John Leggatt & Co, Solicitors
35 Windmill Road   16 Vinter Street
Edinburgh   London
UK   SE23 1JF
                                                                       UK

4 May 2004

For the attention of the Director of Legal Affairs

Dear Sirs

RemCureCo Ltd: distribution agreement

We thank you for your letter of 21 April and enclosures.

Unfortunately, having reviewed the case with our client, we are unable to agree with your contention that no actionable breach of paragraph 7(b) has occurred. We are fortified in this conclusion by the House of Lords' recent decision in the case of *Lynch-Ross v Dannone*. We enclose a copy of the initial case report which appeared in *The Times* on 15 April for your consideration.

In the circumstances, we look forward to receiving your proposals for settlement within the course of the next 14 days, in the absence of which we will advise our client to instruct us to commence proceedings.

Yours faithfully

[Signature]

John Leggatt & Co, Solicitors

Enc

cc James Thorpe, RemCureCo Ltd

7.6 Checklist

The following self-editing checklist may be useful when drafting letters and emails.

Purpose

• What is the purpose of the communication?
• Have I adapted style and content to suit the reader's needs?
• Have I dealt with the issues?
• Have I answered all the questions?
• Have I answered them in enough depth?

Content

• Is the information accurate?
• Is it relevant?

Humanity

• Will my tone produce the desired response?
• Is it friendly, courteous, helpful, frank, forceful?

Layout

• Is the layout appropriate for the purpose and content?
• Is it set out in manageable blocks?

Structure

• Are the sentences short enough?
• Does the order of sentences and paragraphs make sense?
• Does each paragraph contain just one main idea?
• Is there a link between each paragraph and the next?
• Are there links between the sentences in each paragraph?
• Does the whole letter have a clear and logical structure?

Language

• Have I used plain language, ie, clear, concise and correct language that can be easily understood by the reader?
• Have I used active verbs instead of nominalisations wherever possible?

- Have I omitted words and phrases which are:
  - infrequently used;
  - inelegant;
  - redundant;
  - unnecessarily technical;
  - verbose; or
  - vague?
- Is the grammar appropriate for the purpose?
- Are punctuation and spelling correct?

8 INTERNAL COMMUNICATIONS

8.1 Memoranda

Uses

Memoranda are essentially internal company documents. They deal with such issues as:

- policies or procedures which the company has decided to implement;
- important announcements;
- decisions about issues which will affect the recipients.

Memoranda may be addressed to one other person or to a number of persons. They are often referred to as *memos*.

Meeting memoranda, also known as *minutes*, record the matters discussed in a meeting and any decisions reached.

Layout and content

Memoranda should state at the top of the first page:

- the person(s) to whom they are addressed;
- the person who wrote the memorandum;
- the date; and
- the subject.

The first paragraph of the memorandum may be used to explain the background to the issue that the memorandum refers to.

The main part of the memorandum should be used to explain concisely:

- what is going to happen;
- why it is going to happen;
- when it is going to happen; and
- how it will affect everyone.

Numbered paragraphs may be used. They are particularly appropriate when the memorandum sets out a procedure to be followed.

The last part should state the person who recipients should contact for further details. The memorandum should be signed by the writer.

Specimen memorandum

Smith, Billings and Co
23 Grange Road
Liverpool

To: All employees   Date: 13 March 2004

From: Michael Empson

Subject: Litigation department move

You have no doubt heard that due to pressures on our office space resulting from the firm's rapid expansion it has become necessary to move some staff members to another location.

The partners have decided that the whole of the litigation department will be moved to new premises at 35 Smithson Avenue, Liverpool. The relevant details of the move are as follows:

(1) The move will take place over the weekend of 12/13 April.

(2) Staff affected by the move are asked to pack their computers, books and other work items into the storage boxes provided by the removal firm no later than 4pm on Friday 11 April. If needed, more boxes can be obtained from Jane Baxter.

(3) An external IT contracting firm will visit the premises at 35 Smithson Avenue on Monday 14 April to set up the computers and establish the internal network. Therefore we will have a training day for the whole firm, details of which will be announced later.

If anyone has any questions regarding the move, please contact me.

[Signature]

Michael Empson, Senior Partner

8.2 Notes

Uses

Notes are commonly used in legal practice. They include the following:

- Attendance notes, used to record the contents of interviews with clients, telephone conversations and discussions with other lawyers.
- Research notes, which set out the results of legal research carried out by lawyers into issues relevant to cases on which they are working.

Layout and content

No particular formalities need to be used for notes, since they are usually created for the writer's own purposes. However, it is useful to specify:

- the date on which the note is written;
- the name of the case to which it relates; and
- the subject of the note.

In addition, an attendance note should set out the following:

- matters discussed between the parties, including any specific information given by either party;
- any advice given by the lawyer (in the case of a note relating to a lawyer-client discussion); and
- any action to be taken as a result of the attendance.

The content of a research note will vary according to the nature of the research to be carried out, but should contain the following:

- the specific sources of the research findings (ie, volume, page and paragraph numbers), so that these can be quickly found again if needed;
- the conclusions of the research; and
- any matters which might cast doubt on the conclusions of the research.

8.3 Reports

Uses

Reports can be used to make announcements, or to explain or recommend policy. They may come from internal sources. Equally they are often commissioned from external agencies, for example, in the case of a report prepared by an external expert which the company has requested to review a particular problem.

Layout and content

A typical report might be structured in the following way:

1 *Introduction* – summarising the findings of the report and the reasons why it was made.
2 *Background* – setting out how the issue which the report deals with came into being, and how it can be changed.
3 *Facts* – the evidence that supports the claims the writer makes.
4 *Conclusions* – the writer's views formed on the basis of the evidence presented.
5 *Recommendations* – following from the conclusions made, which suggest the ways in which the current situation can be improved.

9 APPLYING FOR LEGAL JOBS

9.1 Job advertisements

Advertisements (often shortened to ads) for employment appear in all the media, including radio, TV and the internet. However, for legal appointments the best place to begin your search for employment may be in a professional legal publication. In most countries the national bar association or law society has its own magazine, which is likely to appear at least monthly. Such magazines generally contain a large section reserved for advertisements for all kinds of legal positions and for legal services.

For the sake of clarity, we have used the word *lawyer* in the example letters given below. You should bear in mind, however, that in England and Wales, the term *solicitor* is more likely to be used, and in the US, the term *attorney* is more likely to be used.

Most advertisements contain a number of abbreviations, which are usually well understood in the profession. They are included primarily to save money on the advertisement. Therefore, a typical advertisement for a general commercial lawyer might read as follows:

Wanted, 3 yrs + PQE gen comm practitioner. Caseload to include Co-Co, comm Prop & IPR. Large city centre practice. Must have own transport. Salary neg FT position, assistant with partner potential. Apply with CV to Mr JM Stokes by 13/04/04.

A full-length version of this would read:

Wanted, a general commercial practitioner with more than three years of post-qualified experience. The caseload will include company commercial, commercial property, and intellectual property rights. Large city centre practice. Must have own transport. Salary negotiable. A full-time position for an assistant lawyer with potential to become a partner. Apply with your curriculum vitae to Mr JM Stokes by 13 April 2004.

9.2 How to apply

There are basically three kinds of job applications that you can make:

- An application for a specific advertised position.
- An application to a recruitment consultant to register your details in case a suitable position arises.
- An unsolicited application – ie, a general application to a firm in circumstances where no specific position has been advertised.

The kind of letter you write will depend on the kind of application you make, but in all cases you should:

- Find out whether the application must be made on a special application form or by sending your curriculum vitae and a covering letter. If an application form is required, telephone or write to the firm to which you are applying to obtain it.
- Find out the name and job title of the person to whom you should send your application. Many job applications are disregarded because they are not addressed to a particular person. Many big law firms nowadays have personnel departments (also called human resources departments) which deal with job applications. If it is not clear to whom an application should be addressed, phone the personnel department to find out.
- Do your research. Find out as much as possible about the firm or organisation you are applying to before sending your application. In this way you can (1) save yourself the trouble of sending out any applications which are highly unlikely to be successful, and (2) adapt your application to the needs of the particular firm or organisation to which you are writing.
- Remember to quote any reference numbers mentioned in the advertisement.

When applying for a legal position, always ensure that your letter and CV or application form are free from grammatical errors and spelling mistakes. Lawyers are trained to pay attention to detail, and mistakes will make a very poor impression.

Application for a specific advertised position

Your letter should have a beginning, middle and end. Generally, the terms *vacancy*, *post*, *position* or *appointment* are used instead of the word *job* in advertisements.

In the beginning of your letter, explain what you are applying for and mention any documents that you have enclosed. For example:

> I wish to apply for the vacancy for a commercial lawyer advertised in this month's edition of Legal News. I enclose a copy of my curriculum vitae OR the relevant application form duly completed.

Use the middle of the letter to state what appeals to you about the position you are applying for, and why you think that you would be particularly well-suited to it. You can use this part of the letter (1) to demonstrate knowledge about the firm or organisation to which you are writing, and (2) to give some indication of your expertise and experience. For example:

> This position is of particular interest to me since I note that your firm is well-known for its work for IT companies. I have had over three years of experience in IT law in my present position, and am keen to develop my expertise in this area further.

At the end of the letter, offer to supply more information if necessary:

> I look forward to hearing from you. However, if there is any further information you require in the meantime, please let me know.

Application to a recruitment consultant to register details

The main purpose of this letter is to indicate what kind of position you are seeking and what kind of previous experience you have. However, it is important to make a good impression on the recruitment consultant to whom you write, since the consultant is only likely to put your name forward to firms looking for new employees if he or she has confidence in your abilities.

When dealing with recruitment consultants it is important to remind them periodically that you are still looking for work. Most consultants have large databases of people who have at one time or other registered their details, and those who have been silent for a long period of time tend to get forgotten. Phone the recruitment consultant either shortly before or shortly after you have sent them your details, and let them know exactly what you are looking for and why you are a suitable candidate. After this initial conversation, if you hear nothing for a week or so, phone again to check on progress.

In your initial letter, state what kind of position you are looking for, the geographical area in which you ideal job should be located, the salary range you are seeking, and mention any documents that you have enclosed. For example:

> I am looking for a position as an assistant commercial lawyer, mainly specialising in company commercial matters, in a large commercially-oriented law firm. Ideally, I would like to remain in the London area, but would be prepared to consider relocating for an exceptional position. I am looking for a salary in the region of £45,000–£55,000 per annum.

You should then state any particular qualities or experience you have that will make you especially attractive to employers. For example:

> I have had over five years of experience in the field of company commercial law and also have significant experience in IT law. I am fluent in German and spent one year during my current employment working at the firm's branch office in Munich, where I headed the company commercial department.

At the end of your letter, you should indicate that you will be proactive in pursuing your job search. A suitably-worded ending will communicate to the recruitment consultant that you are a serious applicant worthy of being strongly marketed to prospective employers. For example:

> If there is any further information you require, please let me know. I am keen to pursue this matter vigorously, and will telephone your Ms Smith on Friday 12 June to discuss progress. I can be contacted at any time on my mobile, number 07339 873192.

An unsolicited application

When sending an unsolicited application, you should start by asking whether the firm you are writing to might have a vacancy that you could fill. For example:

> I am writing to enquire whether you might have a vacancy in your company commercial department for an assistant lawyer. I enclose a copy of my curriculum vitae.

If someone associated with the firm you are writing to suggested that you write to them, mention this in your opening:

> I was recommended by Clive Enright, who has a long association with your firm, to contact you regarding a possible position in your company's commercial department.

In any event, you should then explain why you are applying to the firm – state what it is about the firm that particularly attracts you, and why you would be a suitable employee for the firm. For example:

> I am particularly interested by the possibility of working for your firm, since I note that you have strong expertise in the field of intellectual property. I have three years post-qualified experience working in the commercial department of my present firm, and have primarily focused on patent and industrial design rights. I am keen to further my expertise and experience in this area.

At the end of the letter, offer to supply more information if necessary:

> I look forward to hearing from you. However, if there is any further information you require in the meantime, please let me know.

9.3 Application letters and CVs

When you receive an application form, always read it through carefully so that you know exactly what information is required. It is a good idea to photocopy it, complete the photocopy and, when you are happy with it, copy the information onto the actual form.

Some firms or organisations prefer a curriculum vitae (CV), which is also known as a *resumé* in American English. A curriculum vitae should contain your personal and working history.

Application forms and CVs may be emailed, faxed or sent by post. It is best to try to find out from the firm or organisation to which you are applying which method they prefer before you send your application.

Curriculum vitae

There are a number of ways of presenting information in a CV. Traditionally, the sequence was name, address, contact details, marital status, education, qualifications, work experience, referees and interests. However, it is now more common to begin with brief personal details, followed by a short profile or description of yourself (sometimes also called a career summary). After that, the most important information is recent employment history, and skills and qualifications. In the interests of completeness, you should account for all years since leaving school, but if the information is irrelevant to the position you are applying for or is some years old, you should summarise it as briefly as possible.

These days, it is generally unnecessary to mention marital status, children, age, health, or current salary unless specifically asked to do so, but this will vary according to the law and customs in different countries. Here is a typical CV for an experienced commercial lawyer.

Roland Hamilton

Address	33 Ardley Street
	Oxford
	OX4 9PT
Telephone	01865 774091
Mobile	07329 761459
Email	*roland.hamilton@elt.com*

Qualifications

1997	Diploma of Legal Practice, College of Law
1996	LLB, University of Bristol

Profile
- Four years' qualified commercial lawyer with wide experience in company commercial and IT law
- Experience of supervising and co-ordinating a team of lawyers
- Excellent communication and client skills
- Analytical, innovative, self-motivating, confident
- Fluent in German and Spanish
- Computer literate

Employment

2000–present   **Clifford and Boodle**

Assistant lawyer, commercial department

Caseload comprised company commercial and IT matters. Worked on several large merger cases under the supervision of the partner in charge of the department. Helped build up the IT law practice and was personally involved in supervising, coordinating and training a team of junior assistant lawyers.

1998–2000   **Bradley, Jones & Peters**

Trainee

Undertook training contract, gaining experience in company commercial, commercial property, commercial litigation and criminal litigation departments. Co-authored article, 'Recent developments in IT law' published in the June 1999 edition of Legal News.

Application letter (1): Application for a specific advertised position

In this letter, notice that the applicant starts off by referring to the job advertisement. He goes on to expand on his present duties and gives other information that he believes to be relevant to the post. He explains why he is applying for this particular vacancy and demonstrates knowledge of the firm to which he is applying. If, on his CV, he gives his current employers as referees, he could also mention that he would prefer Smith & Hutton not to approach them until after an interview.

---

23 Wakefield Terrace
Cambridge
CB2 1AP

16 May 2004

Ms G Summers
Human Resources Co-ordinator
Smith & Hatton
12 Gables Road
Oxford
OX1 3NE

Your Ref: GS 345/09

Dear Ms Summers

I wish to apply for the vacancy advertised in Legal News on 10 May 2004 for an assistant commercial lawyer. I enclose a copy of my curriculum vitae.

I am currently employed as an assistant lawyer at Bring & Fewster in Cambridge and have had three years of post-qualified experience, primarily in company commercial and IT law. In addition to handling a substantial caseload, I am also heavily involved in helping to co-ordinate my firm's marketing strategy with regard to IT clients. I am particularly interested by the position on offer at your firm, since I am aware that the firm has extensive expertise in this area.

I speak fluent German, and use the language daily in the course of my work.

If there is any further information you require, please contact me. I look forward to hearing from you.

Yours sincerely

Michael Arthurs

Enc CV

Application letter (2): Application to a recruitment consultant to register details

In this letter, notice that the applicant gives specific information about the kind of post she is looking for. In this way, she ensures both that the recruitment consultants will not waste her time by suggesting her for posts that do not meet her expectations, and she also makes the recruitment consultant's job easier by defining the terms of the employment that they should try to find for her. The applicant signals her seriousness about the job search by telephoning the recruitment consultants before sending her letter and by promising to phone again soon to check on progress.

Recruitment consultants do not usually send written acknowledgments that they have received applicants' details, but may telephone to discuss any aspects of the application that need to be clarified. They may also make alterations to the presentation (but not to the content) of applicants' CVs in order to maximise their chances of obtaining suitable posts.

---

23 The Glebe
Wantage
OX12 9PZ

10 September 2004

Ms MR Talbot
A1 Legal Recruiting
17A March Street
London
WC1 4HS
BY FAX: 020 456 2389

Dear Ms Talbot

I refer to our telephone conversation this morning and now enclose a copy of my curriculum vitae.

As discussed, I am looking for a position as an assistant lawyer in the company commercial department of a commercially-oriented practice in the south-east of the UK. I have three years of post-qualified experience in the commercial department of Hamble, Jones & Partners in Oxford, and have particular expertise in the fields of corporate acquisitions and IT law. I am strongly motivated, have advanced computer skills and I also have experience of supervising other lawyers and trainees. I seek a salary in the range £40,000–£55,000 and am seeking a post with real partnership potential.

I will telephone you on Friday 28 September to check on progress.

Yours sincerely

Vanessa Ledworth

Application letter (3): An unsolicited application

Notice in this letter how the applicant first mentions how he knows of Thompson & Grimes, gives brief details about his education and experience, and then requests an application form. Of course, he could also include a CV with the letter, but in this case he knows that the firm's practice is to send application forms.

14 Grenville Road
Coventry
CVI 5PT

27 May 2005

Mr JC Norton
Thompson & Grimes
35 Anfield Way
Coventry
CVI 9RS

Dear Mr Norton

I am writing to you on the recommendation of Jill Masterton, assistant lawyer in your commercial litigation department. We met last month on a legal skills training course in London and she suggested that I should contact your firm and mention her name.

I am at present employed as a trainee at Burns, Gartner & Co in Warwick. My training contract is due to finish in September of this year, and I am seeking a post as an assistant solicitor. During the course of my training contract I have gained experience in various types of commercial work, including company commercial, commercial litigation and commercial property. I am keen to specialise in commercial property in my future career and am particularly interested in applying to your firm since I am aware that the firm has a strong national reputation in this area of work and is seeking to expand its commercial property team.

I am a strongly motivated person with good academic credentials. I graduated in law from Southampton University with a 2:1 and speak fluent German and Swedish. During the course of my training contract I have handled a number of important commercial property cases on my own, and have particular experience in drafting commercial leases and options. I have also co-written articles on commercial leases which have appeared in Legal News, and have assisted in creating a library of commercial precedents for in-house use at my present firm.

I would be grateful if you could send me an application form and further information about the posts currently available. If you require any further information, I can be contacted by email on *james.thorne@aatco.co.uk* or telephone on 05678 699221.

Yours sincerely

James Thorne

9.4   Attending an interview

If you are invited to an interview, remember the following:

- Make sure you know in advance where the venue for the interview is and how you are going to get there. Leave yourself plenty of time – arriving late will create a very bad impression.

- Look the part. When applying for most legal jobs, you will be expected to be smartly but conservatively dressed.

- Do your research: find out as much about the firm or organisation to which you have applied, and the position you are seeking, as possible.

- Review your application. Be prepared for things you have mentioned in your application to be brought up and questioned by the interviewer. Therefore, do not mention anything in your application unless it can be supported by solid evidence.

- Be prepared for difficult questions. Always answer all questions frankly and fully. Try to discern the underlying objective of the interviewer in asking certain questions. The following questions are interview favourites:

  - *Where do you see yourself in five years' time?*

    The interviewer is testing your ambition, sense of purpose and career planning.

  - *Why do you want to work for us?*

    The interviewer is checking for motivation AND your understanding of the position on offer.

  - *Tell me about yourself.*

    The interviewer is checking mainly for confident self-presentation and for your ability to present relevant information succinctly.

  - *Why do you want to leave your current job?*

    The interviewer is looking for positive motivation. Never say that you want to leave in order to obtain a better-paid position or that your job is boring (even if either of those are true), and avoid direct criticism of your present or past employers or colleagues.

- If you do not get the job after being interviewed, do not be scared to telephone the firm to which you applied to ask the reason for this. If there is something in your style of presentation that you can correct, it is worth learning about it. Most reasonable firms are prepared to discuss over the telephone with candidates the reason why they were rejected.

SPEAKING LEGAL ENGLISH

1 ASPECTS OF SPOKEN ENGLISH

1.1 Spoken and written English compared

Compared to written English, spoken English is both more and less clear.

When reading a piece of written English, all the information in the communication is in the text. It is usually presented in a finished state and contains full, grammatically complete sentences. Some care will have been taken to structure and present the document effectively. The needs of the reader will have been considered to some extent. The document exists in a permanent form and can be read at leisure as many times as necessary.

By contrast, when speaking English with another person, the meaning of the dialogue only emerges gradually. The conversation is likely to be filled with unfinished sentences, interruptions, repetitions, pauses and meaningless phrases and words (such as 'er', 'um', 'you know?', 'if you see what I mean'). The course of the dialogue is unpredictable and infinitely flexible.

However, when speaking English with another person, you receive all kinds of clues, which cannot be found in written English, as to what the other person is really thinking or feeling. These include:

- body language;
- tone of voice; and
- vocal emphasis (sometimes called *stress*).

When you are involved in a conversation with another person you instinctively read the meaning of these clues. You also give such clues to the person you are speaking to.

Conversation also allows you to use a range of techniques which can only be used to a limited extent in writing. These include:

- humour;
- implying,
- euphemisms;
- rhetorical questions;
- open questions;
- narrow and closed questions;
- simple and conditional forms;
- choice of terminology;

- diplomatic language; and
- metaphors and similes.

These issues are discussed in detail in Chapter 1.6.

1.2 Small talk

Some people say that they have no time for small talk. What they mean is that they have no time to get involved in pointless discussions about irrelevant subjects. This view is understandable, but it entirely misunderstands the value of small talk.

It should also be noted that the huge technological advances of the past 10–15 years have made small talk something of a dying art. Many people prefer to send and receive emails than speak directly to another person. However, there is no substitute for a face-to-face meeting.

Why bother with small talk?

The value of small talk is that it is a means of establishing a basis for communication with people whom you do not know well. By starting discussions with some neutral topic, the people involved can get to know each other, trust each other and find their common ground. It is an important phase of any negotiation with strangers. If this phase goes well, a solid basis for negotiating matters of importance will have been established.

It should be acknowledged that not all cultures value small talk. When opening discussions with Germans or Finns, it can be kept to a minimum. Other cultures, including English-speaking ones, value small talk as a way of putting people at their ease and establishing common ground.

The secrets of successful small talk

When engaging in small talk, try to remember that it involves more than the mechanical repetition of a few pleasant platitudes. In fact this kind of thing should be kept to a minimum. It is necessary but basically boring. The secret of successful small talk is to find out what the other person is interested in and let them talk about it. All you need then do is demonstrate a genuine appreciation of those things. While excessive talkativeness may be viewed with suspicion in certain cultures, the feeling that someone is really interested in you and your thoughts and opinions is almost always a positive one. Remember that:

- nobody enjoys listening to someone talking about something that doesn't interest them; but
- everyone enjoys being given the chance to talk about something that interests them, particularly when they have an appreciative audience.

Consequently, the more you can discover about the other person's interests and views prior to your meeting, the better. By building up something of a mental picture of the person you will be speaking to, you are likely to find it easier to talk to them about things that interest them. You will then find some common ground more quickly and this will significantly assist your negotiations with that person. You should also pay attention to any clues given by the person's appearance. For example, if someone walks into the office, puts down their set of golf clubs in a corner, and removes their Ferrari cap, it is pretty likely that golf and motor sports will be successful topics of conversation.

When talking to another person, consider the non-verbal signs you are sending to the other person. Are you presenting yourself as a normal, sociable and friendly person? Try to smile as much as possible: smiles are reassuring.

Which topics can be discussed?

In the absence of such helpful clues as described above, try to engage the other person on a neutral but reasonably interesting and relevant topic. Avoid any topic that might be taboo for the other person, or anything which might lead to violent disagreement (religion and politics are difficult subjects in this respect). Also think carefully about what the choice of topic conveys to the other person about you personally. Safe neutral subjects include the following:

- Conventional greeting ('Hello. How are you?'/'Nice to meet you', etc).
- Weather ('The weather's been great/awful recently, hasn't it?').
- Current events, so long as they are not of a politically sensitive nature.
- Sport ('Did you see the Formula 1 race at the weekend? Great to see Montoya get another win!').
- Personal interests.
- Family, particularly if you know the other person slightly ('How's Jane getting on? And the children? Wonderful!').
- What they did at the weekend ('Did you manage to get out in the sunshine at the weekend?').
- What they are going to do at the weekend ('What have you got planned for the weekend?').
- The other person's journey to your office ('Did you have a good journey here? I hope you managed to find us alright?').
- Show the other person around your office, commenting on key features and introducing key people ('This is my office'/'I'd like you to meet Daniel Jones, our finance director').
- (If arriving at someone else's office) praise the location and facilities ('Great location you have here – right in the centre of town!'/'That looks like a very useful piece of equipment').
- Offer refreshments to your guest (tea, coffee, water, orange juice, etc) ('Try one of these. It's a local speciality').

When approaching small talk it is important to try to sound interested, to avoid being too intrusive, and to recognise the point at which it is time to move on to more meaningful discussions.

1.3 Body language

Body language refers to the way in which people show their feelings by body movements or positions. Whilst it is relatively easy to control your speech, controlling your body language is remarkably difficult. For this reason, it is well worth paying attention to the body language of the people you are talking to – it will tell you a lot about how they feel about what you are saying. Perhaps most significantly, a careful reading of someone's body language will tell you whether what they feel or think differs from what they say they feel or think.

When considering body language, it is worth bearing in mind that the culture from which a person comes will have some effect on the way they use body language. To take an obvious example, an Italian negotiator is much more likely than a Finnish negotiator to use expansive arm and hand gestures.

In addition, certain aspects of body language have defined meanings in particular cultures. For example, in Pakistan extending a clenched fist towards someone represents an obscene insult. If an American executive leans back in his chair and links his fingers behind his head whilst speaking to you this is probably a bad sign. It means that he has decided that he does not need to demonstrate eagerness or attention towards you.

Some examples of body language, together with their possible meanings are given below:

Arms crossed. This usually represents defensiveness, arrogance, dislike or disagreement.

Eyebrows raised. Raised eyebrows generally mean uncertainty, disbelief, surprise or exasperation.

Fist clenched. A clenched fist usually accompanies an aroused emotional state (eg, anger or fear). In a business meeting a clenched fist often denotes anxiety or unstated disagreement.

Hands on hips. This usually indicates a preparedness to take action (eg, to take charge of the organisation of an event). It may also be used to signal a threat against others, or defensiveness against a perceived threat.

Hands behind head. This usually reflects negative thoughts or feelings. It can be taken as a sign of uncertainty, conflict, disagreement, frustration or anger.

Head tilted back. When someone has their head tilted back and is looking at you down their nose, this is a clear sign that they feel themselves to be superior to you.

Head tilted to one side. This can mean different things according to the situation in which it is used. It often indicates friendliness and rapport (for example, in the course of negotiations). It may also be a gesture of submissiveness (when showing respect to a superior). It can also be used to show coyness (when flirting).

Looking down. This usually accompanies feelings of defeat, guilt, shame or submission. It may indicate that the person is lying.

Palm down. A gesture made in which the hand is extended with the palm tilted down is usually a sign of confidence, assertiveness or dominance.

Palm up. A gesture made in which the hands are extended with the palm tilted up is usually a sign of friendliness, permissiveness or humility. It represents non-aggressiveness and vulnerability. A gesture in which both hands are extended together with the palms up can simply mean, 'I don't know'.

Shoulder shrug. A shrugged shoulder is usually a sign of uncertainty and submissiveness. It can simply mean, 'I don't know'.

Steeple. The steeple involves the placing together of the fingertips of both hands whilst speaking or listening. It is generally used to show that you are listening thoughtfully or thinking deeply.

Stroking chin. This gesture usually indicates that you are considering a point.

1.4 Tone of voice

A lot can be learned about someone's attitude or mood by the tone in which they speak. This of course does not register in written English. Attitude or mood in written English can usually only be ascertained from specific statements, and even then it is hard to differentiate between genuine expressions of attitude and conventional formal expressions. For example, the phrase 'we are pleased to send you the documents you requested' tells you nothing about whether the writer is really pleased or not.

The English written in legal contexts is usually neutral as to the feelings of the writer. For example, the words 'we cannot agree to that proposal' seen in writing simply tells you that the proposal cannot be accepted. It gives you no clue as to why the proposal cannot be accepted. In speech, the words 'we cannot agree to that proposal' could be spoken in a variety of different tones, each of which would tell you something different about the attitude of the speaker. For example:

Bored tone: the whole discussion is of little importance to the speaker.

Angry tone: the speaker is insulted by the proposal.

Dismissive tone: the proposal is not worth considering.

Thoughtful tone: the proposal is worth considering but ultimately is not acceptable. The stress in this version of the sentence might well be upon the word *that*, implying that although the speaker cannot agree to the particular proposal made, he or she might agree to a different proposal.

Conciliatory tone: the speaker does not want to antagonise the person who has made the proposal.

Condescending tone: the speaker believes that the person making the proposal is inferior or lacks credibility.

Incredulous tone: the speaker is amazed that such a proposal has been made.

Embarrassed tone: the speaker has to reject the proposal but is not comfortable with the fact that this has to be done.

1.5 Emphasis

One of the interesting aspects of spoken English is that the meaning of a statement which would seem perfectly clear when written down can be altered dramatically if the speaker places emphasis on a particular word or particular words in the statement. When speaking to someone in English you should pay attention both to the emphasis the other person places on particular words and to your own emphasis, otherwise misunderstandings can easily arise.

This point can be illustrated with this simple sentence:

The contract must be signed today.

This sentence could mean (emphasis in italics):

1 '*The* contract must be signed today.'
  It is a particular contract that must be signed today.
2 'The *contract* must be signed today.'
  It is the contract that must be signed, and not something else.
3 'The contract *must* be signed today.'
  There is an obligation that the contract be signed.
4 'The contract must be *signed* today.'
  The important thing is that the contract be signed (not drafted, agreed, etc).
5 'The contract must be signed *today*.'
  The important thing is that the signing of the contract happens today.
6 'The contract must be signed today' (with upward inflection of voice).
  Must the contract be signed today?

1.6 Techniques

There is always more than one way of approaching a discussion and there is always more than one way of saying something in English. The methods you choose will depend upon the subject you are discussing, with whom you are discussing it and what you want to achieve. The following chapters deal with certain well-known techniques which you will find useful when conducting interviews and negotiations with other lawyers and clients.

Humour

Humour can be very useful, particularly when making a presentation. It breaks the ice and establishes a warmer atmosphere. If a speaker can make an audience laugh, the audience will like the speaker more. Consequently, the audience will be more open to the speaker's ideas and therefore easier to persuade.

In a negotiation situation, the use of humour can be used to reduce the degree of opposition and mistrust between the parties negotiating against each other. The establishment of a warmer atmosphere will increase co-operation between the negotiators, making it more likely that mutually acceptable terms will be reached.

Implying

Implying means to suggest rather than to state directly. It can be a helpful tactic during negotiations, when you wish to choose language which will allow the discussions to continue so that positions can be explored. For example, you might wish to state your position on a subject but imply that if certain concessions were made by your opponent, you might be prepared to take a different view. In this situation it would be more helpful to say:

> £10,000 is the most we can offer based on our current understanding of your position.

rather than:

> We're not offering more than £10,000.

The first sentence states a position but implies that if certain unspecified concessions were to be made by the opponent, a better price might be offered. It provides an impetus for negotiations to continue. The second sentence states a position which the opponent can either accept or reject, but it provides no impetus for further negotiation.

Rhetorical questions

Rhetorical questions are questions asked in order to highlight an issue or argument rather than to obtain an answer. For example:

> Who would deny that a person who has suffered injury as a result of the negligence of others should be entitled to damages?

Rhetorical questions should not be over-used, but in moderation can be an effective way to illustrate a point.

Open questions

Open questions are those which can be answered in a variety of ways, where the response is left open to the person to whom you are speaking. They are a useful form of questioning in the early stages of an interview, when you wish to obtain information from the client, or in the early stages of a negotiation, when you wish to explore your opponent's position.

Most conversations taking place in a legal context involve a gradual move from an open-ended, exploratory questioning style towards a more closed, focused style. For example, when negotiating with another lawyer you might start with open-ended questions, such as 'What's your position on ...?'. This style is likely to be accompanied by the use of conditional verb forms; for example, when airing certain possible solutions at an early stage. You might say, for example, 'one possibility *might* be ...'. At the same time, you are likely to use neutral language. For example, you are likely to say, 'I'm *not sure* that is acceptable'.

Narrow and closed questions

Narrow questions seek specific information and only require short answers. For example:

> What's your best offer?

Closed questions are questions which can only be answered with a yes or a no. For example:

> Did you accept that offer?

Leading questions are a particular kind of closed question in which the question contains the answer. For example:

> You sold a batch of this product to Clamp Ltd at a unit price of 150 last month didn't you?

These kinds of questions are useful in client interviews when you require specific information or admissions of specific facts from the client. They are also useful when trying to bring negotiations to a close.

Simple or conditional forms?

Simple forms are always the best kind to use when asking a question to which you require a direct and factual answer ('What is your best price?') or when giving a final response to a question ('We can't accept that proposal').

The main drawback to using simple forms is that they do not usually help the dialogue to flow. They are therefore employed to best effect when closing a negotiation or interview, but are not helpful in the early stages when options are being explored. When suggesting a compromise or formulating a hypothesis, for example, conditional forms are indispensable:

We might agree to ... if you were prepared to ...

The use of *might* indicates to the other party that there is still room for discussion but does not commit you to any particular course of action. The negotiations can continue.

Conditional forms can also be used in a general way to soften the impact of what is being said. For example, in some situations it would be better to say, 'the right solution might be to ...' (which seems respectful and humble) rather than to say, 'the right solution is to ...' (which seems arrogant and presumptuous).

Choice of terminology

English contains a large number of synonyms. Consequently, you are likely to have a wide choice of different words all meaning roughly the same thing at your disposal in any given situation. You should pay close attention to your choice of words – they are not all neutral, but laden with values and connotations. For example, consider this list of words, all of which refer to making a living:

- calling
- career
- profession
- employment
- job
- work
- occupation
- vocation

Whilst all of these words basically refer to the same thing, they have different connotations. Words like *calling* and *vocation* imply an elevated sense of a person's ultimate role in life, whereas *job* implies little more than work done in return for money. *Employment* is the most neutral term in the list.

Diplomatic language

When dealing with difficult or sensitive subjects – or difficult or sensitive people – it is sensible to choose your words carefully. The following suggestions indicate how to soften the way in which you express yourself:

- Using *would, could* or *might* to make what you say sound more tentative. For example, you might say, 'this could be a problem' instead of 'this is a problem' in order to leave open the possibility that it may be possible to find a solution to the problem.

- Presenting your view as a question not a statement. For example, you might say, 'how about offering them £10,000?' instead of 'we'll offer them £10,000' in order to leave the matter open for further discussion.

- Using an introductory phrase to prepare the listener for your message. For example, 'Here's one possibility. Suppose we ...' OR 'We'd like to make an offer to settle this case. This is what we were thinking ...'.

- Adding *I'm afraid* to make clear that you recognise the unhelpfulness of your response. For example, 'That's the most we can offer I'm afraid'.

- Using words which qualify or restrict what you say to make your position more flexible (*a bit difficult, a slight problem*). For example, you might say, 'We have a slight problem with that proposal. We don't like clause seven'. This leaves greater room for flexibility than saying: 'We can't accept clause seven.'

- Using *not* with a positive word instead of the obvious negative word. For example, *not very convenient* = I don't agree.

- Using a comparative (*better, more convenient*) to soften your message. For example, 'It would be better if you could agree to ...' instead of 'This proposal is not acceptable. We want ...'.

- Using a continuous form (*I was wondering*) instead of a simple form (*I wondered*) to make a suggestion more flexible. For example, 'we were wondering if you'd like to make a proposal at this point'.

Metaphors and similes

A metaphor is a figure of speech in which a word or phrase is used to stand for something else, for example, *food for thought*.

A simile is a figure of speech in which one thing is compared to another of a different kind, using the words *as* or *like* (*like a rolling stone, as safe as houses*).

Both of these techniques can be useful ways of illustrating a point. A good example is Winston Churchill's phrase *the Iron Curtain*, used to devastating effect to create a mental picture of the divide created by the USSR's influence in eastern Europe. However, metaphors and similes must be carefully handled. Clichéd expressions should be avoided. The figure of speech being used must be relevant to the matter being discussed.

2 INTERVIEWING AND ADVISING

2.1 Purpose and content

An interview is a conversation designed to achieve a purpose. It is an art rather than a science. However, some suggestions can be made as to how the interviewer should handle the interview so that it is effective.

The essence of an interview between a lawyer and a client is an exchange of information and views. The lawyer requires certain information from the client in order to advise the client. The client wants advice from the lawyer. The lawyer and the client must then jointly decide what should be done to progress the case, and what each of them must do to contribute to this process. In addition, the lawyer must ensure that the client has been informed of and understands certain vital points. These include:

- How much the client will have to pay for the lawyer's services.
- What the lawyer can and cannot do for the client.
- What further information the lawyer needs from the client and why this information is needed.
- What steps the lawyer proposes to take on the client's behalf.
- The timeframe within which these steps will be taken.
- The prospects of success in the client's case (and the strengths and weaknesses of the client's case).

There may be other vital factors according to the type of case being handled and the client's own expectations. Establishing clear understanding with the client is crucial – if the client has not clearly understood these important issues, there is a strong likelihood that he or she may become frustrated or angry at a later stage if the case does not proceed according to his or her expectations. These expectations may of course be wildly unrealistic – it is the lawyer's role to 'manage the client's expectations'.

Overall, the importance of good communication cannot be over-stressed. Research carried out in the UK by the Royal Commission on Legal Services in the early 1990s cited poor communication as the main reason for clients' dissatisfaction with their legal advisers.

2.2 Preparation

Preparation is of fundamental importance. Here are some tips:

- Determine, if possible, the purpose of the meeting. When dealing with the first interview with a new client, it is helpful to instruct staff who book client interviews to obtain as much information from the client as possible about the nature of the legal issue on which they want your advice. If possible, handle the first enquiry from the prospective client yourself.
- Consider the most appropriate structure for the meeting.
- Plan an agenda.
- If the client has been referred from a colleague, speak to that colleague about the work being carried out for the client.
- If dealing with a corporate client, carry out some research into the client's company.
- If dealing with an old client of the firm, retrieve the old files for the client and refresh your memory about the cases that the firm has handled for the client.
- Prepare the physical setting – clear your desk to avoid that omnipresent law firm panic/chaos look. A physical setting that is informal, friendly and private will help make the client feel relaxed and comfortable. If you need access to your computer during the meeting, have it started and readily accessible.
- Avoid interruptions – particularly avoid having to take phone calls mid-interview.
- Be prepared to offer the client refreshments – coffee, tea, water, etc.
- If the client has special needs (eg, is disabled, blind, requires a translator) ensure that the appropriate arrangements are made beforehand.

Certain types of case lend themselves to the use of checklists and factsheets. Using these will help ensure that you obtain the most important facts in respect of the client's case during the first interview. They can be completed in the client's presence during the course of the interview. Some care should be taken about the making of notes – whilst it is important to obtain all the relevant facts, the client will not like it if you spend all your time staring down at your notebook. Try to maintain eye contact with the client and do not allow your note-taking to impede the flow of conversation.

2.3 Conducting the interview

The purpose of the interview is for the lawyer and client to work together to identify the client's interests and achieve the client's aims. Ideally, the lawyer should know the topic of the interview in advance. This will allow him or her to determine what is relevant and to structure the interview so that all the relevant information is obtained.

However, the structure of the interview should not be too rigid. The lawyer must ensure that a natural flow of conversation, involving a genuine exchange of views, occurs. The interview should flow naturally from one topic to the next. It should feel comfortable and positive – it should not be marked by a series of highly specific questions. Clients do not enjoy being interrogated!

Language

Lawyers must try to avoid using legal jargon when speaking to clients. Jargon has its uses within the legal community – it is a shared language full of familiar terms and common expressions – but it is likely to mystify and alienate the client. Its use also helps perpetuate the unhelpful idea that the law is profoundly complex and completely beyond the understanding of ordinary people.

Try to speak plainly, using everyday terms. Find alternatives for legal jargon. For example, do not say, 'We will effect postal service upon the defendant company'. Say instead:

> We will send the documents to Acme Ltd by post.

Where the use of legal jargon is inevitable, ensure that you explain its meaning to the client. For example:

> This is a retention of title clause. A retention of title clause is a clause in the contract which specifies the circumstances under which ownership of the goods passes from company X to company Y.

Listening

Listening is different from hearing and is actually quite difficult. Hearing is the process of receiving information. Listening is the mental processing of what you have heard. You need to pay attention not only to what is said, but also to what is left unsaid, and to the body language which accompanies what is said.

The average rate of speech is between 125 to 175 words per minute, and the average rate at which information is processed is between 400 to 800 words per minute. The listener should therefore be able to assimilate thoughts, organise them and respond to the speaker and have time spare to deal with other unrelated mental processes.

Questioning

Different kinds of questions should be used in different situations and stages of the interview. Open questions are useful when seeking general information about the case from the client. They are particularly suitable when the facts lend themselves to narrative or chronological development, for example, in many litigation scenarios ('Tell me more about that?', 'What happened next?').

Open questions do not pressure the client into responding to specific lines of questioning, and are therefore useful when dealing with sensitive subjects. However, open questions used in isolation are unlikely to provide the interviewer with sufficient specific information.

Narrow or closed questions are useful when you need specific information from the client ('What time was it when that happened?'). They should not be overused, however, as the client will soon begin to feel that he or she is being forced into a passive position in the conversation.

Leading questions are a type of narrow question in which the question contains its own answer ('The weather is lovely today, isn't it?'). They can be used aggressively ('Isn't it true that you drank eight vodkas before you drove home?'). However, such questions may also be used to express empathy with the client ('You're feeling depressed because you worked so hard to get your business going and now it looks as if you might go bankrupt?').

This style of questioning can also be employed to show acceptance by the lawyer of the client's behaviour. Kinsey, who carried out extensive research into sexual behaviour, used this style of questioning to obtain information for precisely this reason. A question like 'When did you have your first homosexual experience?' takes the behaviour for granted, leaving the person being interviewed to confirm the interviewer's expectations.

Feedback

Feedback falls into two parts. Firstly, it may be used with the intention of allowing the lawyer to summarise what he or she has been told by the client and clarify it with the client. The lawyer might say, 'So let's see if I've got this right. You told me that ...', or 'OK, we've identified about five or so issues which we need to look at a bit more'. This process allows the lawyer to investigate further the matters being summarised and invite the client to expand upon or clarify certain issues.

Secondly, feedback may be used to encourage the client to communicate with the lawyer, for example, when the client seems to lack confidence about the relevance of an issue ('I'm not sure if this is relevant, but ...'). Giving positive feedback at this stage ('Please tell me what's on your mind. I'm here to listen and help as much as I can.') enables the lawyer to obtain fuller information from the client than might otherwise be possible. It is also important to give continuous feedback to the client in the form of short phrases which tell the client that you are listening carefully. You should encourage the client to speak by using phrases and words like 'I see', 'that's interesting', 'go on', 'right', 'yes', etc. Even meaningless encouraging noises ('mmm', 'uh-huh', etc) can be helpful in this context. They signal to the client that you are still listening.

Body language

It is important to demonstrate interest in the client and in what the client is telling you. Pay attention to your body language in this regard. The skills needed can be summed up by the acronym S-O-L-E-R:

S   – Face the client Squarely, adopting a posture that indicates involvement.

O   – Adopt an Open posture, one which suggests that you are receptive to the client.

L – Lean slightly forward; not aggressively, but enough to show that you are interested in the client.

E – Maintain Eye contact, but do not stare. Use your eyes to show interest, but vary your eye contact in response to the flow of the questioning.

R – Stay Relaxed. Do not fidget, try to be natural in your expressions.

Identifying the client's aims

What does the client really want? The answer may be simple – the client may have told you at the outset. Sometimes, however, it is necessary to dig a little deeper. What are the client's underlying concerns? What would he or she regard as a satisfactory result? Is the client in dispute with another business with which the client has an ongoing relationship? Is the health of the long-term relationship of more value than the short-term breach?

It may also become clear in the course of your discussions with the client that the client has other problems of which he or she may be unaware, or may not have regarded as problematic. You will need to point these matters out in an appropriate way and either advise the client upon them or arrange for the client to be referred to one of your colleagues on the matter.

Perceived irrelevance

A common problem in interviews is that the client may become confused or frustrated because he or she cannot see the connection between the questions you are asking and the issue on which he or she has sought your advice. The client is unlikely to be a lawyer and will not think like a lawyer, and may therefore perceive your questions as irrelevant. The client's perception of relevance and need may not, in short, match your own.

This problem highlights the importance of lawyer-client communication. The only way to tackle the issue is to explain carefully to the client why the question is relevant to the issue on which your advice has been sought. For example, 'I need to ask you a couple of questions about ... because ...'.

2.4 Checklist

This checklist is designed to help you to prepare for and structure a client interview.

Preparation

- Purpose of meeting?
- Structure?
- Agenda?

- Ongoing work for client? Which lawyer is handling it?
- Client company researched?
- Previous files retrieved?
- Any special needs of client?

Opening

Greet client, offer refreshments, preliminary small talk.

- Obtain the client's account, concerns and goals.
- Explain preliminary matters including fees, retainer, what can and can't be done for the client, and the nature and proposed structure of the interview.

Listening and questioning

- Listen actively to the client's account and show understanding of it.
- Use appropriate questioning techniques (open, closed and leading questions) where necessary to:
  - prompt,
  - clarify,
  - prevent deviation, and
  - probe.
- Pay attention to body language – S-O-L-E-R.
- Identify aims of the client.
- Take notes discreetly (use checklist if appropriate).
- Give feedback.

Summarising

- Summarise the client's account, concerns and goals.
- Identify the relevant facts.
- Identify deficiencies in the available facts.
- Avoid giving premature legal advice.
- Seek further information from the client.

Advising

- Give a brief introduction to the advising process.
- Give a brief outline of the relevant law.
- Apply the law to the client's problem.
- Outline the available legal and non-legal options.
- Discuss the available options with the client and help him or her reach a decision if appropriate.

Concluding

- Confirm whether lawyer is to be retained.
- Describe clearly follow-up action to be taken by lawyer.
- Describe clearly follow-up action to be taken by client.
- Give clear timeframes for action and future meetings.
- Confirm the follow-up procedures with the client.
- Conclude interview appropriately.

Throughout

- Establish and maintain rapport with client.
- Use appropriate language.
- Maintain professional courtesy.
- Move smoothly between interview stages.
- Deal appropriately with any issues of professional conduct or ethics.

2.5 Suggested language

Opening

Making introductions

> Good morning/good afternoon ... I am ... and this is my colleague
> Mr/Miss/Ms/Mrs ...

Ice-breaking

> Is this your first visit to ...?
>
> I hope that you had no trouble finding our office?
>
> It looks as if the weather is going to improve/get worse.
>
> Would you like a cup of tea/coffee?
>
> [If you know the client slightly] How was your weekend?
>
> OR
>
> How is/how are ...[mention wife/husband/girlfriend/boyfriend/children/colleague]?

Opening the discussion

How can I help you?

OR

[If you know what topic the client wants to discuss] I understand that you would like some advice on ...? Perhaps you could tell me a bit about the background.

Advising as to the structure of the interview

OK, perhaps we should start with you giving me some information about the case. After that we can discuss what might be done and then we can think about the way forward. Do you mind if I make a few notes as we're talking?

OR

I think we should start with ... Then we can go on to look at ... Is that OK with you?

Advising about fees

I should mention at this point how this firm's charging system works. We charge by the hour and my hourly rate is ...

OR

I should start by letting you know what our charges are likely to be. A realistic estimate for carrying out this kind of work would be ...

Listening and questioning

Obtaining information from client

Perhaps you could tell me a bit about ...

OR

Maybe you could give me some background information ...

OR

OK, perhaps you could tell me what happened ...

Focusing on a particular issue

Tell me more about that.

OR

What happened next?

OR

You told me that ...

Summarising

Let me see if I've got this right. You told me that ...

OR

OK, we've identified about three or four issues which we need to focus on. These are ...

OR

To sum up, there seems to be ...

Clarifying

Perhaps I should make that clearer by saying ...

OR

Perhaps we should just go over that issue again ...

Preventing deviation

That's an interesting point. However, I'm not sure it's strictly relevant to the issues we need to discuss. I think it would be better to focus on ... Perhaps you could tell me about ...

OR

That's interesting. Perhaps we could come back to that point in a moment.

Interrupting

If I might just interrupt you for a moment, I'd like to …

OR

I'm sorry, you've lost me there. You were saying …?

OR

Can I just stop you there a moment? I'd like to clarify …

Stopping interruptions

If I could just finish what I was saying …

Moving to the next point

OK, I think we've covered that point. Let's move on to the question of …

OR

Let's leave this point for a moment and move on to …

OR

We'll come back to this issue in a while, but let's move on to …

OR

OK, I think I understand that issue. Perhaps you could tell me about …

Highlighting relevant facts

OK, I think the key points are …

OR

What you told me about … seems to me to be important.

OR

The central issues are …

Advising

Identifying the client's aims

> What would be an ideal outcome for you?
>
> OR
>
> Perhaps you could let me know what your priorities are in this matter.
>
> OR
>
> What would you like me to do for you, ideally?

Giving information on the advising process

> OK, we've been over the key issues in this matter. I think it would be helpful now to look at what your legal and non-legal options might be. I'll give you a quick rundown of the applicable law and how it relates to your case. Then we can discuss what we should do to move things forward.

Advising on the relevant law

> The legal position is as follows ...
>
> OR
>
> This question is governed by the law of ...

Outlining the client's options

> You have two or three options here. The first is ...
>
> OR
>
> The best thing to do, from a legal point of view, would be to ... However, we should also consider the non-legal factors such as ...
>
> OR
>
> [Indicating merits of options] Your first option would be to ... The main benefit of taking that course is ... There are some issues to consider and these are ...

Pointing out legal issues overlooked by the client

Incidentally, you should also consider the question of ... I am not a specialist in that field, but my colleague ... would be very happy to advise you on it. Would you like me to arrange an appointment for you?

OR

One issue which I would advise you to give some thought to is ... My advice on that matter is ...

Concluding

Confirming whether lawyer is to be retained

I would be more than happy to handle this case for you. Perhaps you could let me know how you wish to proceed?

Describing follow-up action to be taken by lawyer

What I will do now is ... [eg, write to X]. I will do this by [date].

OR

These are the steps we are going to take ... These will be completed by [date]. Then we will ...

Describing follow-up action to be taken by client, and timeframe

Could you let us have [eg, the following documents] ... by [date].

OR

[Stressing that nothing can be done until client provides further information] As soon as I have heard from you with/received from you the ... then I will be in a position to ...

Concluding interview

OK, I think that covers everything we need to discuss today, unless there's anything else you'd like to discuss?

OR

That seems to cover everything. Are there any other matters you'd like to discuss/any matters you'd like further information about?

Getting rid of clients who seem unwilling to leave

I think we've covered all of the issues now. We do make a point of trying to keep clients' legal costs down at this firm, so with that in mind perhaps we could bring this meeting to conclusion. Don't hesitate to phone or email me if you have any further questions at a later stage.

OR

I'm sorry, but I have another appointment at ... [mention rapidly-approaching time] in ... [mention faraway place].

OR

OK, I don't want to waste any more of your valuable time.

Another good ploy (if you know that you are dealing with a time-wasting client) is to ask your secretary/assistant/colleague to phone you if the meeting runs on past a certain time with news of an 'emergency' which you will have to rush off to deal with.

Seeing the client out

Thanks for coming in to see us today. Don't hesitate to phone or send me an email if you have any questions you'd like to ask/need any information on anything. If I'm out, my secretary/assistant/colleague Mr/Mrs/Ms ... would be glad to help you.

3 NEGOTIATION

3.1 Negotiation styles and strategies

Negotiation style refers to the personal behaviour the negotiator uses to carry out the strategy that he or she has chosen. Three main styles of negotiation have been identified, and these are usually referred to as co-operative, adversarial and problem-solving.

Negotiation strategy refers to the specific goals to be achieved and the pattern of conduct that should improve the chances of achieving those goals.

Research has found that all effective negotiators have a number of features in common – they prepare on the facts, prepare on the law, take satisfaction in using their legal skills, are effective trial advocates and are self-controlled.

The main features of the the three main styles of negotiation are summarised below:

Co-operative	Adversarial	Problem-solving
Participants are friends	Participants are opponents	Participants are problem-solvers
The aim is agreement	The aim is victory	The aim is a wise outcome reached efficiently and amicably
Make concessions to cultivate the relationship	Demand concessions as a condition of the relationship	Separate the people from the problem
Be soft on the people and the problem	Be hard on the people and the problem	Be soft on the people, hard on the problem
Trust others	Distrust others	Proceed independent of trust
Change your position easily	Stick to your position	Focus on interests, not positions
Make offers	Make threats	Explore interests
Reveal your bottom line	Mislead as to your bottom line	Avoid having a bottom line

Accept one-sided losses to reach agreement	Demand one-sided gains as the price of agreement	Invent options for mutual gain
Search for the single answer: the one they will accept	Search for the single answer: the one you will accept	Develop multiple options to choose from; decide later
Insist on agreement	Insist on your position	Insist on objective criteria
Try to avoid a contest of will	Try to win a contest of will	Try to reach a result based on standards independent of will
Yield to pressure	Apply pressure	Reason and be open to reason; yield to principle not pressure

Adversarial/co-operative

Adversarial and co-operative styles of negotiation can be regarded as different forms of positional bargaining. In effect, both styles draw on the principle that the negotiators are opponents. The difference between them is the degree to which the co-operative negotiator is prepared to work with the other side in resolving the differences between them.

By contrast, the stereotypical adversarial negotiator is a tough and aggressive advocate whose aim is victory by defeating the opponent, in much the same manner as he or she might do in court.

Problem-solving

The problem-solving style can be characterised as a form of principled bargaining. Problem-solving negotiators 'separate the people from the problem' and seek to negotiate in a non-confrontational and non-judgmental way, by applying standards of fairness and reasonableness.

Fisher and Murray summarise the essentials of this approach in their book *Getting to Yes*:

> In most instances, to ask a negotiator 'who's winning?' is as inappropriate as to ask who's winning a marriage. If you ask that question about your marriage, you have already lost the most important negotiation – the one about what kind of game to play, about the way you deal with each other and your shared and differing interests.

Negotiation strategies compared

Competitive/Adversarial	Problem-solving
The negotiator	**The negotiator**
Tries to maximise resource gains for own client	Tries to maximise returns for own client including any joint gains available
Makes high opening demands and is slow to concede	Focuses on common interests of parties
Uses threats, confrontation, argument	Tries to understand the merits as objectively as possible
Manipulates people and the process	Uses non-confrontational debating techniques
Is not open to persuasion on substance	Is open to persuasion on substance
Is oriented to qualitative and competitive goals	Is oriented to qualitative goals: fair, wise, durable agreement
Negotiator's assumptions	**Negotiator's assumptions**
Motivation is competitive/antagonistic	Common interests valued
Limited resources	Limited resources with unlimited variation and personal preferences
Independent choices: tomorrow's decision unaffected materially by today's decision	Interdependence recognised
Goal	**Goal**
Win as much as possible and especially more than the other side	Mutually agreeable solution that is fair and efficient for all parties
Weaknesses	**Weaknesses**
Strong bias towards confrontation, encouraging the use of coercion and emotional pressure as persuasive means: hard on relationships, breeding mistrust, feelings of separateness, frustration and anger,	Strong bias towards co-operation, creating internal pressures to compromise and accommodate

resulting in more frequent breakdowns in negotiations; distorting communications, producing misinformation and misjudgments	
Guards against responsiveness and openness to opponent, thereby restricting possibility of joint gains	Avoid strategies that are confrontational because they risk impasse, which is viewed as failure
Encourages breakdown by creating many opportunities for impasse	Focuses on being sensitive to other's perceived interests; increases vulnerability to deception and manipulation by a competitive opponent. Increases possibility that settlement may be more favourable to other side than may be fair
Increases difficulty in predicting responses of opponent because reliance is on manipulation and confrontation	Increases difficulty in establishing definite aspiration level and bottom lines because of reliance on qualitative goals
Contributes to over-estimation of return possible through all alternatives (court, arbitration) because it does not focus on a relatively objective analysis of substantive merits as standard for resolution	Requires substantial skill and knowledge of process to do well
	Requires strong confidence in own assessment powers regarding interest/needs of other side and other's payoff schedule

3.2 Differences in negotiation language between USA and UK

In section 5 of the Introduction we saw that there are certain differences between American and British English. These are relatively minor in comparison to the differences which exist in the mentality and cultural values of the two countries. This chapter briefly summarises how these differences affect the way American and British people use English in negotiations. Note that the USA and UK are selected here purely on the basis that they are the most prominent English-speaking countries. Differences also exist in the way in which other English-speaking countries, such as Australia, New Zealand, Canada and South Africa, use the language in negotiations.

British	American
Formal and reserved on first meeting (informal later on)	Informal and friendly from the start (but initial friendliness may be forced)
Prefer to use indirect language ('I'm not quite with you on that')	Prefer to use direct language ('You're talking bullshit')
Tend to use understatement ('that might be a bit difficult')	Tend to exaggerate ('this is the best deal you'll ever get')
Use irony	May misunderstand irony
Rarely disagree openly (but will qualify agreement or use non-committal terms to indicate lack of enthusiasm about a proposal)	Will disagree openly if necessary
Use humour as a tactic in itself (to break tension, speed up discussion, criticise someone or introduce a new idea)	Use humour to break the ice
Insular but have some cultural awareness	Insular, may be culturally naïve
Use vagueness as a tactic (to confuse or delay)	Dislike tactics to delay negotiations but use vagueness to confuse
Dislike making decision during first meeting	Will press for decision on main points during first meeting (and work out details later)
Generally interested in long-term relationships rather than making a quick buck	Interested in getting the deal
Patient	Impatient ('time is money')
May not reveal bottom line (may be plotting against you)	Likely to place cards on the table and work towards a deal by exchange of offer and counter-offer
Do not usually respond well to hard sell tactics	Require and expect hard sell
Often use woolly, old-fashioned phrasing (may be trying to trick you into underestimating their abilities)	Enthusiastic use of latest business jargon
Apparent formality may conceal more individualistic tendencies	Apparent informality and friendliness may conceal deeply conservative beliefs

Appear to 'muddle through' without clear aims (but known for lateral thinking)	Have a plan and pursue it aggressively, persistently and consistently
May resort to sarcasm when angry ('That's a fantastic idea! You must be a genius!')	May resort to threats when angry, particularly a threat to end the negotiations there and then if progress is not being made ('I can see these talks are going nowhere')

American business and legal people have the reputation of being the world's toughest, most aggressive negotiators. However, they are relatively consistent and rarely renege once a deal has been struck. They are also often naïve about the culture of other countries. This means you have one important advantage over them: you know a lot more about them than they know about you. This can be exploited by at times negotiating on the American wavelength and at other times shifting to the cultural norms of your own countries.

British negotiators often like to present themselves as diplomatic amateurs. They often appear to 'muddle through' negotiations without any clear idea of what they wish to achieve. However, do not underestimate the British love of plotting (evidenced by the fact that one of Britain's national heroes, Guy Fawkes, was a man who plotted to blow up Parliament). Be aware that the woolly exterior may in fact conceal a considerable capacity for ruthlessness when needed. However, like American negotiators they rarely renege once a deal has been struck. The apparent disorganisation of some British negotiators is often viewed as a weak point by Americans and they may instinctively increase the aggressiveness of their approach when confronted with this style in order to 'break' their counterpart.

3.3 The qualities of a good negotiator

The qualities of a good negotiator are as follows:

- The ability to listen and observe.
- The ability to assess any change in power.
- The ability to be persuasive.
- Assertiveness – distinguish from aggressiveness.
- Total commitment to the client's case.
- Patience and remaining cool under pressure.
- Maintaining self-control.
- Knowing the value to the client of each item to be negotiated – and, if possible, to the other side.
- Flexibility – thinking laterally – and imagination.
- Avoiding cornering your opponent – and avoiding impasse.
- Knowing when to conclude.

- Being realistic, rational and reasonable.
- The ability to self-evaluate.
- 'Put yourself in the other side's shoes – but don't stay there too long.'

3.4 Preparation: five-step plan

Step 1: Research facts and law

Without a sound grasp of the facts and the applicable law, effective negotiation is impossible. Before the negotiation you should do the following:

- Review the case file.
- Consider the history and development of the case and identify the relevant facts.
- Identify the legal issues for each set of facts.
- Review agreements similar to those that will be the subject of the negotiation.
- Review the position of your opponents. How do they view the facts, what interpretations of the law favour their standpoint, what strengths and weaknesses are there in their case? You then need to prepare a balance sheet matching the strengths and weaknesses in each side's case.

Step 2: Establish the client's aims and agree a strategy

You need to explore the full range of options that might be available to you, discuss these with your client, and then develop specific objectives for achieving these in the context of a particular negotiation.

The client needs to be advised that sticking at a certain point could lead to deadlock. A client who intends to adopt a co-operative strategy also needs to be warned that this could provide an opportunity for exploitation by the other side.

Step 3: Identify the client's BATNA (best alternative to a negotiated agreement)

Negotiation is one of several means that might be used to achieve your client's aims. The best test of any proposed joint agreement is whether it offers better value than any other solution outside of an agreement.

You should always seek to identify your client's best alternative to a negotiated agreement (BATNA). Your client's BATNA is the standard against which any proposed agreement is measured. Developing a BATNA protects your client from accepting terms that are too unfavourable and from rejecting terms that it would be in the client's best interests to accept. It provides a realistic measure against which you can measure all offers.

Alternatives to an agreement might involve:

- Agreement with another party.

- Unilateral action.
- Mediation or arbitration.
- Going to court.

Working out a BATNA should provide you with a feel for what may be acceptable and what is not. To work out a BATNA you should construct a list of actions that your client might take if no agreement is reached, then select the option that seems best. You should then measure all proposed settlements against this alternative option.

Step 4: Decide what information you need to obtain

Information is continually exchanged during negotiations, and as this process occurs each party learns more and more about its opponent.

You should identify the following in advance of the meeting:

- The information that you need from the negotiation.
- The information that the other side is likely to protect.
- Any information that you want to give to the other side.

Step 5: Plan the agenda

An agenda should identify and illustrate the issues in dispute. It should distinguish three different dimensions of the negotiation:

- Content: the range of topics to be settled.
- Procedures: the manner in which the negotiation will take place, the control of the meetings, the matters to be discussed, the preliminaries, the timing of the different phases of the meeting.
- Personal interaction: the manner in which the individuals involved in negotiating interact with each other.

3.5   Conducting a negotiation

Approaching the negotiation meeting

Negotiation meetings tend to follow a basic pattern:

1   The parties meet.
2   The parties explore each other's positions.
3   They then start a process of persuasion. Offers are made and considered and information is exchanged.
4   The parties then begin to narrow their differences – some issues are agreed and further problems are identified.
5   The negotiation is brought to conclusion.

The way in which this process is handled will depend on the negotiation strategy each party is using.

A problem-solving negotiator will aim to identify mutual needs and produce solutions that satisfy both parties. He or she will seek to expand the options available to each party in a win/win negotiation.

An adversarial negotiator will try to maximise the gain to his or her client in a win/lose situation. He or she will seek the best for the client by denying options to the other side, and will only make concessions if absolutely necessary. The adversarial style can lead to deadlock and adversarial negotiators may have to switch to a more co-operative style towards the end of the negotiation.

Opening

Problem-solving negotiator. A problem-solving negotiator will aim to create an atmosphere that is cordial, collaborative but businesslike. He or she will start with some neutral non-business topic and will avoid sitting opposite the opponent – this can set up a face-to-face confrontation from the start. A problem-solver is likely to have prepared an outline agenda prepared and may start by seeking agreement with the other side about the procedure to be followed.

Adversarial negotiator. An adversarial negotiator is likely to keep the opening phases of the negotiation short and try to use it to project power and establish a psychologically dominant position. The negotiator will engage in initial ice-breaking, to establish a basis for communication, but will be brisk and businesslike. He or she will then move swiftly on to business, without discussing the procedures to be followed.

Exploring positions

Problem-solving negotiator. A problem-solving negotiator will wish to tackle each of the issues across a broad front. This leads to a process in which the overall pattern is cleared and some progress is made on some of the issues. Then the discussion moves on to consider each aspect of the broad pattern. Finally, the parties move into more detailed discussion of the issues. The object of structuring the discussion is to facilitate agreement.

In a problem-solving situation, each party will make a brief opening statement which should present their view of the overall negotiation, identify the party's interest, specify how each party can contribute to achieving a solution for mutual gain and stress those areas in which agreement has already been reached. The parties will then try to identify issues for mutual gain.

Adversarial negotiator. An adversarial negotiator will consider whether to start with the most difficult issues or the least difficult issues.

A co-operative negotiator might wish to start with the least difficult issues, since this is likely to lead to success for both parties in the early stages, thus creating a good working relationship. The negotiator may then be able to gain concessions on bigger and more difficult issues.

A competitive negotiator may wish to start with big and difficult issues. In this way he or she issues a challenge to the opponent and destroys the expectation that the early stages of the negotiation may be marked by civility and trust.

Persuading and making offers

Problem-solving negotiator. A problem-solving negotiator may wish to generate solutions by making hypothetical suggestions instead of concrete offers. He or she may introduce a proposal on a 'what if?' basis, and invite the other side to develop it further. Neither side is obliged to make any commitment or oppose the idea. A more relaxed discussion can then follow, with adjustments to the original idea arising as a result of the joint discussion.

The problem-solving negotiator will try to make it as easy as possible for the other side to shift their position and agree on a compromise. This is achieved by stressing the benefits that a proposed solution offers the other party.

Adversarial negotiator. An adversarial negotiator is more likely to make a concrete offer. He or she is likely to make it at an early stage – by making the first offer, the adversarial negotiator seizes the agenda and clarifies the issues at stake. The offer should be made as soon as the negotiator has assessed the other side's strengths, weaknesses and bargaining positions.

All offers should be justified. By articulating a justification, commitment to that position is conveyed. The other side are forced to confront the justification.

When making an offer, the adversarial negotiator will start with a high opening position. There is a high correlation between the amount of the negotiator's original demand and the ultimate payoff. But the offer should be reasonable – if it is unreasonable, the other side may conclude that the parties are so far apart that it is not worth negotiating further.

The initial proposals must be made firmly. The offer should be specific so as to create commitment. The sum proposed should be exact – not 'around about' or 'in the region of'.

The offer should also be justified. The negotiator should express commitment to his or her offer to show that it is not negotiable.

Narrowing differences

Problem-solving negotiator. Problem-solvers will take care to ensure that the creative possibilities of any hypothetical or concrete proposals are fully explored before taking any decision. They will ask themselves questions like:

- Can a proposal actually achieve a wider benefit than first seems possible?
- Can a new condition be introduced to compensate for the disadvantage of any concession that may be made?
- Can agreement on an apparently minor issue create a useful precedent for use at some later stage?

- Can the negotiation and its outcome be used to create or improve a favourable, more general, relationship with the other party?

Adversarial negotiator. When trying to achieve agreement, the adversarial negotiator is likely to use certain tactics designed to force the opponent to accept his or her offer. For example, the negotiator may seek to 'educate' the other side by expressing anger, using threats and presenting arguments. He or she may also seek to enhance his or her own power by releasing information which suggests that there is no clear alternative to settlement.

As each party learns more about the other's position, the differences between them are likely to narrow. Eventually the adversarial negotiator may switch to a more co-operative style to avoid deadlock. This may lead to certain concessions being made, although an adversarial negotiator will seek to reach agreement whilst making as few concessions as possible. Concessions are only made in response to concessions from the other side.

Closing the negotiation

Once agreement has been reached, it is essential to record all the elements of the agreement in a summary. You should check for clarification and confirm the details of the agreement in writing. Heads of agreement can be useful in this situation.

Where the parties cannot reach agreement on every detail, a draft agreement can be drawn up as a basis for agreement. The idea is that an initial draft is produced, which does not purport to be complete. It is acknowledged to have faults, but is to be used as a basis for further negotiation. Each party is encouraged to make suggestions for improvement. These suggestions are noted and agreed suggestions are incorporated into the text.

3.6 Negotiation ploys

A ploy is defined in the Oxford English Dictionary as 'a cunning act performed to gain an advantage'. A number of standard ploys are often used in commercial negotiations. They are worth knowing about – you may not wish to use such tactics yourself but you will certainly wish to know when your opponent is using a ploy against you. Here are some of the more common ploys.

The bogey

This is a buyer's ploy. The buyer assures the seller that he or she loves the product but has a very limited budget, so that in order for a sale to occur the seller must reduce the price.

The idea is to test the credibility of the seller's price. The seller might react positively by revealing information about costing, so that you can force the price downwards. It may also provoke the seller to look at your real needs.

'I am only a simple grocer'

The idea of this ploy is to make your opponent believe they are dealing with an inexperienced negotiator because he or she claims to be 'only a simple grocer'. They may then relax too much and commit indiscretions about their objectives, tactics and intentions. In fact, although you claim to be 'only a simple grocer', you are the managing director of the world's largest chain of grocery stores.

'I'm sorry I've made a mistake'

This is an irritating and rather dishonest ploy used by sellers. You order some goods at £4.55 per item. The seller then calls you back claiming that he or she has made a mistake in the arithmetic of the order you placed. Instead of the products costing £4.55 each, they actually cost £4.95 each. The seller then claims that he or she cannot sell them at £4.55 because his or her boss will not authorise the sale.

   If you believe the seller to be genuine, you agree to the higher price. If you do not, you cancel the order. Buyers usually submit to the ploy.

Minimum order ploy

This is a ploy used by the seller whereby the seller maximises the value of the order by placing restrictions or conditions on the order the buyer has placed. Examples include:

These are only sold in packs of 12.

If we represent you in the purchase of the building, we must also act as letting agents if you acquire it.

Over and under ploy

This ploy is a handy response to a demand made by your opponent. For example, your opponent might demand that you reduce your price by 5% if they pay your invoice within seven days. You could respond with an 'over and under': 'if you agree to a 5% premium for late payment'.

Quivering quill

This is a ploy used by buyers in which the buyer demands concessions at the very point of closing the deal. At this point, the buyer is about to sign the contract and suddenly demands, for example, 3% off the purchase price. When the seller expresses unwillingness to agree, the buyer threatens not to sign the contract. A typical result is that the seller is pressured into giving a 1.5% reduction on the purchase price.

Shock opening

This is a negotiation ploy designed to pressure the opponent. The other negotiator starts with a price that is much higher than you expected. You are shocked into silence. If – but only if – they back up their opening price with a credible reason for it, you have to review your expectations.

Tough guy/nice guy

This is a ploy that sometimes works on intimidated negotiators. It is an act in which two negotiators alternate between a tough, uncompromising, adversarial style and a softer, more co-operative style.

You prefer to deal with the apparently softer negotiator but he or she claims to be unable to act without the approval of the tougher colleague. He or she wants to help you but needs you to give concessions in return. You end up moving a lot closer to his or her position than you intended, but are comforted by the illusion that this is a lot less far than you would have had to go to satisfy the 'tough guy'. You have been tricked – the act was a set-up to make you concede.

Waking up the dead

This is a risky ploy. It is used where you are dealing with a team of negotiators and are making little progress. The idea behind the ploy is to try to exploit any differences of opinion in the opposing team. You invite a member of the other team who has remained silent throughout to comment:

What do you think, Mr Linden?

Do you have any suggestions on how we might break this impasse, Ms Yardleyo?

You are taking a risk, as the other negotiators may resent your interference and react by hardening their position. The ploy is unlikely to succeed against a disciplined team.

What do you know?

This is a ploy used to try to obtain information.

The other negotiators open the discussion with the question 'What do you know?'. If you tell them, you might end up revealing more about the state of your knowledge than would be wise at that stage of the negotiation. The best response is to say: 'Not much. Perhaps you could go over the issues for me?'

3.7 Checklist

Caution: This model should not be followed slavishly. Not all elements of the model are applicable to each type of negotiation.

NAME(S):
CASE:
NAME OF OPPONENT:

Relevant facts

- Summary of client instructions.
- Summary of facts relevant to each issue.
- Further information needed.
- What information you might reveal.

Interest

- Identify the client's interests which are achievable by negotiation.
- Consider the possible interests of the other side which are achievable by negotiation.
- Consider the extent to which both sides' interests can be achieved in the negotiation.

Client's aims

- Identify aims which are achievable by negotiation. Distinguish between those aims which must be achieved and those the client would ideally like to achieve.
- Identify areas of potential disagreement between the parties. Identify objective criteria for resolving conflicting interests.

Relevant law

- Give a brief summary of the relevant law and how it might be applied to the negotiation.

BATNA (best alternative to a negotiated agreement)

- Identify the client's BATNA.
- Consider the other side's possible BATNA.

Agenda

- Identify issues for negotiation and order them in priority.
- Draft an agenda for a meeting.

Negotiation strategy

- Choose a strategy to suit the negotiation and your opponent's likely tactics.

Professional conduct

- Pursue the negotiation in a professional manner.
- Pursue the negotiation in a courteous manner.

3.8 Suggested language

Opening

Making introductions

> Good morning. I am ... and this is my colleague Mr/Miss/Ms/Mrs ...

Ice-breaking

> Is this your first visit to ...?
>
> I hope that you had no trouble finding our office?
>
> It looks as if the weather is going to improve/get worse.
>
> Would you like a cup of tea/coffee?
>
> [If you know the other party slightly] How was your weekend?
>
> OR
>
> How is/how are [mention wife/husband/girlfriend/boyfriend/children/colleague]?

Setting an agenda

> Are we agreed that today's meeting should be used to cover the following ...?
>
> OR
>
> We would like to use this meeting to ... [eg, explore each other's position, to exchange information]. Is that OK with you?
>
> Possible response:
>
> Yes, we'd like to exchange views, but I think we'd like to move towards an agreement on some of the issues.
>
> Reply:
>
> That's fine. I assumed this meeting would last for an hour. Shall we see if we can agree on a timetable?

Opening the discussion

> Perhaps we could start with the issue of ...
>
> OR
>
> There are three/several/a number of points I'd like to make ...
>
> OR
>
> Perhaps you'd care to give us your thoughts on this matter.

Exploring positions

Investigating options

> [Opening the questioning process] How do you see this matter?
>
> OR
>
> Right, I think we are clear on how we both see the position. Let's look at the creative possibilities.
>
> OR
>
> Another way of looking at this question might be ...

Moving to the next point

> OK, I think we've covered that point. Let's move on to the question of ...
>
> OR
>
> Let's leave this point for a moment and move on to ...
>
> OR
>
> We'll come back to this issue in a while, but let's move on to ...
>
> OR
>
> OK, we seem to be in agreement on that point. Let's move on to ...

Asking for an opinion

> What's your position/view on ...
>
> OR
>
> How do you see this issue?

Giving an opinion

[Tentative, subjective] I believe/think/feel that ...

OR

My view is ...

OR

[Firm] It is clear that ...

Stating a position

[Firm] Our position on this issue is that ...

OR

[Neutral] We believe/think ...

OR

[Indirect] We are approaching this question on the basis that ...

Persuading and making offers

Putting forward a legal analysis

[Tentative] Our analysis of the law relating to this matter is that ...

[Firm] The law is very clear on this issue. It says that ...

Making offers and concessions

We are prepared to make an offer in the following terms to settle this matter ...

OR

We are prepared to concede on the question of ...

Rejecting an offer

[Firm, unequivocal rejection] I'm afraid that is out of the question ...

OR

[Firm, but indicating willingness to consider revised offers without specifying what is expected] You are going to have to do better than that ...

OR

[Neutral] We are unable to accept that ...

Rejecting an offer and making a counter-offer

We can't accept that proposal in its current form. However, if you were prepared to compromise on the question of ...

OR

We can't accept that. However, we would accept ...

OR

We would be prepared to agree on ... if you were prepared to agree on ...

Defending an offer

That is the best offer we can make in the light of the facts as we understand them at the moment. We might be inclined to take a different view if new facts were to emerge which affected the position. Perhaps you could give us some more information on your situation?

Offering a compromise

[Committing oneself if certain conditions are met] We are prepared to ..., on condition that ...

OR

[Not committing oneself if certain conditions are met] We might agree to ... if you accept that ...

OR

We might be inclined to take a different view if ...

Checking understanding

What's your view on that?

OR

Am I making myself clear?

OR

Are there any questions you want to ask about that?

OR

If I understand you correctly you'd like to ...

OR

Let me see if I'm following. What you are saying is ...

Bringing others into the discussion

[Formal] Allow me to give the floor to ...

[Informal] Perhaps I could bring in X at this point. X, what's your view on this?

[Addressing a member of other side's negotiating team] What's your view on this, Mr/Miss/Ms/Mrs Y?

Entering the discussion

Could/May I come in at this point?

OR

Let me just add that ...

Agreeing

I think we are in agreement on that.

OR

Yes, we take the same view on that issue.

OR

We agree.

OR

Agreed.

Agreeing partially

I would tend to agree with you on that.

OR

I basically agree. However, I have the following reservations ...

OR

I basically agree. However, have you taken into account the fact that ...

Disagreeing tactfully

I agree up to a point, but ...

OR

There's some truth in what you say, but ...

Disagreeing

[Politely] That's not a view I share, I'm afraid.

OR

[Forcefully] With all due respect I must disagree.

OR

[Dismissively] Oh, that's nonsense!

Expressing outrage

[Polite] That suggestion entirely lacks merit/credibility.

OR

[Forceful] That is an outrageous suggestion!

OR

[Dismissive] That's absurd!

OR

[Dismissive] Rubbish!/ridiculous!/nonsense!

Accepting an offer

[Enthusiastically] We would be more than happy to accept that …

OR

[Neutrally] Yes, I think we are prepared to accept that …

OR

[Less enthusiastically] Yes, I think we could probably live with that …

Refusing an offer

[Forcefully] No, I'm afraid that's totally unacceptable.

OR

[Neutrally] No, we can't accept that offer.

OR

[Regretfully] Unfortunately, we are unable to accept that.

Playing for time

I'm afraid I'm not in a position to comment on that just yet.

OR

I'm afraid I don't have authority to accept that without checking with …

OR

I'll need to discuss that with … and get back to you.

OR

Perhaps I could suggest we take a short break?

OR

Could you just go over that proposal again? I want to make sure I've understood it properly.

OR

We'll have to think a bit more about that and get back to you.

Interrupting

If I might just interrupt you for a moment, I'd like to …

OR

I'm sorry, you've lost me there. You were saying …?

OR

Can I just stop you there a moment? I'd like to clarify …

Stopping interruptions

[Forceful] Just hear me out on this.

OR

[Polite] If I could just finish what I was saying …

Deflecting an unwanted line of questioning

What exactly are you getting at?

OR

Where is this line of thought leading to exactly?

Narrowing differences

Summarising

To sum up then, there seems to be …

OR

The key issues are …

Correcting misunderstandings

Perhaps I should make that clearer by saying ...

OR

Let me just repeat, in case there is any confusion, that ...

OR

[Responding to mistaken impression of other party] You seem to have misunderstood what I was saying. What I meant was ...

Asking for further information

Could you be a little more specific/precise?

OR

You mentioned something about ... Perhaps you could just tell me a little more about ...

OR

That sounds interesting. Perhaps you could give us a few more details.

Seeking clarification

Am I right in thinking that ...?

OR

Could you just go over the ... again? I'm not quite sure how it was supposed to work.

Making recommendations, proposals and suggestions

I recommend/suggest/propose that ...

OR

Can I suggest something?

OR

[Breaking a deadlock] OK, we seem to have reached an impasse. Perhaps I could suggest something?

Sketching a hypothesis

Let's suppose for a moment that ...

OR

One way of looking at this matter would be ...

OR

What if ...

Projecting false naivety

Correct me if I'm wrong but ...

OR

This is obviously not my field, but ...

Expressing support

I'm in favour of ...

OR

I like that idea. Tell me more about it.

Expressing opposition

I can see many problems in adopting this.

OR

I'm not sure how realistic this proposal is.

OR

If this matter were to be tested in court, the court would never make such an order ...

Closing

Persuading

[Mentioning certain factors to influence the other party] Have you taken into account ...?

OR

[Casting the issue in a new light] Look at it this way. Suppose that ...

OR

[Demonstrating empathy] If I were in your shoes, I would be very interested in ...

Pressuring for a decision

[Threatening a deadline] We are going to have to ask you to make a quick decision. The deadline is ...

OR

We can't keep this offer open for longer than ... There are other interested parties.

OR

[Stressing simplicity of matter] The issues are very simple. There's no reason why this can't be decided by ...

OR

[Keeping up the pressure] I'll phone you tomorrow morning to see what progress has been made.

OR

[Threat] Either you accept this or ... /If you don't accept our demands, we'll ...

Emphasising

I particularly want to emphasise/stress/highlight the fact that ...

OR

A point that we need particularly to bear in mind is ...

OR

The fundamental point is ...

Reaching an agreement

OK, we are in agreement that ...

OR

We have agreed on the following ...

Closing the negotiation

[Adjourning to another day] OK, I think we've done as much as we can today. Let's adjourn to ...

OR

[Reaching deadlock] We seem to have reached deadlock today. Let's wrap this meeting up.

OR

[Agreement reached] We seem to be in agreement on all major points. Can we agree that a memorandum of understanding will be prepared by ... for circulation on ...

Concluding

In conclusion, I would like to say ...

OR

I'd like to finish by saying ...

Saying goodbye

Let me get your coat ...

It's been a pleasure doing business with you. Have a safe journey home.

4 CHAIRING A FORMAL MEETING

4.1 The role of the chair

It is likely that during the course of your working life you will be called upon fairly regularly to chair meetings. The nature of the role you play as the chair[4] will vary slightly according to the degree of formality the meeting requires, what matters are being discussed and who is discussing them. However, in all cases the chair must:

- control and co-ordinate the meeting;
- ensure that all matters under discussion are properly presented;
- allow participants to comment on the matters being discussed;
- ensure that the meeting is not dominated by a single individual;
- move from one issue to the next;
- ensure that business is transacted efficiently;
- ensure that the necessary decisions are made;
- not allow the meeting to exceed the time allotted; and
- see that all necessary minutes and records are kept.

4.2 Structure and language

Most formal meetings commence with the reading of the minutes of the previous meeting and the presentation of the agenda for the current meeting. The matters set out on the agenda are then introduced and discussed by the participants. Towards the end of the meeting, motions are proposed and votes are taken on the matters proposed as motions. The participants then deal with any other business (often marked as 'AOB' on meeting agendas) which needs to be dealt with at that point, and the meeting is then closed.

A typical meeting structure is as follows:

- the chair opens the meeting;
- the minutes are read;
- the agenda is introduced;

---

4   The word 'chair' has replaced 'chairman' in modern English usage, as 'chairman' is regarded as a sexist term. 'Chairperson' is another option. However, this is a rather clumsy word.

- the first subject is introduced;
- the chair gives the floor to a participant;
- another speaker takes the floor;
- the chair keeps order;
- the chair moves the discussion to a new subject;
- the chair directs the discussion;
- participants propose new motions;
- the chair moves to a vote;
- voting occurs;
- consensus is reached;
- any other business is dealt with;
- the meeting is closed.

The language of formal meetings, particularly the language used by the chair, can be rather stylised. The meeting itself is likely to follow a fairly fixed schedule. The language suggestions set out below cover the kinds of language employed at formal meetings. Where relevant, alternatives are given for formal and less formal language. To a great extent, the language used during the meeting will depend on what is being discussed. Refer to Chapter 3.8 for further language suggestions in this respect.

4.3 Suggested language

Opening

Opening the meeting

[Very formal] Ladies and gentlemen, I declare the meeting open.

[Less formal] Right, shall we get started?

OR

Let's get down to business shall we?

The minutes

[Very formal] May I read the minutes?

OR

Would someone move that the minutes of the last meeting be accepted?

[Less formal] Has everyone seen the minutes?

OR

Can we take the minutes as read?

The agenda

Has everyone received a copy of the agenda?

OR

Has everyone got the agenda in front of them?

[Introducing first item] The first item on the agenda today is …

[Amending agenda] I would like to add an item to the agenda.

The subject

The purpose of today's meeting is …

OR

The first problem we have to consider is …

OR

Perhaps we could first look at …

Discussing

Giving the floor

[Very formal] I'd like to give the floor to Mr Lee.

OR

Ms Sanchez, do you have any views on this/would you like to say something about this?

OR

Mr Steiner, I think you know something about this matter.

[Less formal] Have you got anything to say, Dieter?

OR

What are your views on this, Maria?

Taking the floor

[Very formal] With the chair's permission, I'd like to take up the point about …

[Less formal] Could I just make a point about …?

OR

Could I say something here, please?

Finishing a point

Has anyone anything further they wish to add before we move on to the next item?

OR

Has anyone anything further to add?

Directing

[Very formal] We seem to be losing sight of the main point. The question is …

OR

This isn't really relevant to our discussion. What we're trying to do is …

[Less formal] Could we stick to the subject, please?

OR

Let's not get sidetracked. The issue under discussion is …

Keeping order

We can't all speak at once; Ms Sanchez, would you like to speak first?

OR

Mr Robertson, would you mind addressing your remarks to the chair, please?

OR

I shall have to call you to order, Mr Ramirez.

Moving to a new point

[Very formal] Could we move on to item 4 on the agenda, please?

[Less formal] Now, I'd like to turn to …

OR

Can we go on now to …

Postponing discussion

[Very formal] Well, ladies and gentlemen, with your approval, I propose to defer this matter until we have more information at our disposal.

OR

If no one has any objections, I suggest that we leave this matter until our next meeting.

OR

Perhaps we could leave this for the time being. We can come back to it on another occasion …

[Less formal] Let's come back to this later on.

OR

We can talk about this next time we meet.

Voting

Proposing

[Very formal] With the chair's permission, I move that …

OR

I would like to propose the motion that …

OR

Would anyone like to second the motion?

[Less formal] I suggest/propose we …

OR

I'm in favour of that.

OR

Is anyone else in favour of that?

Moving to a vote

[Very formal] Perhaps we should take a formal vote?

OR

Can I ask for a show of hands?

OR

Let's put it to the vote.

OR

Could we take a vote on it?

OR

Can we move to a vote on this?

[Less formal] Should we vote?

Voting

[Very formal]

In the event of a tie, I would like to remind you that I have a casting vote.

Those for the motion, please?

Those against?

Any abstentions?

The motion is carried unanimously.

OR

The motion has been rejected by six votes to five.

[Less formal]

If there's a tie, I have the deciding vote.

Who's in favour?

Who's against?

Abstentions?

Everyone was in favour.

OR

The motion was rejected.

Seeking consensus

Would everyone agree if …

OR

I'd be interested to know if anyone has any objections, but shall we try …

OR

Am I right in thinking that …

Consensus

[Very formal] It seems that we have a consensus.

Can I take it everyone's in favour?

[Less formal] We're all agreed.

OR

I think we all agree on that.

Any other business

[Very formal] Is there any other business?

[Less formal] Any further points?

OR

Is there anything else to discuss?

Closing

[Very formal] I declare the meeting closed. Thank you ladies and gentlemen.

That concludes our business for today. Thank you.

[Less formal] Well, I think that covers everything.

OR

That's all for today. Thank you.

5 MAKING A PRESENTATION

5.1 Preparation

It has been said that the greatest speeches have two things in common:

- The speaker cared about the topic.
- The audience cared about the topic.

When considering your presentation, therefore, you should try to pick a topic that you care about and that the people you will be making the presentation to care about. You may not, of course, have the luxury of being able to pick any topic you wish to speak about. However, you should try to find those aspects of the given topic which interest you and which are likely to interest your audience.

Try to divide your speech into a few manageable sections (say two to five) which cover the main parts of your presentation and make it easy for the audience to follow you. These sections should be logically ordered and should support the main theme of the presentation.

When preparing, make notes but do not write everything down. Brief, clear notes will stop you getting lost, but if you write everything down your style will become very boring and your presentation will be less flexible.

Look the part. Do not turn up in jeans and a T-shirt if everyone in your audience is going to be wearing a business suit.

Consider the following points when preparing your presentation:

- You should not talk too long. Mark Twain once remarked that few sinners are saved after the first 20 minutes of a sermon. If you go on too long, people will gradually switch off and will end up understanding less, not more of what you have said.

- Are you going to use any visual aids? If so, what kind? Check that the room in which you will make the presentation has the facilities you will need Prepare your materials and place them in the correct order for the presentation. Only use visual aids if they will actually help illustrate the points you want to make.

- What will you do if there is a power cut? Ensure that your presentation can be given even if your audio-visual props are not available.

- How big is the room in which you will give your presentation? Remember that you will need to project your voice effectively. Think about using a microphone if necessary.

- Think about the kind of audience you are going to address and tailor your speech to that audience's interests and needs.
- Don't be afraid of repetition – if you are going to tell the audience something you want them to remember, you are going to have to say it several times to get it into their heads. Use illustrations and examples where possible.

5.2   Giving the presentation

Structure

Your presentation should have a clear beginning, middle and end. An effective way of presenting an argument is to start by indicating the theme of your presentation and the points you are going to make in support of that theme. Then make those points. Then at the conclusion of your presentation, summarise the points you've made and explain how they support your theme.

This technique is sometimes characterised as the 'tell them what you're going to say, say it and then tell them you've said it' approach. The main benefits of this approach are (1) clarity and (2) that it gives the opportunity to make each point at least three times in different ways, so that the audience is likely to remember at least the main points made.

Beginning

The introduction should be used to:

- make an impact – you should try to say something immediately that will make the audience want to continue to listen to you (eg, 'What I'm going to tell you today will fundamentally change the way this firm treats its clients');
- contain a preview of what you're going to talk about (eg, 'in my talk today I will show you that the firm's profits have increased by 30 % compared to last year');
- show appreciation and respect to the audience (eg, 'I'd like to thank X for inviting me to come here today. I must say I've been very impressed by how friendly and professional everyone here is').

Middle

In the middle of your speech, you should present and develop your main points:

- The middle of your presentation should be divided into a few manageable sections, each including arguments, examples and supporting statistics.
- These should be presented logically so that each point you make leads naturally to the next point (see checklist).
- Use verbal tagging. This is a technique in which you use a neat mental image that summarises your main points. Winston Churchill's use of the phrase 'Iron Curtain' is an excellent example of this technique. In a presentation on a particular area of the law, one might say something like:

> So as you see, the present law is like a dam with holes in it. The law reforms the government is proposing will plug those holes.

End

The end of your presentation should be used to summarise the main points that you have made:

- You should signal to the audience that you are coming to the end of your presentation. If anyone has fallen asleep, the words 'and finally' or 'in conclusion, I'd like to say' will wake them up.

- Summarise the points you have made. Show how they support the main theme of your presentation.

- End on a high note. Say something that the audience will remember – an insight based on the theme of your presentation ('Remember this. All this points to one thing. That is …') or a call to action ('This shows very clearly the need for us to …'). Never end weakly with words like, 'Well, that's about it I suppose'.

- Invite questions from the floor. Deal with all questioners with respect and answer all questions fully, no matter how ridiculous they are.

Content

The techniques you use to make and illustrate your points can be decisive as to whether you persuade or alienate your audience. Much will depend on the nature of your audience and subject. Here are some useful tips:

- Use terms that the audience can relate to and agree with. People like to hear stated in general terms what they already believe in a particular connection. They feel justified in their beliefs. A bond between the speaker and the audience is established. Relate your arguments to things that matter to the audience.

- Relate the points you make to the main theme of the presentation. The separate points should contribute to the whole.

- Use different kinds of arguments and different kinds of evidence to make your points – different people respond better to different kinds of argument.

- Use quotations and statistics wisely. Only use them when they will genuinely support the points you are making. They should not be used as a substitute for argument.

- Use humour, but only if it can be introduced in a natural and relevant way. It is seldom essential. It must fit the context.

- Simple comparisons can be a good way to illustrate a point, but make sure that they will withstand attack. Do not compare things that are not comparable (for example, 'if we can't trust Clinton to be faithful to his wife, then how can we trust him with the economy' is an irrelevant use of this device).

Language

When giving a presentation, the language you use to make your arguments is at least as important as the arguments themselves. Here are a few tips:

*   Use simple and clear language. The small words are easier to say and often more powerful than the long words ('I love you', 'it's a boy', 'she's dead').

*   Consider the level of understanding of your audience. For example, when addressing non-lawyers do not use legal jargon. If you have to use jargon, be sure to explain it in layman's terms. For example:

> This is what is known as a contractual waiver. A contractual waiver occurs when one party to a contract agrees with the other party not to insist on something specified in the original contract being done.

*   Avoid using language that is sexist, racist or ageist. In particular, do not use *he* when referring to a hypothetical person who could be either male or female. For example, do not say: 'if a lawyer wants to compete effectively in today's market he must understand information technology.' Say instead: 'the lawyer who wants to compete effectively in today's market must understand information technology.'

*   Think carefully about what how your choice of language colours what you are saying about an issue and what it says about your own attitudes. To use a well-known example, when referring to the same militant group, you might refer to *terrorists* or *freedom fighters*. The term you use will influence the audience's perception of your subject and of you personally.

What to avoid

The following should be avoided:

Waffle. Waffle is talking in a vague or trivial way. Your audience will lose patience with you rapidly if you indulge in it. If you have nothing more to say, stop.

Truisms. A truism is something so obvious that it is not worth repeating ('war is a bad thing').

Misinformation. If you are unsure about the truth or accuracy of a statistic or other piece of information, avoid using it. Someone is bound to notice if you use it.

Assertion. Do not state that something is true without backing it up with evidence.

Contradictions. A presentation that contains inconsistencies can be easily dismissed as being poorly thought out. It is also vulnerable to attack. Obvious factual inconsistencies should be easy to remove. Where contradictions exist in the underlying principles on which your speech is based, the position is more complex. In such a situation, if the contradiction is really unavoidable, the best course is to soften the degree of contradiction or even point out and explain the contradiction.

Mumbling. Always speak clearly, project your voice and try to appear self-confident. If you appear to be doubtful about what you are saying, you can hardly expect to persuade your audience.

Unnecessary apologies. Don't apologise for what you are saying (never say things like 'I'm sorry if this is a bit boring, but ...').

5.3 Checklist

Preparation

- Consider your audience. What are they interested in? What do they need to know? What is the best way of presenting it to them?
- Prepare the room in which the presentation is to be given. Is it big enough? Does it have all the equipment you need (eg, flipchart, computer terminals, microphone, overhead projector, television/video)?
- Consider what visual aids you will be using (eg, Powerpoint presentation, transparencies, slides, handout materials). Make sure they will actually improve your speech and are not simply distractions.
- Place your materials in the order you need them to be in for the presentation.

Beginning

- Make an impact – say something that will make the audience want to listen to you.
- Give a preview of the argument you are going to present.
- Establish a relationship with the audience. Thank anyone who should be thanked. Use humour if appropriate.

Middle

- Divide speech into a few manageable points.
- Place them in a logical order. For example, when discussing a problem:
  - What's the problem?
  - What are we currently doing about it?
  - Why this isn't working?
  - What should we be doing about it?
- Demonstrate how each point contributes to the main theme of the presentation.
- Use verbal tagging.

End

- Indicate that you have reached the end part of your presentation ('and finally').
- Summarise the key points of your presentation.
- End with a clear, decisive statement.

Dealing with questions

- Show respect to the questioner, however stupid or aggressive the question.
- Always answer the question in sufficient detail.

Throughout

- Project your voice so that everyone can hear you.
- Maintain eye contact with your audience.
- Use visual aids to illustrate your points. Do not use them excessively.
- Try to avoid contradicting yourself.
- Do not waffle.
- Do not assert that something is true without backing it up with evidence.

5.4 Suggested language

Beginning

Introducing yourself

> Good morning/afternoon/evening. I'm/my name is ... I'm going to speak to you today about ...

Establishing rapport

> It's very nice to see so many people here. I must say I've been impressed at how friendly and professional everyone here is ...
>
> OR
>
> As all of us involved in the business of ... know, this question of ... is one of the biggest challenges facing the business.

Thanking people

> I'd like to thank X for inviting me here today.
>
> OR
>
> I'd like to thank X who's done a great job of getting us all here today/organising this event …

Introducing theme of presentation

> In my talk today I'm going to show that …
>
> OR
>
> I'm going to talk today about the important new developments in … I know a lot of you will have heard something about them and will be thinking 'how does this affect me exactly?'.

Giving a preview of the points you are going to make

> I'm going to make a couple of points/three/four/five points today. Briefly, these are …

Middle

Introducing a controversial point

> Many people blindly assume that X is the case. The truth of the matter is rather different.

Signalling conclusion

> And finally …
>
> OR
>
> In conclusion I'd like to say …
>
> OR
>
> By way of summary …

End
Giving an insight

> 'So, what does all this mean?' I hear you asking. What it means is …
>
> OR
>
> The most important effect of all of this is …

Making a call to action

> What we must now do is …
>
> OR
>
> We must take a number of steps. These are …

Inviting questions

> I'm sure some of you would like to ask questions. I'd be happy to answer them.
>
> OR
>
> Any questions?

Acknowledging a question

> That's an interesting point …
>
> OR
>
> That's a good question …
>
> OR
>
> I see what you mean.

6.1 Considerations

Most lawyers use the telephone many times during a typical working day. There is nothing especially different about using English on the telephone to using any other language on the telephone. However, there are a number of common phrases which people tend to use when speaking on the telephone. Knowing what these are, what they mean and how they are used should help make communication easier.

One of the particular problems with telephoning is that you cannot see the person you are speaking to. You therefore do not have the benefit of the non-verbal clues given by body language which assist communication in face-to-face situations. This makes it especially important for both parties to speak clearly and use simple terms.

An additional consideration for lawyers is that what is said over the telephone is likely to be noted down and recorded in a case file by the person to whom you are speaking. You should do the same. It is therefore important that you do not accidentally reveal something about your client's case that should be kept confidential, or say anything that might be misunderstood. If you are unsure, write a letter, fax or email instead. Always make a note of the contents of all discussions with other lawyers over the telephone immediately after the call is made – in that way, if the other lawyer has misunderstood what you have said, you have the evidence to show that this is the case and put the matter straight.

6.2 Suggested language

There are a number of phrases that are only used when telephoning. Some examples are contained in this dialogue:

Receptionist: Hello, Smith Ltd. How can I help you?

Juan Ramirez: This is Juan Ramirez from [company name]. Could I speak to Clare Peters please?/Could I have extension 736?

Receptionist: Certainly Mr Ramirez, hold on a minute, I'll put you through ...

Clare Peters' office: Tim Brown speaking.

Juan Ramirez: Hello. This is Juan Ramirez calling. Is Clare in?

Tim Brown: I'm afraid she's out at the moment/in a meeting/with a client/not taking any calls/on holiday until Thursday/on a business trip [etc]. Can I take a message?

Juan Ramirez: Yes, this is Juan Ramirez from [company name]. Could you ask Clare to call me as soon as she gets a chance? My number is +34 9 456 8965. I need to talk to her about the Statchem case, it's urgent.

Tim Brown: Could you repeat the number please?

Juan Ramirez: Yes, that's +34 9 456 8965 and my name is Juan Ramirez.

Tim Brown: Could you tell me how you spell 'Ramirez'?

Juan Ramirez: It's R-A-M-I-R-E-Z.

Tim Brown: Thank you Mr Ramirez. I'll make sure Clare gets this ASAP.

Juan Ramirez: Thanks, bye.

Tim Brown: Bye.

The language used during telephone calls is usually informal and differs in some respects to everyday English. Here are some typical language functions and suggested language.

Introducing yourself

This is Anna Lindgren.

OR

Anna Lindgren speaking.

OR

Anna Lindgren here.

Asking who is on the telephone

Excuse me, who is this?

OR

Can I ask who is calling, please?

OR

[When putting a call through to someone] Who shall I say is calling, please?

Asking for someone

[Formal] May I speak to ...?

OR

[Informal] Can I speak to ...?

OR

[Very informal] I need to speak to ...

OR

Is ... in? [informal phrase meaning 'is ... in the office?']

Connecting someone

Hold on a minute, I'll put you through [put through – phrasal verb meaning 'connect'].

OR

Can you hold the line?

OR

Can you hold on a moment?

OR

I'm just connecting you now.

How to reply when someone is not available

I'm afraid ... is in a meeting at the moment/is with a client/is out of the office/is not available at the moment.

OR

[When the extension requested is being used] The line is busy.

Asking for someone else

OK. Is ... there by any chance?

OR

I see. Perhaps I could speak to ... instead?

OR

Could I have extension 971 instead?

Offering to help when the requested person is unavailable

I'm afraid ... is not available/is out of the office/is in a meeting with a client. Can I help you?

Offering to connect the caller to someone else

Would you like to speak to ... he/she also deals with these issues?

OR

I'm sure ... could help you with this. Hold the line and I'll put you through.

Explaining why you're calling

I'm calling about ...

OR

I wanted to speak to ... about ...

OR

It's about the ...

OR

I wanted to ask about ...

OR

I need some advice on ...

Taking a message

Can I take a message?

OR

Would you like to leave a message?

Leaving a message

Perhaps you could tell ... I called and ask him/her to call me back on [give number]. I'll be in the office until ...

OR

Could you tell ... that I called. I'll try him/her again tomorrow.

Clarifying that your number has been noted correctly

> Perhaps you could just read the number back to me?

Stressing importance

> Please tell ... that this is an urgent matter and I need to hear from him/her ...
>
> OR
>
> It's crucial that I hear from ... no later than ...

Stating a deadline

> I need to hear from ... by ... because ...

Concluding the call

> OK. Thanks for your help. Bye.
>
> OR
>
> OK. Many thanks. Bye.

6.3 Leaving a message on an answering machine

Occasionally, there will be no one available to answer the telephone and you will need to leave a message. Here is an outline which covers all the information the person being called might need.

Introduction

> Hello, this is Suzanne Dubois.
>
> OR
>
> [More formal] My name is Suzanne Dubois.
>
> OR
>
> [If you know the person well] Hi, it's Suzanne here. How are you?

State the time of day and the reason for calling

It's 11 am on Tuesday 6 November. I'm phoning [calling, ringing] to find out if .../to see if .../to let you know that.../to tell you that ...

OR

[When replying to a previous telephone message] I got the message you left for me. Thanks for calling. You asked about ... The answer is ...

Make a request

Could you call [ring, phone] me back?

OR

Would you mind calling me back?

Leave your telephone number

My number is ...

OR

You can reach/call me at ...

State a good time to call (if appropriate)

The best time to get hold of me is ...

OR

I'll be on that number until ...

OR

[Indicating times to avoid] I'm in a meeting from 2 to 4 pm but you can get hold of me before or after that.

Ending message

Thanks a lot, bye.

OR

I'll talk to you later, bye.

6.4 Making people speak more slowly

Native English speakers, especially business people, tend to speak very quickly on the telephone. They may also use slang and jargon which you may not be familiar with. These factors can cause difficulties for non-native speakers of English.

Here are some tactics you can use to make people speak more slowly on the telephone:

- Immediately ask the person to speak slowly.

- When taking note of a name or important information, repeat each piece of information as the person speaks. By repeating each important piece of information or each number or letter as they spell or give you a telephone number, you automatically slow the speaker down.

- If you have not understood, do not be afraid to say so. Ask the person to repeat until you have understood.

- If the person does not slow down, begin speaking your own language! A sentence or two of another language spoken quickly will remind the person how lucky they are that they do not need to speak a foreign language to communicate. Used carefully, this exercise in humbling the other speaker can be very effective.

CONTRACTUAL LEGAL ENGLISH

1 BASIC CONCEPTS OF ANGLO-AMERICAN CONTRACT LAW

1.1 The relevance of common law

The basic principles of contract law in the USA, the UK and in those countries formerly under British colonial influence derive from English common law. Common law can be roughly defined as law derived from custom and the precedents set by judgments in previous cases, as opposed to law created by a law-making body and codified in legislation. Common law is in essence made by judges. It is relevant in the countries listed below. Note that in a number of these countries, the legal system used derives from a mixture of different legal traditions, of which common law is only one:

American Samoa	Kiribati
Antigua and Barbuda	Lesotho
Australia	Malawi
Bangladesh	Malaysia
Barbados	Maldives
Belize	Malta
Botswana	Marshall Islands
Cameroon	Mauritius
Canada	Mozambique
Cook Islands	Namibia
Cyprus	Nauru
Dominica	New Zealand
Federated States of Micronesia	Nigeria
Fiji Islands	Niue
Ghana	Pakistan
Grenada	Papua New Guinea
Guyana	Samoa

Hong Kong	Seychelles
India	Sierra Leone
Ireland	Singapore
Israel	Solomon Islands
Jamaica	South Africa
Kenya	Sri Lanka
Swaziland	Tuvali
Tanzania	Uganda
Thailand	UK
Tokelau	USA
Tonga	Vanautu
Trinidad & Tobago	Western Samoa
Tristan da Cunha	Zambia
Turks & Caicos	Zimbabwe

Naturally, contract law has evolved to deal with specific national issues in each of the countries in which the common law system is used. Increasingly, also, common law concepts relating to contract law have been codified in legislation in these countries. However, an understanding of the common law principles of contract provides a starting-point to understanding contract law in the countries in which the national law of contract derives from common law.

In addition, given the economic power of the USA and the dominance of English as the main language of international business relations, it is no surprise that many common law concepts relating to contract law have found their way into the way in which the international business community approaches the composition of business contracts.

It should be remembered of course that many international business contracts written in English are based on terminology and principles drawn from civil law jurisdictions to which common law has no relevance. It is beyond the scope of this book to deal with the differences between common law and civil law terminology. However, the applicability of civil law concepts should be considered when assessing any international contracts involving civil law jurisdictions.

1.2 Elements of contract

In common law, a contract need not be in any particular form. A contract made in spoken words (known as an oral contract) is just as enforceable as a written contract. The only advantage of a written contract over an oral contract is that there is clear evidence of its terms in a permanent form.

Contracts can only be made between *legal persons*. Legal persons include both natural persons and corporations.

There are essentially four elements involved in the formation of a contract:

- offer;
- acceptance;
- consideration; and
- intention to create legal relations.

Offer

All contractual relationships commence with one party offering something to another party in return for something else. This offer must consist of a definite promise to accept a legally binding obligation, provided certain specified terms are met. The *offeror* (the party making the offer) must indicate that he or she is ready to carry out a contractual obligation on certain terms. The offer must be clear and must contain the details of the contract. It must be communicated to the *offeree* (the party to whom the offer is made).

The offeree must be able to accept or refuse the offer made. This will only be possible if the terms of the offer are sufficiently clear. If the offeree is unable to accept the offer in its original form, then he or she may either refuse the offer altogether, or make a *counter-offer*, ie, an offer made by the offeree to the offeror in different terms to the original offer.

An offer must be differentiated from a mere offer to negotiate or an offer to receive offers. The legal terminology for this kind of offer is an *invitation to treat*. A real estate agent's advertisement of a property for sale in a local newspaper is, technically, an invitation to treat. The estate agent provides a guide price, but the prospective purchaser is invited to make an offer to purchase the property.

Acceptance

The offeree's acceptance of the offer must match the offer exactly and must be communicated to the offeror. If the acceptance does not exactly match the terms of the offer, then it must be regarded as a counter-offer. It must be a fact that the offeree has accepted and it must be communicated to the offeror.

In simple transactions the offer and acceptance can be defined quite easily. For example:

---

(1) Peter to Mary:'Will you buy my car for $2,000?' (the offer).

(2) Mary to Peter:'Yes' (the acceptance).

But even in some relatively simple transactions, the position is not so straightforward. For example, in the English case of *Harvey v Facey* [1893] AC 552:

> (1)   Harvey telegraphs Facey:'Will you sell us Bumper Hall Pen?
>   Telegraph lowest cash price.'
>
> (2)   Facey telegraphs Harvey:'Lowest cash price to buy Bumper Hall Pen £900.'
>
> (3)   Harvey telegraphs Facey:'We agree to buy Bumper Hall Pen at £900 asked
>   by you.'

One analysis of this exchange could be that (2) was an offer to sell Bumper Hall
Pen for £900, and that (3) was an acceptance of that offer. However, the court
held that (2) was merely a statement of the price and that (3) was an offer to buy
Bumper Hall Pen which Facey was free to accept or reject.

Consideration

Consideration is defined in the Oxford Dictionary of Law as:

> *an act, forbearance, or promise by one party to a contract that constitutes the price for
> which that party buys the promise of another.*

Consideration usually means the reciprocal promises made by the parties to a
contract. For example:

A promises to sell a car to party B.

B promises to pay £2,000 to A for the car.

Therefore:

A's consideration is the promise to transfer the car to B.

B's consideration is the promise to pay £2,000 to A for the car.

In any contractual situation, it is required that the promise made by each party
must have some economic value. However, there is no requirement that it must
constitute a realistic price for the promise it buys. Thus, a contract made to sell a
property worth £200,000 for the sum of £10,000 is legally valid. It would
therefore be said to be *legally binding*, ie, enforceable.

The main effect of the requirement of consideration is that gratuitous
promises made by one party to another (ie, where one party makes a promise to
another party but no promises are made in return) do not give rise to
contractual obligations. However, it should be noted that in many jurisdictions
this requirement has been displaced by legislation in respect of certain kinds of
contract. In English law there is also the concept of a deed. A deed is a written
document that is used to give legal effect in circumstances where one party
makes a gratuitous promise to another.

Intention to create legal relations

It is a requirement for the valid creation of a contract that the parties must have
the intention to create legal relations. They must intend that the contract they

enter into has legally binding effect, so that they would be entitled to sue on the contract if the other party breaches it. This requirement is designed to exclude trivial, social, family or other domestic agreements.

In business transactions there is a *rebuttable presumption* that parties do intend to create legal relations. A rebuttable presumption is one that can be reversed if evidence to the contrary is produced. In this context it means that the law presumes that legal relations are intended to be created, but this presumption may be proved to be false (ie, it may be rebutted) if evidence is produced which shows that the creation of legal relations was not intended by the parties.

1.3   Privity of contract

An important element of contract law is the doctrine of *privity of contract*. This doctrine states that only those persons who are parties to a contract have legal rights and duties in respect of it, and only those persons can sue the other party if that party breaches the contract. Therefore, third parties have no legal rights or duties in respect of a contract. This means that if a contract exists between A and B to provide services to C, this contract cannot be enforced by C. However, the absoluteness of the doctrine is qualified by legal rules contained in certain statutes designed to protect the rights of third parties, and by judicial decisions in a number of recent cases.

1.4   Agency agreements

An agency agreement is a type of contract in which a person known as the *agent* is appointed to act by another person known as the *principal* to act on behalf of the principal within the limits of the authority agreed between them. An agent might be used, for example, to negotiate a contract between the principal and a third party. Agency agreements are common in the retail sphere in which the principal company might, for example, give authority to the agent to sell its goods in a specified territory on specified terms.

The principal is legally bound by those acts of the agent which are incidental to the ordinary conduct of the agent's business or the effective performance of the agent's duties. The principal may also choose to *ratify* (ie, accept as binding the principal) a previously unauthorised contract.

1.5   Failure of contracts

There are a number of reasons why a contract may fail, by which is meant that a court of law correctly applying Anglo-American contract law principles would decide that the contract was unenforceable. The main reasons for failure are described below.

In addition, if a party to a contract fails to carry out a major term of the contract which he or she has agreed to carry out, then that party is said to have *breached* the contract. The other party will then be entitled to *rescind* (ie, cancel) the contract and claim damages.

Indefiniteness

A contract may fail because it does not contain clear obligations by each party to the contract. This may arise when the language used by the parties is so vague or ambiguous that it is impossible to determine their intent. It may also arise when the language used does not indicate a genuine exchange of promises, in which case there will be no valid consideration.

Capacity

Where it can be shown that one of the parties to a contract lacked capacity to enter into a contract, that contract can be set aside. Capacity to contract means the competence to enter into legally binding agreements. Most common law jurisdictions presume that everyone has capacity except:

- **Minors**: those under 18.
- **Mentally disordered persons**: it is up to a person claiming that they did not have capacity to enter into a contract due to mental disorder to prove (1) that as a result of their mental condition they did not know what they were doing, and (2) that the other party was aware of the incapacity. The *burden of proof* is on them.
- **Intoxicated or drunken persons**: the burden of proof is similar to that which applies to mentally disordered persons.

Mistake

Mistake applies to a situation in which one or both of the parties to the contract have a mistaken belief about an important fact relating to the contract. A mistake can result in a contract being void. It must be a mistake about the facts of the contract, not one about the laws which govern the contract. Depending on the particular provisions enacted in the common law jurisdiction in question, two kinds of mistake may void a contract:

- **Mutual mistake**: where both the parties entered into the contract in the mistaken belief that some fact that is fundamental to the contract is true.
- **Unilateral mistake**: where there is no correspondence between offer and acceptance – where one party makes an offer to the other party but the other party tries to accept this offer in a different sense from that intended by the offeror. Where this occurs, the contract may be void.

Frustration

Frustration of contracts arises when a change of circumstances which occurs after the formation of the contract makes it impossible to fulfil the contract, or changes the performance of the contract into a very different obligation from that agreed to in the contract.

Examples include the destruction of the goods which are the subject matter of the contract, outbreak of war rendering one party to the contract an enemy alien, and industrial action. These situations are those which *force majeure* provisions in contracts are designed to cover.

The effect of frustration is to bring the contract to an immediate end. Both parties are released from further performance, but any legal rights already acquired or payments made as a result of the contract are usually left undisturbed.

Misrepresentation

Misrepresentation is a false statement of fact made by the *representor* (the party making the representation) to the *representee* (the party to whom the representation is made) in the course of negotiating a contract that induces the representee to enter into the contract. This must be fact rather than law or opinion (although it's often difficult to distinguish opinion from fact in these situations; for example, the statement 'this is an excellent racehorse' may be either). There are three categories of misrepresentation:

* **Fraudulent misrepresentation**: the false statement is made knowingly or *recklessly*. Recklessness means that the person making the statement did not know for sure that it was untrue but knew that there was a risk that it might be untrue and made no real effort to find out whether this was the case. The representee may *rescind* the contract and seek damages.

* **Negligent misrepresentation**: the false statement is made carelessly. This occurs when the representor believed the statement was true but had no reasonable grounds to do so. The representee may rescind the contract and seek damages.

* **Innocent misrepresentation**: the false statement was made neither knowingly nor recklessly; ie, the representor believed it to be true. The representee is entitled to rescind the contract.

In all cases of misrepresentation, the affected contract is held to be *voidable* rather than void. This means that the party whose interests are prejudiced by the misrepresentation can decide to affirm the validity of the contract despite the misrepresentation.

Duress

Duress refers to the situation in which a party to a contract has been put under pressure or threats have been made against him or her to force them into making the contract. Alternatively, *economic duress* refers to the situation in which economic pressure is used in an unfair manner to force someone into a contract.

Where duress is found to have existed, the contract in question will be held voidable and can be set aside.

Undue influence

Undue influence refers to the situation in which influence is exerted upon someone in such a way that prevents that person from exercising independent judgment in respect of a transaction. Usually it is up to the party claiming to have been subjected to undue influence to prove that this was the case. However, in certain relationships (husband and wife, doctor and patient, parent and child, etc), undue influence is presumed to exist unless evidence is shown to the contrary – there is a rebuttable presumption that it exists.

As with duress, a finding of undue influence renders the contract voidable. The contract can therefore be set aside.

Fraud

Fraud in contract law falls into two categories. The first is a concealment or false statement made in the course of contractual negotiations that causes harm to another party. This amounts to fraudulent misrepresentation (see 'Misrepresentation' above).

The second category is also known as *non est factum* or *fraud in the factum*. This occurs where a party has been misled into executing a deed or signing a document essentially different from that which the party intended to sign or execute. The Latin *non est factum* literally means 'not my deed'.

In such situations, the contract will be void.

Illegal contracts

Illegal contracts are those that are prohibited by statute or illegal at common law on the grounds of public policy. A good example in the UK is contracts made in respect of gambling (known as *gaming contracts*) which cannot be enforced.

A further category are those contracts which may be described as unfair or unconscionable according to the legislation of the country the laws of which govern the contract. For example, in UK employment and other contracts, parties may not exclude liability for serious injury.

1.6   Performance of contracts

The general rule is that a party must perform exactly what he or she undertook to do in the contract. Contracts may, however, be varied by mutual agreement. Alternatively, where a party agrees to a request of the other party to the contract not to insist on performance of part of the contract, that second party is said to have *waived* his or her right to insist on performance in the manner originally agreed. The parties are then bound by the terms of the waiver and no consideration is necessary to support this.

2 CONTRACTUAL LANGUAGE

2.1 Peculiarities of contractual language

The English used in legal contracts has traditionally been rather old-fashioned and somewhat different to ordinary English. There are several reasons for this, which can be summarised as follows:

- The mixture of languages (English, Latin and French) from which the vocabulary used in legal English is drawn.
- The desire to avoid ambiguity in the use of language.
- Familiarity and habit: lawyers tend to be innately conservative and prefer to use forms and words that have been used before and seem to be effective.
- The tradition of using precedent documents in drafting, which results in lack of change in drafting practices over time.
- Pressure to conform to accepted professional standards.

Some of the peculiar features of contract language are explained in the following sections.

Doublets and triplets

Legal English has a strange habit of not using just one word to say something but two or three strung together (eg, *null and void*). There are some valid reasons why these formulations continue to be used in modern legal English. For example, in the phrase *give, devise and bequeath*, used in wills, the word *devise* meant to give land as inheritance, and the word *bequeath* meant to give personal property or money as inheritance. In addition, the habit of stringing together two or more words is a way of adding rhetorical emphasis to the legal idea being outlined.

The obvious problem with using such doublets and triplets is that they make documents longer and more difficult to read. Modern practice is to avoid these old forms and use one appropriate word instead. For example, the phrase *give, devise and bequeath* could be replaced by the single word *give* without serious loss of meaning.

The argument used by lawyers who wish to continue to use such old-fashioned words and phrases is that there is a valid reason for such words and phrases to be used, which is that they have been tried and tested in the courts and all lawyers know what they mean. Advocates of plain English drafting concede that while certain words and phrases have defined legal meanings, lawyers have a duty to their clients to use plain and simple language wherever possible.

It seems that drafting practices are now moving further towards a plain English style. However, the pace of this change is slow, and as a result it is still quite common to see certain typical doublets and triplets in certain legal documents. Some of the most common of these are listed below:

Able and willing (=able)

Agree and covenant (=agree)

All and sundry (=all)

Authorise and direct (=authorise)

Cancelled and set aside (=cancelled)

Custom and usage (=custom)

Deem and consider (=deem)

Do and perform (=perform)

Due and owing (=owing)

Fit and proper (=fit)

Full and complete (=complete)

Goods and chattels (=goods)

Keep and maintain (=maintain)

Known and described as (=known as)

Legal and valid (=valid)

Null and void (=void)

Object and purpose (=object OR purpose)

Order and direct (=order)

Over and above (=exceeding)

Part and parcel (=part)

Perform and discharge (=perform OR discharge)

Repair and make good (=repair)

Sole and exclusive (=sole OR exclusive)

Terms and conditions (=terms)

Touch and concern (=concern)

Uphold and support (=uphold)

Cancel, annul and set aside (=cancel)

Communicate, indicate or suggest (=communicate)

Dispute, controversy or claim (=dispute)

Give, devise and bequeath (=give)

Hold, possess, and enjoy (=hold)

Pay, satisfy, and discharge (=pay)

Possession, custody and control (=possession OR custody OR control)

Promise, agree and covenant (=promise OR agree)

Repair, uphold and maintain (=repair OR uphold OR maintain)

Way, shape or form (=way)

Deeming

The word *deem* is frequently used in contracts. In its legal sense it means to treat a thing as being something that it is not, or as possessing certain characteristics which it does not in fact possess. This meaning is employed in contracts and in legislation to create the idea that something mentioned in the contract is *deemed* (treated) to be something else. Consequently, although it would seem absurd to a layperson, from the point of view of common law drafting practices it would be perfectly acceptable to write in a contract:

> In this agreement dogs shall be deemed to be cats.

More typically, one might find *deemed* being used in this sort of clause:

> Notice shall be deemed served 72 hours after having been posted.

The purpose of such a clause is to indicate that for the purposes of the contract the parties agree to regard a notice as having been served once 72 hours has passed after the notice was posted.

In ordinary language, *deem* is simply an old-fashioned term meaning to consider in a specified way. It is a synonym for *think* or *judge*.

Unusual word order

In old-fashioned contracts one frequently sees sentences and phrases in which the order of words is distinctly strange. Here are some examples:

---

the provisions for termination hereinafter appearing

will at the cost of the borrower forthwith comply with the same

neither party may assign its rights hereunder without the prior written consent of the other party, which consent may not be withheld arbitrarily

the title above mentioned

such information as the buyer is required by law to provide

There is no single reason which explains this phenomenon. However, one clear factor is the influence of French upon the development of legal English. French was the language of legal proceedings in England for a period of about 300 years following the Norman invasion of England in 1066, with the result that many words in current legal use have their roots in this period. These include *property*, *estate*, *chattel*, *lease*, *executor* and *tenant*.

Although the Statute of Pleading of 1356 provided that all legal proceedings should be in English, the use of French in legal pleadings persisted into the 17th century in some areas of the law. The legacy of French in the form of French-derived words and unusual grammatical structures remains a significant influence on legal English.

Another likely factor is that the old practice of not using punctuation in legal documents meant that lawyers were forced to adopt peculiar styles of phrasing in order to avoid ambiguity in the documents they were drafting.

Here-, there- and where- words

Words like *hereof*, *thereof* and *whereof* are not used often in ordinary English. However, they appear frequently in contracts. They are generally used as a way of avoiding the repetition of names of things in the contract. For example:

---

the parties **hereto**

instead of:

the parties to this contract

---

or:

---

the provisions contained **hereinafter**

instead of:

the provisions referred to later on in this contract

However, in most cases the use of such words is strictly unnecessary or can be rendered unnecessary by the use of definitions. For example, if there is likely to be doubt about the matter, *the parties* can be defined, in a definitions section, as 'the parties to this contract'. In most cases, however, the meaning of words and phrases can be gathered from the context in which they are placed. *Here-*, *there-* and *where-* words persist in modern legal usage largely as a consequence of legal tradition rather than usefulness.

Here is a list of some of these words and the way in which they are used. It should be noted that the list is not exhaustive:

Hereafter means 'from now on or at some time in the future'. For example, 'the contract is effective hereafter'.

Hereat means (1) 'at this place or point' or (2) 'on account of or after this'. For example, 'hereat the stream divided'.

Hereby means 'by this means; as a result of this'. For example, 'the parties hereby declare'.

Herefrom means 'from this place or point'. For example, 'the goods shall be collected herefrom'.

Herein means 'in this document or matter'. For example, 'the terms referred to herein'.

Hereinabove means 'previously in this document or matter'. For example, 'the products hereinabove described'.

Hereinafter means 'later referred to in this matter or document'. For example, 'hereinafter referred to as the Company'.

Hereinbefore means 'previously in this document or matter'. For example, 'the products hereinbefore described'.

Hereof means 'of this matter or document'. For example, 'the parties hereof'.

Hereto means 'to this place or to this matter or document'. For example, 'the parties hereto'.

Heretofore means 'before now'. For example, 'the parties have had no business dealings heretofore'.

Hereunder means 'later referred to in this matter or document'. For example, 'the exemptions referred to hereunder'.

Herewith means 'with this letter'. For example, 'I enclose herewith the plan'.

Thereof means 'of the thing just mentioned'. For example, 'The contract was signed on 1 May 1999. The parties thereof ...'.

Thereafter means 'after that time'. For example, 'The products shall be transported to The Grange. Thereafter, they shall be stored in a warehouse'.

Thereat means (1) at that place or (2) on account of or after that. For example, 'thereat, payments shall cease'.

Thereby means 'by that means; as a result of that'. For example, 'the parties thereby agree'.

Therein means 'in that place, document or respect'. For example, 'The parties shall refer to the contract dated 1 May 1999. It is agreed therein that …'.

Thereinafter means 'later referred to in that matter or document'. For example, 'thereinafter, it is agreed that …'.

Thereof means 'of the thing just mentioned'. For example, 'Reference is made in paragraph 5 to the contract dated 1 May 1999. The parties thereof agreed that …'.

Thereon means 'on or following from the thing just mentioned'. For example, 'The machine rests on a wooden block. There is placed thereon a metal bracket …'.

Thereto means 'to that place or to that matter or document'. For example, 'the parties thereto'.

Therefor means 'for that'. For example, 'the equipment shall be delivered on 13 September 2003. The Company agrees to pay therefor the sum of £150,000'.

Therefor should not be confused with 'therefore' which means 'for that reason'.

Thereupon means 'immediately or shortly after that'. For example, 'delivery shall take place on 13 September 2003. Thereupon the equipment shall be stored in the Company's warehouse'.

Whereabouts means 'the place where someone or something is'. For example, 'the Company shall be kept informed as to the whereabouts of the products'.

Whereat means 'at which'. 'The seller attempted to charge extra interest on late payment, whereat the buyer objected'.

Whereby means 'by which'. For example, 'the contract dated 1 May 1999, whereby the Company agreed to purchase the products'.

Wherefore means 'as a result of which'. For example, 'the buyer breached the contract, wherefore the seller suffered damage'.

Wherein means (1) in which, or (2) in which place or respect. For example, 'the contract dated 1 May 1999, wherein it is stated that …'.

Whereof means 'of what or of which'. For example, 'the Company one of the directors whereof is a foreign national'.

Whereupon means 'immediately after which'. For example, 'The sum of $15,000 shall be paid by the buyer to the seller on 13 September 2003, whereupon the buyer's liability to the seller shall be discharged'.

Whatsoever, wheresoever and howsoever

Whatsoever is an old-fashioned word meaning 'whatever', ie, 'no matter what' in contractual contexts.

Wheresoever is an old-fashioned word meaning 'wherever', ie, 'in or to whatever place' in contractual contexts.

Howsoever is an old-fashioned word meaning 'however', ie, 'in whatever way or to whatever extent'.

These words can often be found in contracts, for example in the following sentence:

> This limitation shall apply in any situation whatsoever, wheresoever and howsoever arising.

The word **whosoever** may also be encountered. This simply means 'whoever'.

Hence, whence and thence

The words *hence*, *whence* and *thence*, and the derivatives *henceforth* and *thenceforth* are all archaic forms in ordinary English which are, however, still occasionally seen in legal English. Their meanings are briefly outlined below:

Hence means (1) for this reason, and (2) from now on. *Henceforth* means from this or that time on.

Whence means (1) from what place or source; (2) from which or from where; (3) to the place from which; or (4) as a consequence of which.

Thence means (1) from a place or source previously mentioned, and (2) as a consequence.

Thenceforth means from that time, place or point onwards.

Synonyms

English contains a large number of synonyms. This poses difficulties in legal language, making it essential for drafters to make efforts to ensure that terminology is used consistently in legal documents. Contract language often contains a number of synonyms which can be confusing to the layperson or non-native English speaker. Some examples are set out below. Note that while the alternative words given are synonyms, the choice of which word to use will be dictated to a large extent by the context:

Assign may be replaced by *deliver, give, hand over, pass, submit, supply, transfer*.

Breach may be replaced by *contravention, failure, infringement, offence, omission, transgression, violation.*

Clause may be replaced by *paragraph, condition, warranty, stipulation, provision, proviso, section, sub-section, part, article.*

Contract may be replaced by *agreement, bargain, commitment, deal, compact, settlement, undertaking, understanding.*

Claim may be replaced by *action, dispute, lawsuit, process, suit.*

Invalid may be replaced by *null and void, unacceptable, ineffective, out-of-date, void.*

Mutual may be replaced by *common, joint, reciprocal, shared.*

Obligation may be replaced by *commitment, compulsion, duty, liability, requirement, responsibility.*

Promise may be replaced by *assurance, commitment, undertaking.*

Valid may be replaced by *allowed, approved, authentic, authorized, current, enforceable, genuine, lawful, legal, legitimate, permissible, proper, ratified.*

-er, -or and -ee names

The English used in contracts contains a large number of names and titles, such as *employer* and *employee,* in which the reciprocal and opposite nature of the relationship is indicated by the use of *-er/-or* endings and *-ee* endings. These endings derive from Latin, which has played a large role in the formation of legal English generally. In the example given here, the employer is the one who employs the employee. Hence, the employee is employed by the employer.

Here are some further examples that you may have encountered:

Assignor is a party who assigns (transfers) something to another party.

Assignee is the party to whom something is assigned.

Donor is a party who donates something to another party.

Donee is the party to whom something is donated.

Interviewer is a person who is interviewing someone.

Interviewee is a person who is being interviewed by the interviewer.

Lessor is a party who grants a lease over a property. He or she is therefore the landlord.

Lessee is the party to whom a lease over a property is granted. He or she is therefore the tenant.

Mortgagor is a lender who lends money to a property owner (the mortgagee) in return for the grant by the mortgagee of a mortgage over the property as security for the loan.

Mortgagee is the property owner to whom money is loaned by the mortgagor in return for the grant of a mortgage over the property.

Offeror is a party who makes a contractual offer to another party.

Offeree is the party to whom a contractual offer is made.

Payer is a party who makes a payment to another party.

Payee is the party to whom payment is made.

Promisor is a party who makes a promise to another party.

Promisee is the party to whom a promise is made.

Representor is a party who makes a contractual representation to another party.

Representee is the party to whom a contractual representation is made.

Transferor is a party who transfers something to another party.

Transferee is the party to whom something is transferred.

One should note that these words are not always used in the way the examples given above might lead one to expect. For example, a *guarantor* is someone who provides a *guarantee*. However, the person to whom a guarantee is given is known technically as the *principal debtor*, not the guarantee. The guarantee is the document by which the secondary agreement that constitutes the guarantee is made.

Obligations, authorisations and conditions

In contracts, it is usual to find the words *shall*, *will*, *must* and *may* used over and over again. The words are used in different contexts.

In the third person *will* refers to the future ('he will go' means he intends to go) whereas *shall* indicates an imperative ('he shall go' means that he is obliged to go). Therefore, in legal documents drafted in the third person, obligations are often expressed using *shall*. *Will* should not be used if the intention is to express an obligation.

Shall is frequently overused to indicate the future. This should be avoided. *Must* is a good replacement for shall when expressing the imperative: 'If X becomes a party to this agreement, he shall [must] immediately pay to Y ...'

May is used in the following situations:

- to express a possibility that something may be done ('the Company may purchase further products');
- to indicate that one has a discretion to do that thing ('the parties to this contract may assign the benefits under this contract'); or
- to indicate a wish ('the parties intend that the signature of this contract may signal the beginning of a mutually beneficial co-operation between them').

The following words are generally used in the contexts suggested:

- *is entitled to* indicates a party's right ('X is entitled to use the office premises');
- *is not entitled to* indicates that a party does not have a right ('X is not entitled to use the office premises');
- *may* indicates a party's discretion to do something ('X may use the office premises');
- *may not* indicates that a party does not have discretion to do something ('X may not use the office premises');
- *must* or *shall* indicates an obligation to do something ('X must/shall pay the rent');
- *shall not* indicates a duty not to do something ('X shall not pay to Y …');
- *must* can also be used to indicate a condition precedent ('in order to qualify for this position, X must …');
- *is not required to* indicates that there is not duty to do something ('X is not required to pay Y to use the office premises').

2.2 Rules of interpretation

The textual approach

The basic method of interpretation traditionally used by common law lawyers is known as the *textual* or *literal* approach. This approach is based on the idea that the meaning and effect of a contract or piece of legislation should be determined solely from the words of the text itself and not from any external evidence.

This method contrasts with the approach to interpretation traditionally used in civil law jurisdictions. In such jurisdictions, the *purposive* or *teleological* approach is used. This is based on the idea that the meaning and effect of a contract or piece of legislation should be determined taking account of object and purpose of the contract or piece of legislation and the intentions of the parties (if a contract) or intention of the drafter (if legislation).

The effect of this approach on the drafting of contracts is that common law lawyers tend to draft contracts in a way which seeks to cover any possible thing which might go wrong in the contract, no matter how remote. This of course leads to long and complicated documents. This tendency is made worse by the fact that many common law countries (particularly the USA and to a lesser extent the UK) have lightly-regulated free-market economies in which parties' freedom to contract is not much affected by legal rules. In such climates there is greater need for remedies and dispute resolution methods to be specifically agreed between the parties in the contract itself.

Specific rules of interpretation

In addition to the basic approach outlined above, some specific rules of interpretation are used in common law jurisdictions. The six primary rules are briefly outlined below.

> The document must be read as a whole

This rule provides that when a reader is seeking to interpret the meaning of a particular clause in a contract, this should not be done without taking into consideration what the rest of the contract says. The exact meaning of a part of the contract should become clear once the whole document has been read.

> Words should be given their ordinary meaning

This rule provides that when reading a contract, one should stick to the ordinary and grammatical sense of the words being used. There are two exceptions to this:

- where the ordinary meaning of a word leads either to absurdity or inconsistency with the rest of the document, the meaning should be modified in the light of the intentions of the parties to avoid such absurdity or inconsistency;

- technical words should be given their technical meanings.

> *Contra proferentem* rule

This rule provides that if an ambiguity in a contract cannot be resolved in any other way, then it must be interpreted against the interests of the party which suggested it.

For example, if a problem arises concerning the extent of cover provided in an insurance contract and one interpretation favours the insurer and the other the insured, the court will use the interpretation which favours the insured.

> *Noscitur a sociis* rule

Noscitur a sociis is Latin meaning 'it is known by its neighbours'. The *noscitur a sociis* rule states that if the meaning of a phrase in a contract is unclear by itself, its meaning should be gathered from the words and phrases associated with it.

Ejusdem generis rule

Ejusdem generis is Latin meaning 'of the same kind'. The *ejusdem generis* rule applies when a list of specific items belonging to the same class is followed by general words; the general words are treated as confined to other items of the same class.

Therefore, if a list reads 'cats, dogs and other animals', the phrase 'other animals' will be interpreted as meaning other *domestic* animals only.

Expressio unius est exclusio alterius rule

Expressio unius est exclusio alterius is Latin meaning 'the inclusion of one is the exclusion of another'. The *expressio unius est exclusio alterius* rule states that when a list of specific items is not followed by general words, it is taken as exhaustive. For example, 'weekends and public holidays' excludes ordinary weekdays.

3 STRUCTURE OF A CONTRACT

Most commercial contracts follow the structure outlined below, although there may be variation in the order in which clauses are presented according to the nature of the contract and the preferences of the drafters:

1   The names and addresses of the parties
2   Recital
3   Definitions
4   Conditions precedent
5   Agreements
6   Representations and warranties
7   Boilerplate clauses
8   Schedules
9   Signature section
10 Appendices

Some brief notes regarding the points listed above are given below.

The names and addresses of the parties

The first section of the contract usually sets out the full names and postal addresses of all the parties to the contract. This section may also specify that a shortened name will be used in the remainder of the contract to denote each of the parties. For example:

Pan-Oceanic Shrimp Packers plc (hereinafter referred to as 'the Company')

The words 'the Company' will then be used in the remainder of the contract in place of Pan-Oceanic Shrimp Packers plc.

Recital

The recital is often referred to as a non-operative part of the contract, since it has no specific legal effect. The purpose of the recital is to explain to the reader the background to the transaction. If necessary, the recital also sets out certain facts which may influence the way in which a court might interpret provisions of the contract.

For example, the background to an exclusion clause might be clarified by relating the decision of both parties to impose the risk of loss on one party rather than the other because this is more economical from an insurance viewpoint.

Definitions

The definitions section contains a list of terms used later in the contract. A definition is given for each term, which represents the way in which the drafters of the contract wish the term to be interpreted as a matter of law. Here is an example of a definition:

'Execution date' shall mean 3 October 2002, the date of execution of this Agreement.

Often the definitions section needs to be read in conjunction with another section of the agreement. For example, a definition may simply state that '... shall have the meaning assigned to that term in section 4.3 of this Agreement'.

Conditions precedent

Conditions precedent are conditions which have to be satisfied before the agreement, or a certain part of the agreement, comes into force. They are generally viewed as being outside the main terms of the contract. One important consequence of this fact is that these conditions are therefore not subject to the *parol evidence rule*. This rule states that where all the terms of a contract are contained in a written document, no external evidence may be added to it to vary the interpretation to be given to the contract. Since the conditions precedent are not regarded as forming part of the main terms of the contract, the parol evidence rule does not apply. Consequently, it follows that external evidence can be added to vary the interpretation of such clauses.

Agreements

The agreements section contains the rights and obligations of the parties. This part reflects the heart of the deal struck between the parties. The drafting of the clauses will therefore depend upon the particular facts of the case at hand. In a simple sale of goods contract, the seller will promise to sell and deliver goods of a certain description and quality. The buyer will promise to pay for them.

In addition, this part of the contract will contain various clauses covering what happens if the seller fails to deliver or the buyer fails to pay.

Representations and warranties

The representations and warranties section contains promises by one or other party that a given statement or set of facts is true. A representation is a statement of fact made by one contracting party to the other which induces the other to enter the contract. A warranty is a contractual promise and if such a promise is broken, the innocent party will be able to claim damages.

Boilerplate clauses

Boilerplate clauses are standard clauses which are inserted as a matter of course into certain types of agreement. The different types of boilerplate clause which may be used are considered in Chapter 4.4.

Schedules

Schedules form part of the substantive agreement. They are a useful place to put detailed substantive provisions. In this way, the logical flow of the contract is not impeded by a mass of detail.

Signature section

The signature section comes after the schedules and before the appendices. Witnesses are not required for most kinds of contract. All parties to the contract are required to sign the document as evidence of their agreement to its terms.

Appendices

Documents referred to in an agreement should be attached as appendices for ease of reference. These may not necessarily form part of the agreement.

4 CONTENT OF A CONTRACT

4.1 Conditions and warranties

The terms of a contract may be divided into two categories: *conditions* and *warranties*.[5]

Conditions are major terms of the contract, those that are of the essence of the contract. Breach of a condition constitutes a fundamental breach of the contract and entitles the injured party to treat the contract as discharged, that is, they no longer have any obligations under the terms of the contract.

Warranties are minor terms of the contract, breach of which will entitle the innocent party to damages but not to treat the contract as discharged. Note, however, that in UK insurance law, a warranty has the same meaning as the definition of a condition given above.

In the USA, the term *warranty* covers both conditions and warranties.

4.2 Implied terms

These are not terms agreed by the parties and do not appear in the contract. However, it is important to know about them.

The phrase *implied term* is the jargon used by common law lawyers to refer to two different matters. These are:

1   Legal rules contained in legislation which apply to the contract in question. For example, if legislation provides that goods sold in any commercial agreement must be of satisfactory quality, it is then an implied term of any contract dealing with the sale of goods that they must be of satisfactory quality.

2   In the event that breach of the contract results in a court case, the phrase 'implied term' is used to indicate an interpretation of the contract made by the court which is intended to by the court to give effect to the presumed intentions of the parties in making the contract.

An implied term may be either a condition or a warranty.

---

5   But note that in the USA and Canada all the terms of the contract are known as warranties.

4.3 Boilerplate clauses

These are standard clauses inserted as a matter of course into all contracts of a certain type. Christou[6] has drawn an analogy between the operation of such clauses and the operation of computer technology: if the conditions which form the heart of the agreement between the parties are the operational software, then the boilerplate clauses are the hardware which govern the internal working of the contract. They are generally classifiable as warranties.

The range of possible boilerplate clauses is wide, and depends on the type of contract in question. However, a certain number tend to appear in most commercial agreements. The most common of these are discussed below.

4.4 Specific clause types

This chapter focuses on the clause types which are often encountered in business contracts. In respect of each clause type:

- the purpose of the clause is explained;
- a specimen clause is given; and
- the meaning of any unusual words or phrases used in the clause is explained.

The first two clauses featured below (status of parties and purpose of contract) come from recitals to contracts. The others may be classified as boilerplate clauses.

Status of parties

Purpose of clause

This clause typically contains the following information:

- who the parties are;
- under what national jurisdiction they are incorporated;
- their business addresses and contact details; and
- what area of business they are engaged in.

This kind of clause has no particular legal effect but contains useful background information. It is usually contained in the recital section.

Specimen clause

The specimen clause given below clause identifies the parties to the contract, confirms that they are valid companies (corporations) and sets out some brief background details about the areas of business the parties are involved in:

---

6   Christou, Richard, *Boilerplate: Practical Clauses*, 1995, London: Sweet & Maxwell, p 1.

Statchem Inc is a corporation duly organized and validly existing under the laws of the State of New York, United States of America, with its principal office located at New York City, New York. Statchem Inc is engaged in the business of producing and selling statistical reports to companies engaged in the production of chemicals used in industrial cleaning processes.

Chem Scourge Ltd is a corporation duly organized and validly existing under the laws of England and Wales, with its principal office located at Reading, UK. Chem Scourge is engaged in the business of producing and selling chemicals used in industrial cleaning processes.

Meaning of words and phrases

Duly organized and validly existing: the companies are organised according to the applicable company regulations, have proper legal status and are not bankrupt.

Principal office: main office or headquarters.

Engaged in the business of: involved in the business of.

Purpose of contract

Purpose of clause

This clause explains the reason the contract has been made and what it is intended to achieve. It forms the main part of the recital. This kind of clause usually has no particular legal effect but may be helpful in interpreting other parts of the contract.

Specimen clause

The specimen clause given below is taken from the recital to a sales representative agreement. It simply records the company's desire to appoint a sales representative and the representative's ability to perform this role:

The Company desires to appoint a Representative for the Territory as hereinafter defined, and the Representative declares it possesses the requisite skills, facilities and financial and physical resources to perform as such Representative for the said Territory and Sales Responsibility and is willing to do so.

Meaning of words and phrases

The Company desires to appoint: the Company wishes to appoint.

The Territory: the specified geographical area within which the representative is authorised by the Company to act under the contract.

As hereinafter defined: as defined later in the contract. These words alert the reader to the likelihood that the contract contains a definitions section in which the words 'the Territory' will be given a defined meaning for the purposes of the contract.

The requisite skills: the skills necessary for acting successfully as a representative.

Condition precedent

Purpose of clause

A condition precedent is usually a clause which provides that a party is required to do something before taking some further action. For example, the seller may be required to send a notice of default to the buyer before seeking a legal remedy against the buyer.

Specimen clause

The specimen clause given below places a condition on the seller's right to seek a remedy if the buyer fails to make payment in time. The seller is not obliged to send a notice, but if he or she does not send one then no remedy can be sought:

If the Buyer fails to make any payment on time, the Seller must send a Notice of Default before seeking any remedy.

Meaning of words and phrases

A Notice of Default: a formal document advising the Buyer that he or she has failed to do something required to be done under the contract.

Remedy: any method available in law to enforce, protect or recover rights, usually available by seeking a court order.

Goods

Purpose of clause

This clause defines the products and/or services being dealt with by the contract. It may refer to a list of products and/or services contained in one of the schedules to the contract. In addition, the clause may provide that the list may be altered by agreement between the parties.

Specimen clause

The specimen clause given below does not list the goods dealt with in the contract, but refers the reader to a schedule in which the goods will be set out in detail. The purpose of putting the list of goods in a schedule is to avoid cluttering the main part of the document with fine detail. The clause also provides that any variation to the range of goods to be dealt with in the contract can only be done with the written agreement of both parties:

> The Products and Services, collectively referred to herein as 'Goods', covered by this Agreement are as described in Schedule 1 hereto and are limited to that as described. They may be subsequently enlarged upon, reduced or otherwise changed by written mutual consent of the parties.

Meaning of words and phrases

Collectively referred to herein: referred to as a group of things in this contract.

Schedule 1 hereto: schedule 1 of this contract.

Limited to that as described: the range of goods dealt with in this contract are solely those listed in the schedule.

Written mutual consent: the written agreement of both parties to the contract.

Prices

Purpose of clause

The prices to be paid for the products and services may actually be contained in a schedule to which the prices clause will refer. In addition to stating the prices at which the products and services are to be sold, the prices clause may also contain the following information:

- the currency in which transactions are to take place;
- the basis for variation of prices; and
- the basis for giving discounts (for example, for large orders).

Specimen clause

The specimen clause given below comes from a distribution agreement and regulates the prices of good supplied to the distributor for resale in a specified territory. The prices are contained in a separate schedule and the main effect of the clause is to give the company the right to vary the prices so long as it gives three months' written notice to the distributor:

> The Company undertakes to supply the Products to the Distributor at the prices currently as per the Price List set out in Schedule 1 hereto PROVIDED ALWAYS that on giving the Distributor not less than 3 months' notice in writing the Company shall be entitled to make any price adjustments which it considers necessary and prudent.

Meaning of words and phrases

Undertakes to supply: agrees to supply.

As per the price list: in accordance with the price list.

Provided always: so long as, if.

Necessary and prudent: sensible in the light of the market conditions. This is a classic doublet (see above).

Terms of payment

Purpose of clause

The terms of payment clause deals with the basis on which payments shall be made. It may contain the following information:

- the time period within which payment must be made;
- the level of interest charged on late payment; and
- any arrangements for credit facilities.

Specimen clause

The specimen clause given below creates an obligation for the distributor to pay the company within a specified time period from receiving the goods:

> The Distributor shall pay the Company for all Products purchased hereunder not later than thirty days from the date of invoice.

Meaning of words and phrases

Purchased hereunder: purchased in accordance with this contract.

Uniqueneness of goods

Purpose of clause

This clause states that goods sold under the contract are unique and cannot be purchased elsewhere. The purpose of this clause is to encourage a court to make an order for *specific performance* in the event that a claim arose due to breach of the contract. Specific performance occurs when the court orders a party to fulfil his or her obligations under the contract. A court may make such an order where the damage suffered by the innocent party would not be satisfactorily compensated by the payment of money.

Specimen clause

> The Seller and Buyer affirm that the goods sold under this contract are unique and cannot be purchased on the open market or manufactured specially.

Meaning of words and phrases

The Seller and Buyer affirm: the seller and buyer confirm and declare.

Commencement and termination

Purpose of clause

The commencement and termination clause sets out when the contract starts and finishes. This may be expressed in terms of specific dates, or it may be expressed on the basis of particular events occurring. Such clauses often also contain provisions dealing with:

- circumstances under which the contract can be extended and for how long;
- any events which would automatically terminate the contract; or
- the manner in which either party may terminate the contract where there has been a material breach by the other party.

Specimen clause

The specimen clause given below provides that the contract will start on the date it is signed and go on for two years. After that it will automatically be renewed for periods of two years if the distributor has sold enough goods to satisfy the company. The clause also indicates that there are other clauses governing termination in the contract and that this clause must be read in conjunction with those other clauses:

> This agreement shall be for a period of two years from the date hereof and shall thereafter be renewed for further successive periods of two years PROVIDED ALWAYS that the Distributor shall have achieved a level of sales to the satisfaction of the Company and also subject to the provisions for termination hereinafter appearing.

Meaning of words and phrases

From the date hereof: from the date this contract is signed.

Renewed for further successive periods of two years: the contract will continue indefinitely in two-year periods following the end of the first two-year period.

The provisions for termination: the clauses governing termination of the contract.

Hereinafter appearing: appearing later in this contract.

Language

Purpose of clause

The language clause states which language is the controlling language for the purposes of interpreting the contract. It may also state which language the parties should use when writing letters to one another.

Specimen clause

The specimen clause given below states that English shall be the operational language for the purposes of the contract and also the dominant language in interpreting it. This may be of importance in international contracts involving different national languages. In such cases it is usual to prepare versions of the contract in both languages. Specifying which language is to be used when interpreting the agreement avoids the possibility of conflict when linguistic differences cause ambiguities to arise:

> The English language shall be the controlling language for the purpose of interpreting this Agreement, and all correspondence between Company and Representative shall be in the English language.

Meaning of words and phrases

Correspondence: letters, memoranda, notes, messages.

Procedures on termination

Purpose of clause

This clause sets out any procedures which the parties agree to follow after the agreement has been terminated. These particularly relate to the return of samples, specimens and technical and advertising material by an agent to a principal in the case of an agency agreement. They may also relate to the destruction of any confidential material acquired in the course of the contract.

Specimen clause

The specimen clause given below simply deals with the administrative acts to be carried out by the distributor following termination of the agreement. It seeks to ensure that the company's property does not remain in the distributor's hands and that the company can obtain the benefit of the distributor's customer list:

> Upon termination of this Agreement, the Distributor shall promptly return to the Company or otherwise dispose of as the Company may instruct all samples, instruction books, technical pamphlets, catalogues, advertising material and other documents and papers whatsoever in the Distributor's possession and also deliver up to the Company a note of the names and addresses of all customers to whom the Products have been supplied during the currency of this Agreement.

Meaning of words and phrases

Other documents and papers whatsoever: any other documents and papers.
Deliver up: deliver, provide.
During the currency of this Agreement: during the period of this contract.

Retention of title

Purpose of clause

The retention of title clause usually specifies that where goods are being transferred from one party to the contract to another, ownership of the goods does not change until the second party pays for the goods.

Specimen clause

The specimen clause given below is intended to ensure that the distributor does not own the goods until they have been paid for in a specified manner:

> Title to the Products shall only pass to the Distributor when payment has been received by the Company in the manner stipulated in paragraph 4 herein.

Meaning of words and phrases

Title: right of ownership.
Pass: be transferred to.
Stipulated: specified.

Service of notices

Purpose of clause

This clause specifies the way in which any notice or other communication that may have to be given by either party in performing the contract is to be sent. Such a clause frequently states that notices may be sent by post or fax, gives the address or fax number to which the notice should be sent, and the name of the persons for whose attention it should be marked.

Specimen clause

The specimen clause given below specifies the ways in which notices required under the contract must be served and sets out the time limits by the expiration of which they will be deemed served:

> Any notice given under this Agreement shall be in writing and signed by or on behalf of the party giving it and may be served by leaving it or sending it by fax, prepaid recorded delivery or registered post to the address and for the attention of the relevant party set out in clause 15.2 (or as otherwise notified from time to time hereunder). Any notice so served by fax or post shall be deemed to have been received:
>
> (a)   in the case of fax, twelve (12) hours after the time of dispatch;
>
> (b)   in the case of recorded delivery or registered post, forty eight (48) hours from the date of posting.

Meaning of words and phrases

Notified from time to time hereunder: advised to the other party when necessary under the terms of this contract.

So served: served in such a way.

The time of dispatch: the time of sending.

Governing law

Purpose of clause

This clause states which national law governs the contract and which court has jurisdiction in the event of disputes arising from the contract. It is an essential clause in cases in which the parties are situated in different countries, since the manner in which a contractual breach is interpreted in the law of one country may differ significantly from the practice in the law of another country.

Specimen clause

The specimen clause given below provides that the law to be used if there is a dispute about the contract is that of England and Wales:

> This Agreement is governed by and shall be construed in accordance with the laws of England and Wales.

Meaning of words and phrases

Construed in accordance with: interpreted according to.

Assignment

Purpose of clause

The assignment clause deals with the circumstances under which the benefit of the contract can be *assigned* (transferred) to a third party by either party to the contract. These clauses usually provide that if assignment is permitted, then the party that wishes to assign the benefit of the contract must inform the other party in writing before carrying out the assignment.

Specimen clause

The purpose of the specimen clause given below is to try to ensure that neither party can transfer (assign) its rights or obligations under the contract without informing the other party and obtaining the other party's written agreement. The clause specifies that the other party should agree to a reasonable request to assign and that if either party tries to make an assignment without the other party's written agreement, this will be ineffective. The inclusion of the section about the agreement not being assigned by operation of law refers to circumstances when a legal obligation beyond the parties' control might result in an assignment being made. The validity of this part of the clause will depend entirely on the legal circumstances:

> Neither party may assign its rights or obligations hereunder without the prior written consent of the other party, which consent may not be withheld arbitrarily, nor may this agreement be assigned by operation of law. Any purported assignment in the absence of such written consent shall be void.

Meaning of words and phrases

Hereunder: in this contract.

Prior written consent: written agreement obtained beforehand.

Which consent may not be withheld arbitrarily: agreement must be given unless there is good reason not to.

Purported assignment: an invalid assignment claimed falsely to be a valid one.

Void: of no legal effect, not legally enforceable.

Indemnity

Purpose of clause

An indemnity is an agreement by one party to a contract (X) made with another party to the contract (Y) to protect Y against liability for any sums owed to a third party (Z). X agrees to assume liability for any sums Y might owe Z. Indemnity clauses are generally designed to protect one or other of the parties to a contract from any liability in respect of claims brought by third parties.

Specimen clause

In the specimen clause given below, the distributor agrees to protect the company by providing it with an indemnity against any court claims or costs arising from sale of the products. This indemnity does not cover claims and costs which result from manufacturing defects in the products:

> The Distributor shall indemnify the Company against all actions, costs, claims and demands arising from the sale of the Products by the Distributor, excluding matters of a product liability nature.

Meaning of words and phrases

Actions, costs, claims and demands: a catch-all definition including court cases, costs, formal demands for payment, etc.

Matters of a product liability nature: claims relating to manufacturing defects in the products.

Arbitration

Purpose of clause

Arbitration clauses generally specify the terms under which any dispute arising from the contract will be settled by arbitration rather than being referred to the court. Arbitration is the settlement of a dispute by one or more independent third parties. These clauses usually name the venue at which arbitration will take place and either appoint the arbitrators or define the way in which arbitrators are to be appointed in the absence of agreement between the parties.

Specimen clause

The specimen clause given below records the parties' agreement that any disputes arising from the agreement will be settled by arbitration. It also indicates the place at which arbitration will take place, the rules of arbitration that will be followed and the status of the arbitrator's decision:

> Any dispute arising out of this agreement shall be finally settled by arbitration in accordance with the arbitration rules of the Committee of Arbitration at the Central Chamber of Commerce in Finland and the arbitration tribunal shall consist of one arbitrator.

Meaning of words and phrases

Finally settled by arbitration: resolved by arbitration with no possibility of taking the dispute further in the event that one of the parties does not like the outcome.

Abitration tribunal: the arbitration court.

Whole agreement/merger clause

Purpose of clause

The whole agreement or merger clause (merger is the USA term, whole agreement the UK term for such clauses) specifies the supremacy of the written contract in recording the agreement between the parties. It may also specify the conditions under which the parties may vary the terms of the agreement. The clause usually specifies that the written contract contains the whole of the agreement between the parties and overrides any previous oral and written agreements. It may also specify that any variation of the terms of the contract must be in the form of a written document.

Specimen clause

The aim of the specimen clause given below is to record the parties' agreement that all the terms of the contract between them are contained solely in the written agreement and not elsewhere. It confirms that the contract is final and complete:

> This agreement is the whole agreement between the parties and supersedes all prior written and oral agreements, understandings and commitments between the parties.

Meaning of words and phrases

Supersedes: takes the place of, overrides.
Oral agreements: agreements made by spoken words.

Severance

Purpose of clause

The purpose of the severance clause is to record the parties' wish that if the court finds that any part of the contract is unenforceable, the remainder of the contract should not be affected by this. The clause accordingly invites the court to 'sever' the unenforceable clause from the rest of the contract.

Specimen clause

The specimen clause given below is a standard example of this type of clause:

> The invalidity, in whole or in part, of any term of this agreement does not affect the validity of the remainder of the agreement.

Meaning of words and phrases

Severance: removing one part of the contract from the rest of the contract.

Invalidity: being void, not legally enforceable.

Waiver

Purpose of clause

A waiver occurs when one party to a contract agrees not to insist on strict performance by the other party of one or more of the terms of the contract. The party therefore refrains from asserting its full legal rights under the contract. The terms of the contract are accordingly varied. A waiver clause usually states the terms under which a waiver is effective and generally provides that it must be in writing and signed by both parties to the contract.

Specimen clause

The specimen clause given below is intended to prevent a waiver of the contract occurring unless both parties have agreed to the variation in writing:

> No variation of this Agreement (or any document entered into pursuant to this Agreement) shall be valid unless it is in writing and signed by or on behalf of each of the parties hereto.

Meaning of words and phrases

Waiver: variation of a term of a contract caused when one party to the contract agrees not to insist on strict performance by the other party of one or more of the terms of the contract.

Pursuant to: in accordance with.

On behalf of: as a representative of.

The parties hereto: the parties to this contract.

Inspection

Purpose of clause

An inspection clause usually records that a party has inspected the goods which are to be sold under the contract and enters into the contract in reliance on that inspection. The intended effect is to prevent the buyer suing the seller in the event that the goods are not in the condition he or she believes them to be in. It involves application of the principle *caveat emptor* (see the Glossary of Foreign Terms Used in Law).

Specimen clause

The aim of the specimen clause given below is to try to ensure that the seller is not liable to pay the buyer any compensation if the facts are not actually as the buyer believes them to be. The buyer accordingly accepts this risk by accepting such a clause in the contract:

> The Buyer has inspected and is familiar with the premises and the physical condition of all the furniture, fixtures and equipment and improvements thereon and therein, and enters into this Agreement on the Buyer's own independent investigation.

Meaning of words and phrases

The premises: the building and land occupied by a business.

Fixtures: a piece of equipment or furniture which is fixed into position.

Improvements thereon and therein: improvements of any kind made to the premises, furniture, fixtures and equipment.

Enters into this Agreement: accepts, signs this contract.

Novation

Purpose of clause

Novation occurs when a contract is replaced by a new one either between the same parties or introducing a new part. The parties specify the circumstances in which and the manner in which a new contract arises as a result of the discharge of an obligation under the original one. Such provisions take effect as subsequent independently drafted variations of the original contract.

Specimen clause

In the specimen clause given below Statchem has agreed to pay the $150,000 debt originally owed by Chem Scourge to the company. This clause accordingly releases Chem Scourge from liability to pay and transfers that liability to Statchem. A contractual obligation is therefore created between Statchem and the company which did not exist before:

> The Company hereby acknowledges that in consideration of Statchem Inc having assumed the liability of Chem Scourge Ltd to pay to the Company $150,000 for Products delivered on 23 September 2003, the Company releases all the claims which it had against Chem Scourge Ltd under the original contract. In lieu of these claims, the Company accepts the liability of Statchem Inc for the obligation of Chem Scourge Ltd under the original contract.

Meaning of words and phrases

The Company hereby acknowledges: the Company accepts as a result of this clause.

In consideration of: as a contractually binding promise made in return for the promise made by the other party.

Releases all the claims: abandons all the claims.

In lieu of: instead of.

Limited warranty

Purpose of clause

A limited warranty is a warranty which is limited in extent or time. For example, in a sales of goods contract, the seller might warrant that the goods sold were free of defects for a period of one year from the date of purchase. The seller might also limit the warranty by, for example, stating that the warranty is only available if the buyer could show that certain manufacturer's recommendations had been followed in using the goods.

Specimen clause

The specimen clause given below is intended to limit the manufacturer's liability to repair or replace any defective part to a certain time period after purchase:

The Manufacturer agrees to repair or replace any defective part during the first 12 months after purchase.

Meaning of words and phrases

Defective part: a broken or faulty component.

Exemption clauses

Purpose of clause

Exemption clauses seek to exclude or reduce the liability of one of the parties in specified circumstances. In common law jurisdictions, courts usually interpret these clauses narrowly by applying the *contra proferentem* rule, which states that in cases of ambiguity, the clause shall be interpreted against the party seeking to rely on it.

Specimen clause

The specimen clause given below is taken from a share purchase agreement. It aims to limit the seller's liability for claims based on matters revealed in the disclosure letter and accounts – information which would have been provided to the buyer before the purchase went ahead:

> The Vendor shall not be liable for any Claim:
>
> (a) in the case of a Claim in respect of a breach of the Warranties, if and to the extent that the fact, matter, event or circumstance giving rise to such claim was fairly and reasonably disclosed in the Disclosure Letter; or
>
> (b) if and to the extent that the matter is specifically disclosed or is specifically provided for in the Accounts.

Meaning of words and phrases

Vendor: seller.

Disclosed: made known, revealed.

Disclosure Letter: a document in which the sellers of a company set out all the facts already revealed to the buyer which breach the warranties contained in the contract. It is usual practice for the buyer then to agree that it cannot sue for breach of warranty caused by this disclosure.

If and to the extent that: if but only so far as; ie, if the full extent of the matter is not made known, the buyer may still have a right to sue.

Confidentiality and disclosure/secrecy clause

Purpose of clause

The aim of this clause is to protect both parties' intellectual property rights and know-how. Such clauses usually provide that neither party may reveal to another party any confidential information about the other party acquired as a result of the contract. This obligation usually endures after the contract is terminated. However, it does not apply to information that is already in the public domain.

Specimen clause

The specimen clause given below is intended to ensure that the distributor must keep the company's methods secret. The aim is to prevent the company's competitors from acquiring such confidential information:

> The Distributor agrees that it will not at any time after the signature of this Agreement disclose any information in relation to the Company's method of manufacture or design or the Distributor's method of distribution in relation to the Products.

Meaning of words and phrases

At any time after the signature of this Agreement: this phrase indicates that no specific time-limit applies to the obligation, meaning that the distributor must never disclose any of the information specified in the clause.

Restraint of trade/anti-competition clause

Purpose of clause

These clauses are designed to prevent one or other of the parties from entering into competition with the other party following the termination of the contract. Such clauses are common in certain kinds of employment contract and in distribution agreements. The clauses typically contain restrictions on the party competing in a specified territory, in a specified business sector for a specified period of time. The extent to which such clauses are enforceable will depend on the law governing the agreement, and the nature of the restriction imposed.

Specimen clause

The specimen clause given below aims to prevent the distributor from competing with the company for which it is the distributor by distributing the same products for another company in the same geographical area during the course of the agreement and for two years after it ends:

The Distributor agrees that it will not during this Agreement or for a period of two years after the termination of this Agreement be involved whether as principal, partner, agent, contractor or employer in the manufacture, sale or distribution in the Territory of any Products which the Distributor has distributed under this Agreement.

Meaning of words and phrases

Whether as principal, partner, agent, contractor or employer: the distributor is not allowed to be involved in distributing these products in any way.

Force majeure

Purpose of clause

Force majeure is French for irresistible compulsion or coercion. A *force majeure* clause specifies circumstances which the parties agree to regard as being beyond their reasonable control. The effect of this is that if one of these circumstances arises, and the contract is breached as a result, neither party can be held liable. Examples of circumstances which are often regarded as constituting *force majeure* include industrial disputes or strikes, outbreak of war and natural disasters.

Specimen clause

The specimen clause given below is a typical example of this type of clause:

> Neither party shall be liable to the other for any failure to perform or delay in performance of the terms of this agreement, other than an obligation to pay monies, caused by any circumstances beyond its reasonable control, including but not limited to defaults of suppliers or subcontractors and all types of industrial disputes, lockouts and strikes.

Meaning of words and phrases

Liable to the other: responsible in law to the other.

Failure to perform: failure to do something that was agreed to be done in the contract.

Circumstances beyond its reasonable control: circumstances which the party could not be expected to have any control over.

Defaults: failures to fulfil an obligation.

Lockouts: situations in which employers refuse to allow employees to enter their place of work until they agree to certain conditions.

Costs

Purpose of clause

Costs clauses state the proportion of the costs of negotiating and drafting the contract to be paid by each party. The normal provision is that each party pays only its own costs. The purpose of this type of clause is to prevent either party trying to claim these costs from the other party at a later stage.

Specimen clause

The specimen clause given below is a typical example of this type of clause, and simply clarifies that each party is responsible for its own costs incurred in relation to the agreement:

> Each party to this Agreement shall bear the costs and expenses incurred by it in relation to the negotiation, drafting and execution of the Agreement.

Meaning of words and phrases

Bear the costs and expenses: pay the costs and expenses.

Negotiation, drafting and execution: all the stages of drawing up the agreement including negotiating it, writing it and signing it so that it becomes legally enforceable.

Currency

Purpose of clause

A currency clause generally states the currency in which any amounts payable under the contract are to be paid.

Specimen clause

The specimen clause given below states the currency which the parties must use when carrying out the transactions provided for in the contract and clarifies that this currency applies to all money amounts stated in the contract unless there is a clear statement to the contrary in the contract. The point of this is to ensure that if a drafting error results in, for example, Italian Lira being written as the applicable currency in one part of the contract, the parties will not be bound by the error:

> Except as expressly provided in this Agreement, all amounts in this Agreement are stated and will be paid in US dollars.

Meaning of words and phrases

Except as expressly provided in this Agreement: unless there is a clear statement to the contrary in some part of the contract.

Amendment

Purpose of clause

An amendment clause deals with the way in which any amendments required to be made to the contract are made. The usual provision is that amendments are ineffective unless made in writing and signed by the authorised representatives of both parties.

Specimen clause

The specimen clause given below seeks to ensure that if any changes need to be made to the contract, these can only be done in writing and must be approved by a person from each party who has been given specific and valid permission to authorise such changes. The purpose of this is to try to ensure that changes which the other party has not agreed to are not introduced into the contract:

> No amendment to this Agreement will have any effect unless it is made in writing and signed by a duly authorised representative of each of the parties.

Meaning of words and phrases

A duly authorised representative: a person who has been given specific and valid permission by a party to do something.

Interpretation

Purpose of clause

An interpretation clause states the way in which certain linguistic features of the contract are to be interpreted. It may, for example, state that reference to a particular gender includes both genders and that reference to a person may also include a limited company. Interpretation clauses may also clarify that any reference to legislation also includes reference to subordinate legislation (ie, legal rules made under the authority of a particular statute).

Specimen clause

The specimen clause given below aims to ensure that the language used in the contract is interpreted in a consistent and predictable way, that it is understood that the schedules form part of the contract, and to clarify that the parties understand that any subordinate legislation will also apply to the contract:

In this Agreement:

(a)   use of the singular includes the plural (and vice versa) and reference to any gender includes all genders;

(b)   any reference to a person shall include a firm or limited company;

(c)   any reference to a clause, schedule or appendix is a reference to that clause, schedule or appendix to this Agreement;

(d)   the annexed schedules form part of this Agreement and a reference to 'this Agreement' includes a reference to the schedules;

(e)   reference to any law or statute includes a reference to that law or statute as from time to time amended and to any orders, statutory instruments or regulations made under that law or statute.

Meaning of words and phrases

Reference to any gender includes all genders: this phrase is the ultimate evidence of lawyers' tendency to be cautious. It foresees the possibility of hermaphrodite involvement in the contract.

That law or statute as from time to time amended: the law or statute and any amendments that are made to it while the contract is still valid.

Statutory instruments: subordinate legislation made under the authority of a statute.

5 SPECIMEN CONTRACT & ANALYSIS

The contract set out below is an example of a fairly typical UK-style share purchase agreement. The schedules have been removed in order to keep the text short. First, a specimen paragraph is given and after it some notes on the paragraph.

The opening paragraphs

THIS AGREEMENT is made on 8 May 2004

Between

(1) Panatella Mimms Limited whose registered office is at 3 Allstreet, London, UK (the Vendor).

(2) Corona Sandbach Limited whose [registered] office is at 55 Bigstreet, London, UK (the Purchaser).

WHEREAS

(A) Stubb Delamere Limited (the Company) is a private company limited by shares incorporated in England. The whole of the issued share capital of the company is beneficially owned by the Vendor.

(B) The Vendor has agreed to sell all of the issued share capital of the Company to the Purchaser for the consideration and upon the terms set out in this Agreement.

The opening paragraphs contain the details of the parties to the contract and then go on to set out brief details of the background to the contract. These details have no legal effect but are useful reference information for the reader.

Paragraph 1

IT IS AGREED as follows:

1.1   In this Agreement, the following expressions shall have the following meanings:

Accounts means the audited balance sheet of the Company as at the Accounts Date and the audited profit and loss account of the Company in respect of the financial year ended on the Accounts Date, together with any notes, reports, statements or documents included in or annexed to them;

Accounts Date means 31 December;

Business Days means days on which Anytown clearing banks are open for business;

Claim means any claim for breach of a Warranty or under the Tax Indemnity;

Companies Act means the Companies Act 1985 as the same may be amended, re-enacted or replaced from time to time;

Completion means completion of the sale and purchase of the Shares under this Agreement;

Costs means all and any legal, accounting and other professional costs, expenses, and fees including managerial time;

Disclosure Letter means the letter in the agreed form from the Vendor to the Purchaser executed and delivered immediately before the entry into of this Agreement;

Financial year shall be construed in accordance with section 223 of the Companies Act;

Intellectual Property Rights means patents, trade marks, service marks, trade names, design rights, copyrights (including rights in computer software), rights in know-how and other intellectual property rights, in each case whether registered or unregistered and including applications for the grant of any of such rights and all rights or forms of protection having equivalent or similar effects anywhere in the world;

Properties means the freehold and leasehold properties of the Group, particulars of which are set out in Schedule 3;

Security interest means any security interest of any nature whatsoever including, without limitation, any mortgage, charge, pledge, lien, assignment by way of security or other encumbrance;

Shares means all the issued shares in the capital of the Company;

Tax Indemnity means the deed of indemnity, in the agreed form, to be entered into on Completion by the Vendor, the Company and the Purchaser;

Tax Warranties means the representations and warranties set out in Part D of Schedule 2;

Warranties means the representations and warranties set out in Schedule 2.

1.2   In this Agreement:

(a)   the headings are inserted for convenience only and shall not affect the construction of this Agreement;

(b)   any statement qualified by the expression to the best knowledge of the Vendor or so far as the Vendor is aware or any similar expression shall be deemed to include an additional statement that it has been made after due and careful enquiry;

(c)   any reference to a document in the agreed form is to the form of the relevant document agreed between the parties and initialled for the purpose of identification.

Paragraph 1 contains the definitions used in the contract. These definitions contain the precise meanings which the parties have agreed to give to certain terms used in the contract. The definitions have legal effect – they specify for the court the nature of the parties' understanding of the terms used.

Paragraph 2

> 2.1 The Vendor as beneficial owner shall sell, and the Purchaser shall purchase, the Shares. The Shares shall be sold free from all security interests, options, equities, claims or other third party rights (including rights of pre-emption) of any nature whatsoever, together with all rights attaching to them.
>
> 2.2 The total price payable by the Purchaser to the Vendor for the Shares shall be the sum of $800,000.

The two parts of paragraph 2 set out the heart of the deal – ie, the agreement to sell the shares and the price to be paid for them. The paragraph contains mutual promises by each party. Consequently, consideration exists.

Paragraph 3

> 3.1 Completion of the sale and purchase of the Shares shall be conditional upon the following conditions having been fulfilled:
>
> (a) The written consent in due form of Anybank plc must be obtained by the Vendor and produced for inspection by the Purchaser.

Paragraph 3 contains a condition precedent which must be fulfilled before the sale and purchase of the shares can be completed.

Paragraph 4

> 4.1 The sale and purchase of the Shares shall be completed immediately after the signing of this Agreement on 16 May 2004. The events referred to in the following provisions of this clause 4 shall take place on Completion.
>
> 4.2 On completion the Vendor shall deliver (or cause to be delivered) to the Purchaser:
>
> (a) duly executed transfers into the name of the Purchaser in respect of all of the Shares, together with the relative share certificates;
>
> (b) an original of the Tax Indemnity duly executed by the Vendor;
>
> (c) the Certificate of Incorporation, Common Seal, Share Register and Share Certificate Books (with any unissued share certificates), all minute books and other statutory books (which shall be written-up to but not including Completion) of the Company;

(d) all such other documents (including any necessary waivers or consents) as may be required to enable the Purchaser to be registered as the holder(s) of the shares;

(e) a letter of resignation in the agreed form duly executed by the existing auditors of the Company in accordance with section 392 of the Companies Act, together with evidence that such letter has been deposited at the registered office of the Company with a statement pursuant to section 394 of the Companies Act, that there are no circumstances connected with such resignation which they consider should be brought to the attention of the members or creditors of the Company;

(f) a letter of resignation in the agreed form duly executed by each of the directors of the Company required to resign by the Purchaser;

(g) a letter of resignation in the agreed form between the Company and Victor Smith duly executed by Victor Smith;

(h) a service agreement in the agreed form between the Company and Sarah Marshall duly executed by Sarah Marshall;

(i) a certificate of title in the agreed form in respect of the Properties.

4.3   The Vendor shall procure the revocation of all authorities to the bankers of the Company relating to bank accounts, giving authority to such persons as the Purchaser may nominate to operate the same.

4.4   The Vendor shall procure that resolutions of the Board of Directors of the Company are passed by which the following business is transacted:

(a) the registration (subject to their being duly stamped) of the transfers in respect of the Shares referred to in clause 4.2 is approved;

(b) the accounting reference date of the Company is changed to 24 April;

(c) the registered office is changed to 55 Bigstreet, London, UK;

(d) the resignations referred to in clause 4.2(g) and (h), are accepted; and

(e) such persons as are nominated by the Purchaser are appointed as directors and/or secretary of the Company.

4.5   The Purchaser shall:

(a) in satisfaction of its obligations under clause 2.2, cause the price to be paid by electronic funds transfer to the Vendor's bank account at Anybank of 22 Allstreets, London, UK, Sort Code 20-78-53, Account No: 65347-2900;

(b) deliver to the Vendor an original of the Tax Indemnity duly executed by the Purchaser;

Any payment made in accordance with clause 4.5(a) shall constitute a good discharge for the Purchaser of its obligations under clause 2.2 and the Purchaser shall not be concerned to see that the funds are applied in payment to the Vendor.

4.6   If the Vendor fails or is unable to perform any material obligation required to be performed by the Vendor pursuant to clause 4.2 by the last date on which Completion is required to occur, the Purchaser shall not be obliged to complete the sale and purchase of the Shares and may, in its absolute discretion, by written notice to the Vendor:

(a) rescind this Agreement without liability on the part of the Purchaser; or

> (b) elect to complete this Agreement on that date, to the extent that the Vendor is ready, able and willing to do so, and specify a later date on which the Vendor shall be obliged to complete the outstanding obligations of the Vendor; or
>
> (c) elect to defer the completion of this Agreement by not more than twenty (20) Business Days to such other date as it may specify in such notice, in which event the provisions of this clause shall apply, *mutatis mutandis*, if the Vendor fails or is unable to perform any such obligations on such other date.

Paragraph 4 sets out the matters which must take place on completion. This paragraph constitutes part of the main agreements between the parties, although it is likely that breach of one or two of these terms alone would not give rise to a right to rescind the contract altogether. Due to the nature of the transaction, by which one company acquires another, there are a large number of obligations to be performed, most of which are of a routine and procedural kind.

Paragraph 5

> 5.1 Neither of the Vendors shall (whether alone or jointly with another and whether directly or indirectly) carry on or be engaged or (except as the owner for investment of securities dealt in on a stock exchange and not exceeding 5 per cent in nominal value of the securities of that class) be interested in any Competing Business during a period of one year after Completion. For this purpose, Competing Business means a business:
>
> (a) which involves any business carried on by the Company as at Completion; and
>
> (b) which is carried on within the area in which the Company carries on business as at Completion.
>
> 5.2 Neither of the Vendors shall within a period of one year after Completion, directly or indirectly, solicit or endeavour to entice away from the Company, offer employment to or employ, or offer or conclude any contract for services with, any person who was employed by the Company in skilled or managerial work at any time during the six months prior to Completion.
>
> 5.3 Except so far as may be required by law and in such circumstances only after prior consultation with the Purchaser, neither of the Vendors shall at any time disclose to any person or use to the detriment of the Company any trade secret or other confidential information of a technical character which he or she holds in relation to the Company or its affairs.
>
> 5.4 Any provision of this Agreement (or of any agreement or arrangement of which it forms part) by virtue of which such agreement or arrangement is subject to registration under the <u>Restrictive Trade Practices Act 1976</u> shall only take effect the day after particulars of such agreement or arrangement have been furnished to the Director General of Fair Trading pursuant to section 24 of that Act.

Paragraph 5 deals with restraint of trade and confidentiality. It prohibits, firstly, the purchasers of the company from competing with the vendors in a similar area of business or geographical territory for a one-year period (5.1). Secondly, it prohibits the purchasers from trying to entice employees and recent ex-employees of the company to work for them during a one-year period (5.2).

Paragraph 5.3 deals with confidentiality. It lays an obligation on the vendors not to disclose trade secrets or confidential information 'of a technical character' to any third parties at any time. The only exception to this obligation is a legal requirement arises to reveal such information. In these circumstances the vendors agree to consult with the purchasers before disclosing any information.

Paragraph 5.4 deals with procedural requirements under English anti-competition legislation.

Paragraph 6

6.1   Each of the Vendors:

    (a) represents and warrants to the Purchaser in the terms of the Warranties and acknowledges that the Purchaser has entered into this Agreement in reliance upon the Warranties;

    (b) undertakes, without limiting the rights of the Purchaser in any way, if there is a breach of any Warranty in respect of the Company, to pay in cash to the Purchaser (or, if so directed by the Purchaser, to the Company) on demand a sum equal to the aggregate of:

       I   the amount which, if received by the Company, would be necessary to put the Company into the position which would have existed had there been no breach of the Warranty in question; and

       II all Costs suffered or incurred by the Purchaser or the Company directly or indirectly, as a result of or in connection with such breach of warranty;

    (c) agrees to waive the benefit of all rights (if any) which he or she may have against the Company, or any present or former officers or employee of the Company, on whom the Vendor may have relied in agreeing to any term of this Agreement or any statement set out in the Disclosure Letter and the Vendor undertakes not to make any claim in respect of such reliance.

6.2   Each of the Warranties shall be construed as a separate Warranty and (save as expressly provided to the contrary) shall not be limited or restricted by reference to or in inference from the terms of any other Warranty or any other term of this Agreement.

6.3   The rights and remedies of the Purchaser in respect of the Warranties shall not be affected by (i) Completion, (ii) any investigation made into the affairs of the Company or any knowledge held or gained of any such affairs by or on behalf of the Purchaser (except for matters fairly and reasonably disclosed in the Disclosure Letter) or (iii) any event or matter whatsoever, other than a specific and duly authorised written waiver or release by the Purchaser.

> 6.4 The Vendors shall procure that (save only as may be necessary to give effect to this Agreement) neither the Vendors nor the Company shall do, allow or procure any act or omission before Completion which would constitute a breach of any of the Warranties if they were given at any and all times from the date hereof down to Completion or which would make any of the Warranties inaccurate or misleading if they were so given.

A contract of this kind would normally contain very detailed warranties, which have been omitted from the specimen contained above. The warranties would be contained in schedules to avoid interruption of the general flow of the agreement with a mass of detail. Paragraph 6 of the contract refers to the warranties and sets out (in 6.1(b)) the intentions of the parties as to the practical consequences of the breach of a warranty; (in 6.1(c)) a waiver of any claims the vendors may have against the company that is being sold to the purchasers; and (in 6.2) agreement that each warranty should be interpreted as being separate from the other warranties.

The paragraph also clarifies (in 6.3) that completion and certain other events shall not affect the purchasers' rights in respect of the warranties, and (in 6.4) the vendors themselves promise not to breach the warranties before completion.

Paragraph 7

> 7.1 The Vendor shall not be liable for any Claim:
>
> (a) unless it receives from the Purchaser written notice containing details of the Claim including the Purchaser's estimate (on a without prejudice basis) of the amount of such Claim;
>
> I   on or before 31 April 2006, in the case of a Claim for breach of any of the Warranties other than the Tax Warranties, the Property Warranties and the Pensions Warranties;
>
> II   on or before 31 December 2005, in the case of a Claim for breach of any of the Tax Warranties or pursuant to the Tax [Indemnity];
>
> III on or before 31 December 2006, in case of a Claim for breach of any of the Property Warranties or the Pensions Warranties;
>
> (b) unless the aggregate amount of the liability of the Vendor for all Claims exceeds $50,000 (in which event the Purchaser shall be entitled to claim the whole of the amount thereof and not merely the excess).
>
> 7.2 The aggregate amount of the liability of the Vendor for all Claims shall not exceed $200,000.
>
> 7.3 None of the limitations contained in clauses 7.1 and 7.2 shall apply to any breach of any Warranty which (or the delay in discovery of which) is the consequence of dishonest, deliberate or reckless mis-statement, concealment or other conduct by any member of the Vendor any officer or employee, or former officer or employee, of the Vendor.

7.4   The Vendor shall not be liable for any Claim:

     (a)   in the case of a Claim in respect of a breach of the Warranties, if and to the extent that the fact, matter, event or circumstance giving rise to such claim was fairly and reasonably disclosed in the Disclosure Letter; or

     (a)   if and to the extent that the matter is specifically disclosed or is specifically provided or reserved for in the Accounts.

7.5   If the Purchaser becomes aware that any claim has been made against the Company by a third party after Completion which is likely to result in the Purchaser being entitled to make a Claim against the Vendor in respect of a breach of any Warranty:

     (a)   the Purchaser shall give notice of such claim to the Vendor as soon as reasonably practicable and shall procure that the Company gives the Vendor all reasonable facilities to investigate any such claim;

     (b)   the Purchaser shall cause the Company to take such action as the Vendor shall reasonably request to avoid, resist or compromise any such claim (subject to the Company being entitled to employ its own legal advisers and being indemnified and secured to its reasonable satisfaction by the Vendor against all losses, costs, damages and expenses, including those of its legal advisers, incurred in connection with such claim);

     (c)   the Purchaser shall cause the Company to consult as fully as is reasonably practicable with the Vendor as regards the conduct of any proceedings arising out of such claim and, if the Vendor so requests, to permit the Vendor to participate in those proceedings at their own expense.

Paragraph 7 imposes certain conditions precedent on the pressing of any claim for breach of warranty by the purchasers. Paragraph 7.1 imposes an obligation for the purchaser to serve written notice within a specified time period in the event of specified breaches, and also imposes a minimum value for all claims, below which it is agreed that no claim can be made (see also paragraph 7.2).

Paragraph 7.3 provides that these limitations on making claims will not apply if a breach of a warranty is found to be the result of the vendors' dishonesty.

Paragraph 7.4 constitutes an exemption clause in relation to breaches of warranty previously revealed to the purchasers.

Paragraph 7.5 sets out the procedures to be followed if the purchaser discovers that a claim is being made by a third party which is likely to result in the purchaser making a claim against the vendor for breach of warranty.

Paragraph 8

8   This Agreement and the Tax Indemnity together constitute the entire agreement and understanding between the parties in connection with the sale and purchase of the Shares.

Paragraph 8 is a typical whole agreement clause which states that the written agreement supersedes any previous agreements between the parties.

Paragraph 9

> 9 No variation of this Agreement (or any document entered into pursuant to this Agreement) shall be valid unless it is in writing and signed by or on behalf of each of the parties hereto.

Paragraph 9 is a waiver clause which sets out the parties' agreement that no waiver of the agreement is allowed unless agreed in writing by both parties.

Paragraph 10

> 10 Neither party shall be entitled to assign the benefit of any provision of this Agreement without the prior written approval of the other party.

Paragraph 10 is an assignment clause. It states that the other parties' written agreement is needed before a party is entitled to assign the benefit of any part of the agreement to another party.

Paragraph 11

> 11 No announcement or circular in connection with the existence or the subject matter of this Agreement shall be made or issued by or on behalf of the Vendor or the Purchaser without the prior written approval of the other (such approval not to be unreasonably withheld or delayed) during any period prior to or within three (3) months after Completion. This shall not affect any announcement or circular required by law or the rules of any stock exchange.

This clause provides that no announcement relating to the acquisition of the company can be made without the written agreement of the other party. However, the clause provides that this approval cannot be unreasonably withheld or delayed, which means that there would need to be a good reason for permission not to be given.

Paragraph 12

> 12 If any provision of this Agreement is held to be invalid or unenforceable, then such provision shall (so far as it is invalid or unenforceable) be given no effect and shall be deemed not to be included in this Agreement but without invalidating any of the remaining provisions of this Agreement.

This is a severance clause, according to which the parties agree that if one part of the contract is regarded by a court to be invalid, this should not affect the rest of the contract. The legal validity of this clause will depend on the circumstances of any claim made.

Paragraph 13

13 The Vendor shall do or procure to be done all such further acts and things, and execute or procure the execution of all such other documents, as the Purchaser may from time to time reasonably require, whether on or after Completion, for the purpose of giving to the Purchaser the full benefit of all the provisions of this Agreement.

Paragraph 13 is a further assistance clause by which the vendor promises to assist the purchaser by doing any further administrative acts in relation to the share transfer which may be required after completion.

Paragraph 14

14.1 Any notice given under this Agreement shall be in writing and signed by or on behalf of the party giving it and may be served by leaving it or sending it by fax, prepaid recorded delivery or registered post to the address and for the attention of the relevant party set out in clause 15.2 (or as otherwise notified from time to time hereunder). Any notice so served by fax or post shall be deemed to have been received:

(a) in the case of fax, twelve (12) hours after the time of dispatch;

(b) in the case of recorded delivery or registered post, forty-eight (48) hours from the date of posting.

14.2 The addresses of the parties for the purpose of clause 14.1 are as follows:

The Vendor:	Panatella Mimms Limited
	3 Allstreet
	London
	UK
For the attention of:	Mr MG Winterley
Fax:	0207 987 654
The Purchaser:	Corona Sandbach Limited
	55 Bigstreet
	London
	UK
For the attention of:	Ms GR Foster
Fax:	0207 123 456

This clause deals with the service of notices. It specifies the ways in which notices may be served in relation to the contract. It also sets out the time periods in which the parties agree to *deem* that service has taken place for the purposes of the contract.

Paragraph 15

> 15 This Agreement is governed by and shall be construed in accordance with the laws of England.
>
> AS WITNESS this Agreement has been signed on behalf of the parties the day and year first before written.

This is a governing law clause. It specifies that the contract shall be interpreted in accordance with English law.

GLOSSARIES

Words Which Are Easily Confused

Many words in English sound and look alike but can have radically different meanings. It is important to be aware of the more common of these false pairs – the consequences of confusing them could be disastrous. If in doubt, consult a good dictionary.

The following is a non-exhaustive list of the most common examples:

Advice is a noun which means guidance or recommendation about future action (eg, 'friends always ask his advice').

Advise is a verb that chiefly means to recommend a course of action (eg, 'we advised him to go home').

Affect is a verb which means to make a difference to (eg, 'the pay cuts will affect everyone').

Effect is used both as a noun meaning a result (eg, 'the substance has a pain-reducing effect') and as a verb meaning to bring about (a result) (eg, 'he effected a cost-cutting exercise').

Anonymous is an adjective which refers to a name that is not known or not made known (eg, 'he wrote anonymously in the newspaper') or which means having no outstanding or individual features (eg, 'the building looked rather anonymous').

Unanimous is an adjective meaning to be fully in agreement (eg, 'the decision was made unanimously').

Ante means 'before' (eg, 'ante-meridiem').

Anti means 'against' (eg, 'anti-nuclear').

Appraise means to assess something (eg, 'we appraised the services offered by the company').

Apprise is to inform somebody about something (eg, 'he apprised me of the news').

Assent means approval or agreement (eg, 'her proposal received the assent of all present').

Ascent means an instance of going up something (eg, 'the first ascent of the Matterhorn').

Aural refers to something which relates to the ear or sense of hearing.

Oral means spoken rather than written.

Biannual refers to something which occurs twice a year.

Biennial refers to something which occurs every two years.

Canvas is a type of material.

Canvass means to seek political support before an election or to seek people's opinions on something (eg, 'I canvassed her opinion on the matter').

Chance means (1) the possibility of something happening (eg, 'there is a chance that it might rain today'); (2) an opportunity (eg, 'you'll have a chance to meet her'); and (3) the way in which things happen without any obvious plan or cause (eg, 'we met entirely by chance').

Change means (1) to make or become different (eg, 'we'll change this provision of the contract'); (2) to exchange a sum of money for the same sum in a different currency (eg, 'she changed her dollars into Euros'); (3) to move from one thing to another (eg, 'he changed jobs often').

Complacent means uncritically satisfied with oneself; smug.

Complaisant indicates a willingness to please others or to accept their behaviour without protest.

Compliment means to politely congratulate or praise (eg, 'he complimented her on her appearance').

Complement means to add in a way that improves (eg, 'she selected a green sweater to complement her blonde hair').

Council means an assembly of people meeting regularly to advise on, discuss or organise something.

Counsel means (1) advice or (2) a barrister conducting a case.

Credible means convincing or believable.

Creditable means deserving recognition and praise.

Curb means a check or restraint (eg, 'curbs on public spending').

Kerb means the edge of a pavement (sidewalk) (eg, 'the car's tyres scraped along the side of the kerb').

Defuse means to remove the fuse from an explosive device (eg, 'the bomb squad defused the device').

Diffuse means spread over a wide area (eg, 'the crowd gradually diffused').

Dependant is a noun which refers to a person who relies on another for financial support (eg, 'she has three dependants').

Dependent is an adjective meaning (1) relying on someone or something for support (eg, 'we are dependent on the services offered by that firm'); (2) determined or influenced by (eg, 'our decision is dependent on the outcome of the arbitration'); or (3) unable to do without (eg, 'my colleague is dependent on strong coffee').

Discreet means careful and judicious (eg, 'she gave discreet advice').

Discrete means separate, distinct (eg, 'that is a discrete issue').

Disinterested means impartial (eg, 'a lawyer is under an obligation to give disinterested advice').

Uninterested means not interested (eg, 'a person uninterested in fame').

Draft means (1) to prepare a preliminary version of a text; (2) a preliminary version of a text; (3) a written order requesting a bank to pay a specified sum; or (4) USA compulsory recruitment for military service.

Draught means (1) a current of cool air indoors; (2) an act of drinking or breathing in; (3) (of beer) served from a cask.

Elicit is a verb meaning to draw out a response or reaction (eg, 'my questioning elicited no response from him').

Illicit is an adjective meaning forbidden or unlawful (eg, 'he was caught trying to smuggle illicit substances into the country').

Eligible means satisfying the conditions to do or receive something (eg, 'you are eligible to enter this competition').

Illegible means not clear enough to be read (eg, 'your handwriting is illegible').

Equable means calm and even-tempered (eg, 'she remained equable at all times').

Equitable means fair and just (eg, 'this is an equitable system').

Flare means (1) a sudden brief burst of flame or light; (2) a device producing a very bright flame as a signal or marker; (3) a gradual widening towards the hem of a garment; or (4) trousers of which the legs widen from the knees.

Flair means (1) natural ability or talent or (2) stylishness.

Flaunt means to display something ostentatiously (eg, 'he flaunted his newly-acquired wealth').

Flout means to disobey a rule or law (eg, 'she flouted the speeding restrictions').

Insidious means proceeding in a gradual and harmful way (eg, 'that is an insidious practice').

Invidious means unacceptable, unfair and likely to arouse resentment or anger in others (eg, 'she was placed in an invidious position').

Loose means not fixed in place or tied up (eg, 'a loose tooth').

Lose means to no longer have or become unable to find.

Omit means to leave something out (eg, 'paragraph 3 should be omitted').

Emit means to discharge something (eg, 'the factory emitted smoke').

Pedal is a noun meaning a foot-operated lever.

Peddle is a verb meaning to sell goods.

Practice is a noun meaning the action of doing something rather than the theories about it. Practice is also the spelling for the verb in American English.

Practise is the British English spelling of the verb (eg, 'I need to practise my French').

Prescribe means to recommend the use of a medicine or treatment or to state officially that something should be done (eg, 'the doctor prescribed a course of treatment').

Proscribe means to forbid or condemn something (eg, 'the statute proscribes the use of dangerous chemicals').

Principal is usually an adjective meaning main or most important (eg, 'the country's principal exports').

Principle is a noun that usually means a truth or general law used as the basis for something (eg, 'the general principles of law').

Stationary is an adjective meaning not moving or changing (eg, 'the car was stationary at the traffic lights').

Stationery is a noun meaning paper and other writing materials (eg, 'the paper is kept in the stationery cupboard').

Story means a tale or account of something (eg, 'we listened to his story with interest').

Storey means the floor of a building (eg, 'the office was on the tenth storey of the building').

Tortious means having the nature of a tort, wrongful (eg, 'he committed a tortious act and is therefore likely to be sued').

Tortuous means (1) full of twists and turns (eg, 'a tortuous route') or (2) excessively complex (eg, 'a tortuous case').

Unexceptional means not out of the ordinary (eg, 'his performance in the examination was unexceptional').

Unexceptionable means not able to be objected to but not particularly new or exciting (eg, 'the hotel was unexceptionable').

Whose means belonging to or associated with which person, or of whom or which (eg, 'whose is this?' or 'she's a woman whose views I respect').

Who's is short for either who is or who has (eg, 'he has a daughter who's a legal secretary' or 'who's arranged the conference?').

Business Abbreviations

Here is a list of some common business abbreviations and their definitions.

ABC	activity-based costing
ACH	automated clearing house
ADR	American depositary receipt
AGM	annual general meeting
AMEX	American Stock Exchange
APR	annualised percentage rate (of interest)
ATM	automated teller machine (cash dispenser)
B2B	business-to-business
B2C	business-to-consumer
CAPM	capital asset pricing model
CCA	current cost accounting
CD	certificate of deposit
CEO	chief executive officer
CFO	chief financial officer
CGT	capital gains tax
COO	chief operating officer
COSA	cost of sales adjustment
CPA	certified public accountant (USA); critical path analysis
CPP	current purchasing power (accounting)
CRC	current replacement cost
CVP	cost-volume-profit analysis
DCF	discounted cash flow
EBIT	earnings before interest and tax
EBITDA	earnings before interest, tax, depreciation and amortization
EDP	electronic data processing
EFT	electronic funds transfer
EFTPOS	electronic funds transfer at point of sale
EMS	European Monetary System
EMU	economic and monetary union
EPS	earnings per share
ESOP	employee stock or share ownership plan

EV	economic value
EVA	economic value added
FASB	Financial Accounting Standards Board (USA)
FDI	Foreign Direct Investment
FIFO	first in, first out (used for valuing stock/inventory)
forex	foreign exchange
FRN	floating rate note
GAAP	generally accepted accounting principles (USA)
GAAS	generally accepted audited standards
IPO	initial public offering
IRR	internal rate of return
IRS	Internal Revenue Service (USA)
LAN	local area network
LIBOR	London Interbank Offered Rate
LIFFE	London International Financial Futures Exchange
LIFO	last in, first out (used for valuing stock/inventory value, popular in the USA)
M & A	mergers and acquisitions
MBI	management buy-in
MBO	management buy-out
MCT	mainstream corporate tax
MLR	minimum lending rate
NASDAQ	National Association of Securities Dealers Automated Quotations System (USA)
NBV	net book value
NPV	net present value; no par value
NRV	net realisable value
Nymex	New York Mercantile Exchange
NYSE	New York Stock Exchange
OTC	over the counter
P&L a/c	profit and loss account (known as the income statement in the USA)
P/E	price/earnings (ratio)
PIN	personal identification number

PPP	purchasing power parity
PSBR	public sector borrowing rate
ROA	return on assets
ROCE	return on capital employed
ROE	return on equity
ROI	return on investment
RONA	return on net assets
ROOA	return on operating assets
ROTA	return on total assets
S&L	Savings and Loan Association (USA)
SDR	special drawing rate (at the IMF)
SEAQ	Stock Exchange Automated Quotations (UK)
SEC	Securities and Exchange Commission (USA)
SET	secure electronic transaction
SIB	Securities and Investments Board (UK)
SITC	standard international trade classification
SME	small and medium-sized enterprises
SRO	self-regulating organization
STRGL	statement of total recognised gains and losses
T-bill	Treasury bill
TQM	total quality management
TSR	total shareholder return
USP	unique selling proposition
VAT	value-added tax
WDV	written down value
WIP	work-in-progress
XBRL	extensible business reporting language
ZBB	zero based budgeting

Phrasal Verbs Used in Legal English

The following is a non-exhaustive list of phrasal verbs used in legal English together with examples of usage:

Abide by means to accept a decision, a law or an agreement and obey it. For example, 'the parties must abide by the terms of the agreement'.

Accede to means to agree to or allow something that someone has asked for, after you have opposed it for a while. For example, 'the company eventually acceded to repeated requests for a price reduction'.

Account for means: (1) to explain how or why something happened. For example, 'how do you account for the fact that the goods were delivered late?'; (2) to be a particular part of something. For example, 'computer sales account for 50% of the company's profits'; (3) to keep a record of how the money in your care will be spent or has been spent. For example, 'every cent in the fund has been accounted for'; (4) to consider particular facts or circumstances when you are making a decision about something. For example, 'the costs of possible litigation were accounted for when calculating the amount of money to be set aside'.

Account to means to make a payment to someone together with an itemised breakdown showing how the payment is calculated. For example, 'the lawyer accounted to her client in respect of the damages received as a result of the litigation'.

Adhere to means to act in the way that a particular law, rule, agreement or set of instructions says that you should. For example, 'the parties have adhered strictly to the terms of the agreement'.

Amount to means: (1) to add up to something or result in a final total of something. For example, 'the overall costs amounted to well over $50,000'; (2) to be equal to or the same as something. For example, 'what they did amounted to a breach of contract'.

Appertain to (or 'pertain to') means to belong to something or be connected with something. For example, 'the duties appertaining to this position'.

Break down means: (1) to separate into different parts to make something easier to discuss, analyse or deal with. For example, 'the figures break down as follows ...'; (2) to fail. For example, 'negotiations between the parties have broken down'.

Break off means: (1) to stop speaking or to stop doing something before you have finished. For example, 'we had to break off the meeting'; (2) to separate something from something else using force, or for something to become separated in this way. For example, 'the handle of the cup just broke off'.

Break up means: (1) the splitting up of a company or an organisation into smaller parts. For example, 'the company was broken up into smaller concerns'; (2) the splitting up of a group of people. For example, 'the conference broke up into discussion groups'.

Call in means: (1) to request the return of something. For example, 'the bank has decided to call in the loan'; (2) to visit a place or person for a short time. For example, 'he called in at the office before going to court this morning'; (3) to telephone your office. For example, 'do you mind if I use your phone? I just want to call in and tell my assistant I'm running late'.

Carry on means to continue something. For example, 'the company carries on its business as a garden furniture retailer'.

Carry out means to do something that you said you would do or that you have been asked to do. For example, 'the lawyer carried out his client's instructions carefully'.

Change over means to stop using one system or thing and start using another. For example, 'The Greeks have changed over to the Euro'.

Consist in means to have something as its main or only feature. For example, 'the strength of this firm consists in its experienced litigation department'.

Consist of means to be formed from the people or things mentioned. For example, 'the team consists of a number of specialists in different areas'.

Cover up means to try hard to stop people finding out about a mistake, a crime or the true state of affairs. For example, 'the company attempted to cover up its trading losses by falsifying its accounts'.

Deal in means to do business, to make money by buying and selling a particular product or kind of goods. For example, 'the company deals in computer hardware'.

Deal with means: (1) to do business regularly with a person or organisation. For example, 'we only deal with reputable suppliers'; (2) to talk to a person or organisation in order to reach an agreement or settle a dispute. For example, 'I like to deal with people I know I can trust'; (3) to solve a problem or carry out a task. For example, 'my lawyers dealt with the company sale very efficiently'; (4) to be about something. For example, 'this article deals with the issues raised by contractual waivers'; (5) to look after, talk to or control people in an appropriate way. For example, 'we sometimes have to deal with very difficult people in this job'; (6) to take appropriate action in a particular situation. For example, 'could you deal with this complaint?'.

Depart from means to behave in a way that is different from what is usual or expected. For example, 'we have departed from usual practice due to the exceptional circumstances of the case'.

Dispose of means: (1) to get rid of or sell something that is not required. For example, 'the company disposed of many of its assets'; (2) to successfully deal with or finish with a problem. For example, 'there remains only the question of funding to dispose of'.

Draw up means: (1) to make or write something that needs careful planning. For example, 'my lawyers will draw up the contract'; (2) to bring something nearer to something else. For example, 'she drew up another chair in order to participate more easily in the discussion'; (3) to come to a stop. For example, 'the car drew up outside the office'.

Draw upon/on means to use something that you have or that is available to help you do something. For example, 'the company will draw upon its reserves of capital to finance the deal'.

Engage in means to be involved in something, to take part in something or to be busy doing something. For example, 'this company is engaged in the manufacture of steel tubes'.

Enlarge on/upon means to say or write more about something you have mentioned. For example, 'Would you care to enlarge on that point?'.

Enter into means: (1) to begin or become involved in a formal agreement. For example, 'the parties entered into an agreement relating to a share sale'; (2) to begin to discuss or deal with something. For example, 'the company agreed to enter into negotiations'.

Entitle to means to give a right to have or do something. For example, 'the parties are entitled to assign the benefit of the agreement on giving notice in writing'.

Factor in means to include a particular fact or situation when you are calculating something or thinking about or planning something. For example, 'you must factor in labour costs when calculating the cost of the repairs'.

File away means to put papers, documents, etc, away in a place where you can find them easily. For example, 'I filed the papers away in the drawer'.

Gear to means to make or change something so that it is suitable for a particular need or an appropriate level or standard. For example, 'it is vital that we gear our service to our clients' needs'.

Gear up means to be prepared, ready and able to do something or to become or make ready and able to do something. For example, 'the firm must gear itself up to be able to cope with these large corporate transactions'.

Hand down means: (1) to give or leave something to a younger person or to pass from one generation to another as an inheritance. For example, 'this house has been handed down from generation to generation'; (2) to announce an official decision (particularly of a court of law). For example, 'the judge handed down a sentence'.

Hand over means: (1) to give somebody else your position of power or authority or to give somebody else the responsibility for dealing with a particular situation. For example, 'he handed over the position to his deputy when he retired'; (2) to give someone else a turn to speak when you have finished talking. For example, 'I'd like to hand over now to our guest speaker'.

Limit to means to make something exist or happen only in a particular place, within a particular group or for a particular purpose. For example, 'limited to industrial use'.

Object to means to say that you disagree with, disapprove of or oppose something. For example, 'we object to further changes being made to the agreement'.

Opt for means to choose something or make a decision about something. For example, 'many clients now opt for this service'.

Opt in means to choose to take part in something. For example, 'all staff members have the chance to opt in to a pension plan offered by the company'.

Opt out means to choose not to take part in something. For example, 'very few staff members have opted out of the company pension plan'.

Pass off means: (1) to pretend that something or somebody is something that they are not. For example, 'the company tried to pass off their copied product as the real thing'; (2) if an event passes off in a particular way, it takes place and is finished in that way. For example, 'the meeting passed off without any trouble'.

Pass up means to decide not to take advantage of an opportunity, offer, etc. For example, 'the company passed up the opportunity to submit a tender for the project'.

Pencil in means to write someone's name for an appointment, or the details of an arrangement, although you know that this might have to be changed later. For example, 'I've pencilled in 5 June for the meeting'.

Point out means: (1) to show somebody which person or thing you are referring to. For example, 'I'll point out the court building when we arrive'; (2) to mention something in order to give somebody information about it or make them notice it. For example, 'I pointed out one or two typing errors in the document'.

Press for means to make repeated and urgent requests for something. For example, 'let's press for a final agreement today'.

Press on means to continue moving forward quickly or to continue to do a task in a determined way. For example, 'the company pressed on with its plans to expand into new markets'.

Proceed against means to start a court case against somebody. For example, 'my client is entitled to proceed against the manufacturer and the retailer'.

Proceed from means to be caused by or be the result of something. For example, 'the dispute proceeded from a misunderstanding between the parties'.

Provide against means to make plans in order to deal with or prevent a bad or unpleasant situation. For example, 'the insurance policy provides against loss of income'.

Provide for means: (1) to make plans or arrangements to deal with something that may happen in the future. For example, 'the contract provides for assignment under certain circumstances'; (2) to give somebody the things that they need to live. For example, 'the family has three children to provide for'.

Put across means to communicate your ideas, feeling, etc, to somebody clearly and successfully. For example, 'he put across his thoughts clearly and forcefully to the audience'.

Put back means: (1) to return something to its usual place. For example, 'he put the papers back in the file'; (2) to move something to a later time or date. For example, 'the meeting has been put back to 11 July'; (3) to cause something to be delayed. For example, 'the strike has put back our deliveries by a fortnight'.

Put down means: (1) to pay part of the cost of something. For example, 'I had to put down a deposit on the purchase of the property'; (2) to criticise somebody and make them feel stupid, especially in front of other people. For example, 'she's always putting other people down'; (3) to place something on the floor or on a surface. For example, 'put your paper down a minute and come and give me a hand with this'; (4) to write something down or make notes about something. For example, 'I've put down a few ideas which we can discuss during our meeting'; (5) to kill an animal because it is old or sick. For example, 'we had to have the horse put down because it was badly injured in an accident'.

Put forward means: (1) to suggest an idea or plan so that it can be discussed. For example, 'an idea put forward during the meeting'; (2) to suggest somebody as a candidate for a job or position. For example, 'three people put themselves forward as candidates'; (3) to move something to an earlier time or date. For example, 'the meeting's been put forward a few hours'.

Put in means: (1) to contribute money to something or pay money into a bank. For example, 'he put in £20,000 of his own money into the business'; (2) to contribute time or effort to something. For example, 'she put in a lot of hours on that case'; (3) to make an official request or claim. For example, 'I've put in a request for a pay rise'; (4) to include something in a letter or document. For example, 'you should put in a paragraph explaining the indemnity provisions to the client'.

Put off means to cancel or delay something. For example, 'we'll have to put off discussion of that issue until our next meeting'.

Reckon on means to rely on something happening. For example, 'we reckon on making a profit of £200,000'.

Reckon up means to add figures or numbers together. For example, 'the total comes to £200 if I've reckoned it up correctly'.

Refer to means: (1) to mention or talk about somebody or something. For example, 'he referred to the case throughout our meeting'; (2) to describe or be connected to something. For example, 'paragraph 7 refers to the question of indemnities'; (3) to look at something for information. For example, 'I'll refer to the textbook to see if paragraph 7 will be valid'; (4) to send somebody or something to a different place or person to get help, advice or a decision. For example, 'the case was referred to arbitration'.

Report to: if you report to someone in a company or organisation, that person is responsible for your work and tells you what to do. For example, 'I report directly to the senior partner of the firm'.

Resort to means to make use of something, especially something bad or unpleasant, as a way of achieving something, often because no other course of action is possible. For example, 'he resorted to threats in order to obtain their agreement'.

Rest on means: (1) to depend on something. For example, 'our chances of winning this contract rest solely on price'; (2) to be based on something. For example, 'her argument seemed to rest on an incorrect assumption'.

Rest with means to be someone's responsibility. For example, 'the final decision rests with the client'.

Result in means to have a particular effect. For example, 'the presentation of the new evidence resulted in us winning the case'.

Revert to means: (1) (of land or property) to return legally to the owner. For example, 'after his death the house reverted to the original owner'; (2) to go back to a previous condition or activity. For example, 'we reverted to our old methods'; (3) to start talking or thinking again about a subject being considered earlier. For example, 'to revert to the question of delivery of the goods'.

Rough out means to draw or write the main parts of something without including all the details. For example, 'I've roughed out the basis of the deal on the back of an envelope'.

Rule in: if somebody rules something in, they decide that it is possible or that it can or should happen or be included. For example, 'the judge ruled in the disputed evidence'.

Rule out: (1) if somebody rules somebody out, this means that they decide it is not possible for that person to do something or to have done something. For example, 'I think we can rule out Linden as a possible candidate'; (2) if somebody rules something out, this means that it is not possible or that it cannot or should not happen. For example, 'I think we can rule out trying to set up an office in Shanghai at this stage'.

Serve upon/on means to give or send somebody an official document, especially one that orders them to appear at court. For example, 'the court served a summons upon the company'.

Set down means: (1) to place an object down on a surface. For example, 'he set the tray down on the table'; (2) to write something down on paper in order to record it. For example, 'I have set down my thoughts on this question in the paper you have in front of you'; (3) to give something as a rule or guideline. For example, 'this firm must set down clear guidelines about what procedures to follow if a client makes a complaint'.

Set forth means to state something clearly or make something known. For example, 'the position is set forth in paragraph 7 of the contract'.

Set up means: (1) to make something ready for use. For example, 'we set up the conference room before the meeting'; (2) to provide someone with the money they need to start a business, buy a home, etc. For example, 'his uncle helped set him up in business'; (3) to create something or start a business. For example, 'setting up a business is not easy'; (4) to trick someone, especially by making them appear to be guilty of something they have not done. For example, 'the police set me up'; (5) to make someone feel healthier, stronger, more active, etc. For example, 'a cup of coffee in the morning helps set me up for the day'; (6) to arrange or organise something. For example, 'we set up a meeting for 10 am tomorrow'.

Settle up means to pay the money you owe. For example, 'we need to settle up with them for the hire of the machinery'.

Sift through means to carefully examine a large amount of something in order to find something important or decide what is useful and what is not. For example, 'we sifted through the evidence looking for weaknesses in their case'.

Skim through means to read something very quickly in order to get a general impression or find a particular point. For example, 'the lawyer skimmed quickly through the report'.

Speak for means to state the wishes or views of someone or to act as a representative for someone. For example, 'I speak for everyone when I say that this conference has been very useful and interesting'.

Speak out means to say what you think clearly and publicly, often criticising or opposing others in a way that needs courage. For example, 'she spoke out against the harsh treatment they had suffered'.

Strike off means to remove someone's name from the list of members of a profession so that they can no longer work in that profession. For example, 'the attorney was struck off after being convicted of a criminal offence'.

Strike out means: (1) the removal by a judge or the court of a case before that court. For example, 'the judge ordered that the case be struck out as an abuse of process'; (2) to remove something from a text by drawing a line through it. For example, 'You should strike out all unnecessary words in the text'; (3) to start being independent and do something new. For example, 'he left the firm and set up his own business'; (4) to aim a violent blow at somebody. For example, 'he struck out with his fist'.

Subject to means: (1) dependent on. For example, 'we agree subject to several conditions'; (2) to make somebody or something experience or be affected by something, usually something unpleasant. For example, 'the products are subjected to rigorous tests'.

Subscribe to means to agree with an opinion, theory, etc. For example, 'I don't subscribe to that point of view I'm afraid'.

Substitute for means to take the place of somebody or something else. For example, 'there is no substitute for good legal advice'.

Sue for means to formally ask for something in a court of law. For example, 'the company sued for damages'.

Sum up means to give the main points of something in a few words. For example, 'to sum up, there are three main points to remember'. The summing-up is the formal speech made by a judge to the jury near the end of a trial, giving the main points of the evidence and the arguments in the case.

Take over means: (1) to gain control of a company by buying its shares (hence *takeover*). For example, 'the company was taken over last year'; (2) to affect so strongly that one is unable to think about or do anything else. For example, 'my job is starting to take over my life'.

Tamper with means to do something to something without permission. For example, 'the agreement expressly prohibits any tampering with the machinery'.

Testify to means to show or be evidence that something is true. For example, 'this contract testifies to Johan's drafting skills'.

Trade down means: (1) to sell something large or expensive and buy something smaller and less expensive. For example, 'she sold her Rolls Royce and traded down to a Toyota Corolla'; (2) to spend less money on things than you used to. For example, 'people are trading down and buying cheaper products'.

Trade in means to give something that you have used to somebody you are buying something new from as part of your payment. For example, 'we traded in our car for a lorry'.

Trade off means to balance two things or situations which are opposed to each other. For example, 'we agreed to trade off sharing information against a price reduction'.

Turn down means: (1) to reject or refuse something. For example, 'we turned down their offer'; (2) to adjust the controls of something in order to reduce the amount of heat, noise, etc. For example, 'the heating should be turned down now that the weather is warmer'.

Weigh up means to think carefully about the different factors involved in an issue before making a decision. For example, 'we weighed up their arguments carefully before responding'.

Wind down means: (1) to bring a business or an activity gradually to an end over a period of time. For example, 'the company is winding down its research programme'; (2) to relax after a period of stress or excitement. For example, 'it took me an hour or two to wind down after a stressful day at work'; (3) if a machine winds down, it goes slowly for a while and then stops. For example, 'the clock has wound right down'; (4) to make the window of a car open and go downwards by turning a handle or pressing a button. For example, 'she wound down the window and asked a passer-by for directions'.

Wind up means: (1) to bring a company to an end and distribute its assets to its creditors. For example, 'the company was wound up last year'; (2) to bring something to an end (eg, a speech, a meeting or a discussion). For example, 'let's wind up the discussion now'; (3) to deliberately make someone angry or annoyed. For example, 'are you trying to wind me up?'; (4) to close a car window and make it go upwards by turning a handle or pressing a button. For example, 'wind up the window, Pete, it's getting cold in here'; (5) to make something mechanical work by turning a handle several times. For example, 'I tried to amuse the cat by winding up the toy mouse and letting it run across the floor'.

Work around means to find a way of doing something in spite of situations, rules, etc, that could prevent you doing it. For example, 'we can't get rid of this problem so we'll just have to work around it'.

Work out means: (1) to happen or develop in a particular way, especially a successful way. For example, 'the plan worked out well'; (2) to calculate. For example, 'I'll work the sums out later'; (3) to understand something. For example, 'I can't work out what their bottom line is in this negotiation'; (4) to organise, plan or resolve something in a satisfactory way. For example, 'they worked out their difficulties'; (5) to continue to work at your job until the end of the period of time mentioned. For example, 'they made him work out his notice' (ie, the period of time that is officially fixed before you can leave your job); (6) to train the body by physical exercise. For example, 'I work out three times per week'.

Wrap up means: (1) to complete something in a satisfactory way. For example, 'let's try to wrap things up by 5 pm'; (2) to be so involved in a person or activity that you do not notice what is happening around you. For example, 'he was so wrapped up in watching the match that he didn't notice me leave'; (3) to cover something in a layer of paper or other material, either to protect it or because you are going to give it as a gift. For example, 'we wrapped up the presents'; (4) to put on warm clothes. For example, 'wrap up warm – it's freezing outside'.

Write off means: (1) to cancel a debt and accept that it will never be paid. For example, 'we wrote off £10,000 in unpaid debts last year'; (2) to consider that somebody or something is a failure or not important. For example, 'I think we can write off any hope that this project will succeed'; (3) to damage a vehicle so severely that it is not worth spending money on to repair. For example, 'that's the second car she's written off this year'; (4) to write to a company or organisation, asking them to send you something. For example, 'I wrote off for their new catalogue'.

Yield up means: (1) to reveal something that has been hidden. For example, 'a thorough investigation of the state of the company yielded up a few interesting facts'; (2) to allow somebody to take something that you own and feel is very important for you. For example, 'he was forced to yield up some precious antiques to his creditors'.

Obscure Words Used in Business Contracts

Here are some relatively obscure words which are often found in business contracts based on British and American drafting standards.

Where the word in question is generally used to mean one thing in legal English and another in ordinary English (eg, *furnish, provision, construction*), only the legal usage meaning is given:

Abet. Encourage or help someone to do something wrong. For example, 'the perpetrators were aided and abetted by the company representative'.

Abstain. To refrain from doing something. For example, 'members have the right to abstain from voting'.

Accrue. Acquire, gain. For example, 'it is anticipated that benefits will accrue to the company as a result of the co-operation agreement'.

Acquiescence. Consent which is implied from conduct. For example, 'the other party signalled their acquiescence by refraining from taking steps to protest'.

Adjudicate. Make a formal judgment on an undecided matter. For example, 'the court adjudicated on the case'.

Ambiguity. Uncertain or inexact meaning. For example, 'this clause is ambiguous and should accordingly be redrafted'.

Annexes. Relevant documents attached to a contract or other legal document for ease of reference.

Annually. Every year.

Annul. To declare a contract to be no longer valid.

Arbitrator. An independent person who is appointed by agreement between parties to a contract or by a court to hear and decide a dispute. The process is known as *arbitration*.

Assent. To agree or concur. For example, 'the company is prepared to assent to that proposal'.

Assign. (1) A person or corporation to which something is transferred (eg, the benefit of a contract); (2) to make an assignment. For example, 'the company and its successors and assigns'.

Barred. Prevented or forbidden. For example, 'the proposed claim is statute-barred'.

Binding. Legally enforceable. For example, 'this clause binds both parties'.

Breach. The infringing or violation of a right, duty or law. For example, 'Statchem have breached paragraph 14 of the contract by their actions'.

Clause. A sentence or paragraph in a contract.

Consent. Agreement or compliance with a course of action or proposal. For example, 'no assignment shall be valid unless both parties have given their consent in writing prior to the proposed assignment being made'.

Consignment. A delivery of goods. For example, 'the first consignment must be delivered on 14 April'.

Construction. Interpretation. For example, 'on proper construction of this clause, it appears to mean that assignment is not permitted under the contract'.

Construed. Interpreted. For example, 'paragraph 16 shall be construed in the light of the provisions of paragraph 17'.

Convene. To call, summon or assemble. For example, 'the parties convened in the meeting room'.

Correspondence. Letters, memoranda, notes, messages. For example, 'there has been considerable correspondence between the parties'.

Corresponding. (1) Communicating by exchanging letters; (2) comparable or equivalent to another thing (eg, 'the corresponding obligations contained in this agreement').

Counterpart. (1) A document that exactly corresponds to the original. For example, 'a counterpart of this agreement shall be prepared'; (2) a person fulfilling a similar role in another organisation. For example, 'I will telephone my counterpart to ask about her client's position in relation to the case'.

Covenant. An agreement or a term in an agreement. For example, 'the covenants contained in the lease agreement'.

Deadlock. A situation in which no progress can be made. For example, 'the negotiations have reached deadlock'.

Default. Failure to fulfil an obligation. For example, 'the company has defaulted on its repayment schedule'.

Delegation. The grant of authority to a person to act on behalf of one or more others for agreed purposes. For example, 'the parties are entitled to delegate authority to subcontractors'.

Derogation means to deviate from something. For example, 'the company derogated from the agreement'.

Designated. (1) Officially give a particular name or status to (eg, 'John was designated "Managing Director"'); (2) appoint to a particular job (eg, 'John was designated Managing Director').

Determine. To decide or resolve. For example, 'this issue shall be determined by means of the procedures which the company has established for that purpose'.

Detriment. Harm or damage. For example, 'the company has acted to its detriment in agreeing to a variation of the original contract'.

Discharge. To release from an obligation. For example, 'the parties shall be discharged from all liability once all the terms of the contract have been performed in full'.

Disclose. Make known, reveal. For example, 'the company disclosed certain information to the distributor'.

Dispose. To sell or transfer (property). For example, 'the company had to dispose of some of its assets in order to pay its debts'.

Elect. Decide, opt. For example, 'the parties may elect to refer the matter to arbitration if the dispute cannot be resolved by other means'.

Enforce. To compel, impose or put into effect. Hence *enforceable* (capable of being enforced). For example, 'the terms of the contract can be enforced if necessary'.

Entice. Attract by offering something pleasant or beneficial. For example, 'the company tried to entice their rival's employees to come and work for them'.

Essence. Something intrinsic or essential. For example, 'the essence of this case is whether or not the defendant was present at the scene'. The *essence of a contract* means the essential conditions without which the contract would not have been agreed.

Exclusive. Restricted to certain parties. Hence *non-exclusive*: not restricted to certain parties. For example, 'Bondark Ltd holds exclusive distribution rights in respect of the product in the defined territory'.

Execution. (1) The carrying out or performance of something (eg, the terms of a contract); (2) the signature of a contract. For example, 'the parties executed the contract'.

Express. Clearly stated. For example, 'the contract contains express warranties'.

Facilitate. To make easy or make easier. For example, 'implementation of the contract was facilitated by the assistance given by expert advisers'.

Fit. Suitable for a particular role or position. For example, 'the judge took the view that Mr Jones was not fit to run a public company'.

Fixture. An item, usually a piece of equipment or furniture, which is fixed into position.

Forbearance. The act of refraining from enforcing a debt. For example, 'the suppliers' forbearance in extending credit to the company meant that the company was able to continue trading'.

Forthwith. Immediately, without delay. For example, 'the goods must be returned forthwith'.

Furnish. To provide or send something. For example, 'the distributor agrees to furnish sales information to the Company'.

Gratuitous. Given freely without anything being given in return. For example, 'he made a gratuitous promise to give her the property'.

Hold. To find as a matter of law. For example, 'the court held that Statchem had breached the contract and were accordingly liable to pay damages'.

Implement. To carry out, perform or put into effect. For example, 'the provisions of paragraph 12 of the contract have now been implemented'.

Imply. To introduce (a term) into a contract as a result of law or to give effect to the intentions of the parties. An implied term is one regarded by the courts as necessary to give effect to the intentions of the parties, or one introduced into the contract by statute.

Induce. Persuade or influence someone to do something. For example, 'the parties were induced to enter into the contract'.

Infringe. To violate or interfere with the rights of another person. For example, 'the company infringed upon another company's intellectual property rights'.

Instrument. A legal document, usually one which directs that certain actions be taken (eg, a contract).

Invalid. Not legally enforceable or legally binding. For example, 'this is an invalid clause'.

Irrevocable. Not able to be revoked, ie, not able to be changed, reversed or recovered. For example, 'the parties made an irrevocable commitment'.

Issue. (1) To print, publish or distribute. For example, 'the company issued shares'. (2) A person's descendants.

Know-how. Practical knowledge or skill.

Liability. An obligation or duty imposed by law, or an amount of money owed to another person. For example, 'the company has liability to pay damages to the employee'.

Lockout. A situation in which an employer refuses to allow employees to enter their place of work until they agree to certain conditions.

Material. Relevant, important, essential. For example, 'breach of a material term of the contract can give the innocent party the right to rescind the contract'.

Mutual. (1) Experienced or done by two or more people equally; (2) (of two or more people) having the same specified relationship to each other; (3) shared by two or more people; (4) joint. For example, 'no assignment may take place without the parties' mutual agreement in writing'.

Nevertheless. Despite. For example, 'nevertheless, the contract remains invalid'.

Notice. Information or warning addressed to a party that something is going to happen or has happened; a notification. See also *due notice* in the next Glossary. For example, 'any notice required to be served under this contract must be served in accordance with paragraph 18'.

Notwithstanding. Despite. For example, 'the parties went ahead with the deal notwithstanding Statchem's financial problems'.

Null. Invalid, having no legal force. For example, 'the contract is null [and void]'.

Omission. A failure to do something that one was supposed to do. For example, 'an omission may render the contract void'.

Onerous. Involving much effort and difficulty. For example, 'the duties laid upon the company are onerous'.

Pass. Transfer to or inherit. For example, 'the property passed to his successors'.

Prefer (charges). To put forward for consideration by a court of law. Usually used with reference to criminal charges. For example, 'charges were preferred'.

Provenance. The origin or early history of something. For example, 'the provenance of this document is uncertain'.

Provision. A term or clause of a contract. For example, 'the contract contains provisions dealing with termination'.

Provisional. Made for present purposes and may be changed later. For example, 'a provisional agreement'.

Purport. Falsely claims to be. For example, 'a purported assignment is one made without the prior written agreement of both parties'.

Reasonable. (1) Fair and sensible; (2) appropriate in a particular situation; (3) fairly good; (4) not too expensive.

Rebut. Oppose by contrary evidence, disprove or contradict something. For example, 'this presumption can be rebutted on the production of evidence to the contrary'.

Reciprocal. Given or done in return, or affecting two parties to a contract equally. For example, 'the contract contains reciprocal obligations regarding payment'.

Recognise. To accept as legally valid. For example, 'the court refused to recognise the judgment made in the foreign court'.

Redemption. Return or payment of property offered as security for a debt. Redemption date is the date upon which this occurs. For example, 'redemption of the mortgage will take place when the last instalment is paid upon it'.

Redress. Legal remedy or relief. For example, 'the innocent party has the right to seek redress'.

Remedy. Any method available in law to enforce, protect or recover rights, usually available by seeking a court order. For example, 'the primary remedy is to claim damages'.

Render. Deliver, provide, present for inspection. For example, 'the company agrees to render the goods for inspection'.

Revoke. To cancel, annul or withdraw. For example, 'we revoked the order we had placed'.

Severance. The removal of one part of the contract from the rest of the contract without affecting the validity of the rest of the contract. For example, 'the severance clause seeks to ensure that the contract will not be rendered wholly invalid if one part of it is deleted'.

Solicit. Ask for or try to obtain something (eg, business) from someone. For example, 'the employee is prohibited from seeking to solicit business from the company'.

Stipulate. Specify, require or demand. Hence *stipulation*. For example, 'the contract stipulates that all payments be made in US dollars'.

Stipulation. An essential term or condition of an agreement. For example, 'the contract contains a stipulation that all payments be made in US dollars'.

Successor. A person or corporation that inherits something (eg, the benefit of a contract) from another person or corporation. For example, 'Statchem is the successor of Alftech and accordingly now has the benefit of Alftech's contracts with third parties'.

Sundry. Of various kinds. For example, 'telephones, televisions and sundry other appliances'.

Supersede. Take the place of, override. For example, 'this contract supersedes all previous agreements between the parties'.

Term. (1) A substantive part of a contract which creates a contractual obligation. For example, 'one of the terms of the contract deals with delivery of the goods'; (2) the period during which a contract is in force. For example, 'the term of this contract shall be five years from the date of execution'.

Transaction. An act or series of acts carried out in the ordinary course of business negotiations. For example, 'the company engaged in a number of transactions'.

Unenforceable. Not capable of being legally enforced, not legally binding. For example, 'this contract is unenforceable'.

Uphold. To confirm (eg, the validity of a decision). For example, 'the appeal court upheld the decision of the lower court'.

Usage: (1) the action of using something or the fact of being used (eg, 'a survey of water usage'); (2) the way in which words are used in a language (eg, 'this word is no longer in common usage').

Vendor. Seller.

Venue. The place at which something occurs or is located. For example, 'the arbitration venue shall be the International Chamber of Commerce in Geneva'.

Void. Having no legal effect. For example, 'the contract is void due to lack of consideration'.

Voidable. Capable of being set aside. For example, 'the contract is voidable as a result of the other party's breach'.

Whereas. While. This word is often used in recitals in contracts. For example, 'whereas the Company is the owner of certain intellectual property rights ...'.

Obscure Phrases Used in Business Contracts

Here are some examples of standard phrases which are commonly encountered in business contracts based on British or American drafting standards:

Accord and satisfaction. The substitution and performance of a new set of obligations under a contract, by means of which the parties to the contract are released from their original obligations.

Act of God. An accident or event which arises independently of human intervention and which is entirely due to natural causes (eg, an earthquake).

Actions, costs, claims and demands. A catch-all definition including court cases, costs, formal demands for payment, etc.

Aggregate amount. An amount calculated by combining different items.

Aggrieved party. A term used to describe a party to the contract in a situation in which that party has the right to bring a claim in respect of breach of contract by the other party to the contract. See also *innocent party*.

An adverse effect. A harmful or prejudicial effect.

Annexed hereto. Attached to this document.

Arising out of. Resulting from.

As contemplated by this agreement. As intended by this agreement.

As hereinafter defined. As defined later in the contract. These words alert the reader to the likelihood that the contract contains a definitions section in which the words 'the Territory' will be given a defined meaning for the purposes of the contract.

As per ... In accordance with ...

At any time after the signature of this Agreement. Ever. The obligation is not time-limited.

Bear the costs of. Be responsible for paying the costs of.

By reason of. Because of.

Capacity to enter into and perform. Legal right to sign a contract so that it becomes legally enforceable and carry out the obligations it contains.

Circumstances beyond reasonable control. Circumstances which the party could not be expected to have any control over.

Collectively referred to herein. Referred to as a group of things in this contract.

Completion date. The date on which the main terms of the contract are carried out and ownership of goods is transferred from one party to another.

Construed in accordance with. Interpreted according to.

Defaulting party. A party to a contract who has defaulted on his or her obligations. See also *non-defaulting party*.

Defective part. A broken or faulty component.

Deliver up. Deliver, provide.

Discharge of contract/liability/obligation. The termination of a contract/liability or obligation usually by performance.

Disclosure letter. A document in which the sellers of a company set out all the facts already revealed to the buyer which breach the warranties contained in the contract. It is usual practice for the buyer then to agree that it cannot sue for breach of warranty caused by this disclosure.

Due and owing. Owed; of money that must be paid by one party to another.

Due notice. Proper notice; notice in accordance with the requirements of the contract and/or the law.

Duly authorised representative. Someone who has been given authority by one of the relevant parties to do certain things, which are usually things which will legally bind that party.

Duly organised and validly existing. (Of a company) organised according to the applicable company regulations, having proper legal status and not being bankrupt.

Duplicate contract. An exact copy of the original contract.

During the currency of this Agreement. During the period of this contract.

Engaged in the business of. Involved in the business of.

Enters into this agreement. Accepts, signs this contract.

Except as expressly provided in this Agreement. Unless there is a clear statement to the contrary in some part of the contract.

Execution date. The date on which a contract is signed.

Execution of documents. The signature of documents so that they become legally enforceable.

Exhibits attached/annexed hereto. Particular relevant documents attached to the contract as 'exhibits'.

Expiration of a time-period/limitation. When a time period/limitation has come to an end or run out.

Failure to perform. Failure to do something that was agreed to be done in the contract.

Finally settled by arbitration. Resolved by arbitration with no possibility of taking the dispute further in the event that one of the parties does not like the outcome.

From the date hereof. From the date this contract is signed.

Furnish with. Provide to (someone).

Give and execute all necessary consents. Provide all agreements that are required and sign and do all things necessary to ensure that they are legally enforceable.

Going concern. A viable, ongoing business which may, for example, be sold as such (therefore the sale price takes into account the value of the goodwill of the business) rather than as a sale of individual assets.

Hold harmless. Indemnify.

In any manner that the parties may determine. In any manner that the parties may decide.

In consideration of. As a contractually binding promise made in return for the promise made by the other party.

Incorporated herein. Contained in this contract or to be treated by the parties as contained in the contract.

Incur expenses/fees. To run up or make oneself liable to pay expenses or fees.

In lieu of. Instead of.

Innocent party. A party to a contract who has not defaulted on his or her contractual obligations in circumstances where the other party has defaulted.

In respect of/in respect thereof. Concerning.

In satisfaction of debts. In payment of debts.

Instrument in writing. A formal written legal document.

In witness whereof. 'To confirm my agreement to the terms of this contract.'

Legally binding. Legally enforceable.

Liable to the other. Responsible in law to the other.

Make good. Repair, replace or renew something.

Material breach. A serious breach of a major term of the contract.

Material term. A significant or important term of the contract.

Matters of a product liability nature. Matters relating to manufacturing defects in the products.

Mutual consent. Both parties agree (to a certain proposition).

Mutual covenants and agreements. Things both parties have agreed in the contract.

Negotiation, drafting and execution. All the stages of drawing up the agreement including negotiating it writing it and signing it so that it becomes legally enforceable.

Non-defaulting party. A party to a contract who has not defaulted on his or her contractual obligations. Also known as the innocent party in circumstances where the other party has defaulted on his or her contractual obligations.

Notice of Default. A formal document advising a party to a contract that he or she has failed to do something required to be done under the contract.

Notice shall be deemed served. Notice shall be treated or regarded for the purposes of this contract as having been served.

Notified from time to time hereunder. Advised to the other party when necessary under the terms of this contract.

Of even date herewith/hereof. Made on the same date as this agreement.

On a without prejudice basis. Refers to an offer made in legal proceedings which is not to be referred to in the final hearing of the claim.

On behalf of. As a representative of.

Other documents and papers whatsoever. Any other documents and papers.

Payment falling due on. Payment becoming due to be made on a specified date.

Principal office. Main office or headquarters.

Prior written consent. Written agreement obtained beforehand.

Provided always that. So long as, if.

Public domain. Accessible to the public, forming part of public knowledge.

Purchased hereunder. Purchased in accordance with this contract.

Purported assignment. An invalid assignment claimed falsely to be a valid one.

Pursuant to. In accordance with.

Reasonable/best endeavours. Appropriate efforts or attempts.

Release all the claims. Abandon all the claims.

Renewed for further successive periods of two years. The contract will continue indefinitely in two-year periods following the end of the first two-year period.

Save as to. Except for.

Schedule 1 hereto. Schedule 1 of this contract.

Sell or otherwise dispose of. To sell or transfer (property) in some other way.

Set aside. Treat as no longer valid.

Set forth herein. Contained in this contract or document.

Settled amicably. (Of a claim or dispute) resolved without the need for court proceedings.

Shall be held by the parties. Shall be regarded by the parties as being such and such.

Shall procure that. Shall ensure that a specified action is done.

So served. Served in such a way.

Subject to the following terms. Dependent on or on the basis of the following terms.

Succeeding period. A period of time following one previously defined.

Take effect. Become legally enforceable.

Take or institute proceedings. To make a claim to a civil court.

That law or statute as from time to time amended. The law or statute and any amendments that are made to it while the contract is still valid.

The Company desires to appoint. The Company wishes to appoint.

The Company hereby acknowledges. The Company accepts as a result of this clause.

The parties acknowledge that. The parties accept (that something is the case).

The parties hereto. The parties to this contract.

The premises. (1) The building and land occupied by a business; (2) the theoretical bases of an argument.

The prevailing party. The party which wins in a court case or arbitration.

The provisions for termination hereinafter appearing. The clauses governing termination of the contract appearing later in this contract.

The Seller and Buyer affirm. The parties declare.

The requisite skills. The skills necessary for performing a particular role or task.

The same/the said/the aforesaid. The thing previously referred to.

The Territory. The specified geographical area within which a party is authorised to act on behalf of the other party to the contract.

The time of dispatch. The time of sending.

Undertakes to supply. Agrees to supply.

Which consent may not be withheld arbitrarily. Agreement must be given unless there is good reason not to.

Without prejudice to the generality of the foregoing. Having no effect on the general meaning of the previous clauses in the contract.

Written mutual consent. The written agreement of both parties to the contract.

Foreign Terms Used in Law

A large number of foreign words and phrases are used in legal and academic texts. These are frequently derived from Latin or French. A number of terms which are frequently encountered in legal texts are set out below. Examples of usage are given in respect of the terms which remain in daily use in legal English. The list is not exhaustive:

A fortiori (Latin): more conclusively.

A priori (Latin): based on deduction rather than experience.

Ab initio (Latin): from the beginning. For example, 'this agreement is void *ab initio*'.

Ad hoc (Latin): made or done for a particular purpose. For example, 'an *ad hoc* tribunal was set up to deal with the claims'.

Ad hominem (Latin): to an individual's interests or passions; used of an argument that takes advantage of the character of the person on the other side.

Ad infinitum (Latin): endlessly; forever. For example, 'this case seems to have dragged on *ad infinitum*'.

Ad referendum (Latin): to be further considered. This often refers to a contract that has been signed although minor points remain to be decided.

Ad valorem (Latin): according to value (as opposed to volume).

Annus et dies (Latin): a year and a day.

Bona fide (Latin): genuine, real. For example, 'a *bona fide* purchaser is interested in buying the company'.

Bona vacantia (Latin): property not distributed by a deceased's will and to which no relative is entitled on intestacy.

Caveat emptor (Latin): the buyer is responsible for checking the quality of goods before purchasing them (literally, 'let the buyer beware').

Circa (Latin): around or about: used for dates and large quantities; can be abbreviated to *c* or *c.*

Cognoscenti (Italian): people who are well-informed about something. For example, 'the *cognoscenti* agree that this decision is unprecedented'.

De facto (Latin): in fact, whether by right or not. For example, 'she has acquired *de facto* control of the company'.

De jure (Latin): rightful, by right (eg, a *de jure* claim to the territory).

Deus ex machina (Latin): an unexpected event that saves an apparently hopeless situation.

Éminence grise (French): a person who has power or influence without holding an official position.

Et al (Latin): and others. This is used as an abbreviation in bibliographies when citing multiple editorship or authorship to save the writer the trouble of writing out all the names. Thus, 'John Smith *et al*, *Textbook on Damages*'.

Ex aequo et bono (Latin): as a result of fair dealing and good conscience.

Ex gratia (Latin): a payment given as a favour rather than because of any legal obligation. For example, 'the executor made an *ex gratia* payment to one of the beneficiaries of the estate'.

Ex officio (Latin): by virtue of one's status or position.

Ex parte (Latin): on the part of one side only. For example, 'the lawyer made an *ex parte* application to the court to obtain an emergency injunction'.

Ex post facto (Latin): by a subsequent act. It describes any legal act, such as a statute, that has retrospective effect.

Flagrante delicto (Latin): in the commission of an offence. For example, 'the accused was caught in *flagrante delicto*. He can have no possible defence'.

Force majeure (French): irresistible compulsion or coercion. Often used in commercial contracts to describe events which may affect the contract but are completely outside the parties' control. For example, 'the contract contains the usual provision regarding situations considered by the parties to constitute *force majeure*'.

In absentia (Latin): while not present. For example, 'as the defendant was abroad at the date of the hearing, the case continued *in absentia*'.

In camera (Latin): in private. For example, 'due to the sensitivity of the case, the proceedings took place *in camera*'.

In extremis (Latin): in an extremely difficult situation; at the point of death. For example, 'the will was clearly made out *in extremis*'.

In loco parentis (Latin): in the place of a parent. For example, 'since the child's parents are deceased, his uncle is acting *in loco parentis*'.

In re (Latin): in the matter of.

In situ (Latin): in the original or appropriate position. For example, 'the wreckage was examined *in situ*'.

Inter alia (Latin): amongst other things. For example, 'the contract provides, *inter alia*, that the company will be sold for the sum of ...'.

Ipso facto (Latin): by that very fact or act.

Jus (Latin): a law or right.

Locus standi (Latin): the legal right to bring an action or challenge some decision. For example, 'the court rejected her application. It ruled that she had no *locus standi* to make an application in these proceedings'.

Mea culpa (Latin): my fault.

Modus operandi (Latin): a way of doing something. For example, 'his *modus operandi* was fascinating to watch'.

Mutatis mutandis (Latin): 'that having been changed which had to be changed' or 'with the necessary changes'. The phrase is used in contracts to indicate that a stipulation contained in one clause should also be applied in another part of the contract once the necessary changes have been made.

Obiter dictum (Latin): a remark made in passing. Something said by a judge while giving judgment that was not essential to the decision in the case but which may be of persuasive authority in future cases. For example, 'the judge said *obiter* that there did appear to be some authority for the argument the defendant had made'.

Pace (Latin): despite.

Pari passu (Latin): in equal step. This term is often seen in venture capital term sheets, and indicates that one series of equity will have the same rights and privileges as another.

Per annum (Latin): for each year. For example, 'the director earned £250,000 *per annum* before tax'.

Per capita (Latin): for each person.

Per se (Latin): by or in itself. For example, 'the government is not opposed to further European integration *per se*, but it does have certain concerns about the manner in which it is done'.

Persona non grata (Latin): a person who is not welcome somewhere.

Per stirpes (Latin): among families. Used by lawyers in connection with the distribution of inheritance.

Post eventum (Latin): after the event.

Post mortem (Latin): after death. Generally used as a noun to describe the clinical investigation of a dead body.

Prima facie (Latin): on the face of things; accepted as so until proved otherwise. For example, '*prima facie* you appear to have a reasonable case, although I will need further information before giving an informed opinion on its merits'.

Pro rata (Latin): proportional; proportionally.

Procès-verbal (French): an informal record or memorandum of international understandings resulting from negotiation.

Quid pro quo (Latin): a favour or advantage given in return for something.

Ratio decidendi (Latin): the reason for deciding; the principles of law on which the court reaches its decision.

Re (Latin): with regard to, in the matter of.

Res ipsa loquitur (Latin): the thing speaks for itself. A principle often applied in the tort of negligence which states that if an accident happens which is of a kind that usually only happens as a result of negligence, and the circumstances that gave rise to the accident were under the control of the defendant, it may be assumed, unless there is evidence to the contrary, that the accident was caused by the defendant's negligence.

Restitutio in integrum (Latin): restoration to the original position which existed before the events which triggered legal proceedings (re damages).

Sic (Latin): thus; used in brackets in quotes to show that the writer has made a mistake. For example, 'Jacques Chirats (*sic*) opposed the plan'.

Sine die (Latin): (of proceedings) adjourned indefinitely.

Sine qua non (Latin): without which, not. Used to refer to anything indispensable, and without which another cannot exist.

Stet (Latin): let it stand or do not delete; cancels an alteration in proofreading; dots are placed under what is to remain.

Sub judice (Latin): being considered by a court of law and therefore not to be publicly discussed elsewhere.

Sub rosa (Latin): literally 'under the rose': used to describe something that is occurring but not on an official basis.

Sui generis (Latin): unique, of its own kind.

Travaux préparatoires (French): preparatory works that provide a background to the enactment of legislation.

Ultra vires (Latin): beyond the powers. This describes an act by a public authority, company or other body which goes beyond the limits of the powers that it has.

Vis-à-vis (French): in relation to; as compared with.

Legal Terminology

The following is a non-exhaustive list of specific legal terminology and terms of art often found in commercial as well as certain other branches of law:

Abandonment. The act of giving up the ownership of something covered by an insurance policy and treating it as if it has been completely lost or destroyed.

Abatement. The proportionate reduction in the payment of debts that takes place if a person's assets are insufficient to settle with his or her creditors in full.

Absolute title. Ownership of a legal estate in registered land with a guarantee by the state that no one has a better right to that estate.

Acceptance. Consent, assent or approval. The acceptance of an offer to create a contract must be unqualified and may be either by word of mouth or by conduct.

Account of profits. A remedy that a litigant can claim as an alternative to damages in certain circumstances, eg, in an action for breach of copyright.

Accumulation. The continual addition of the income of a fund so that the fund grows indefinitely.

Agency. The relationship of principal and agent where the principal is bound by contracts entered into by the agent with third parties.

Agent. A person who is employed to act on behalf of another person who is known as the principal. The work of an agent is to conclude contracts with third parties on behalf of the principal.

Allotment. A method of acquiring previously unissued shares in a limited company in exchange for a capital contribution.

Appurtenant. Attached or annexed to land and enhancing the land or its use.

Articles of association. Regulations for the management of registered companies. They form, together with the provisions of the memorandum of association, the company's constitution.

Asset. Property; anything which can be turned into cash.

Assignment. The transfer of a legal right by one legal person to another.

Audit. A detailed inspection of a company's accounts by outside accountants usually in connection with the preparation of the annual accounts of the company at the end of the year.

Authorised capital (nominal capital). The total value of the shares that a registered company is authorised to issue in order to raise capital.

Bailment. The transfer of the possession of goods by the owner (the *bailor*) to another (the *bailee*) for a particular purpose, eg, the hiring or loan of goods.

Balance sheet. A document presenting in summary form a true and fair view of a company's financial position at a particular time.

Bearer. A person in possession of a bill of exchange or promissory note that is payable to the bearer.

Bill of exchange. An unconditional order in writing, addressed by one person (the *drawer*) to another (the *drawee*) and signed by the person giving it, requiring the drawee to pay on demand a specified sum of money to a specified person (the *payee*) or to the bearer.

Bill of lading. A document acknowledging the shipment of a consignor's goods for carriage by sea.

Bond. (1) A document issued by a government, local authority or other public body undertaking to repay long-term debt with interest; (2) a deed by which one person (the *obligor*) commits himself or herself to do something or refrain from doing something.

Bonus issue (capitalisation issue). A method of increasing a company's issued capital by issuing further shares to existing company members.

Burden of proof. The duty of a party to litigation to prove a fact in issue. Generally, the burden of proof falls on the party who relies on the truth of a particular fact to support their argument.

Capacity. The legal competence to enter into and be bound by the terms of a contract.

Capital (share capital). A fund which represents the nominal value of shares issued by a company.

Capital allowance. A tax allowance for businesses on capital expenditure on particular items (eg, plants and equipment).

Cargo. Goods other than the personal luggage of passengers carried by a ship or aircraft.

Cartel. A national or international association of independent enterprises formed to create a monopoly in a given industry.

Charge. (1) An interest in land securing the payment of money (see also *mortgage*); (2) an interest in company property created in favour of a creditor to secure the amount owing.

Charterparty. A written contract in which a person (the *charterer*) hires from a shipowner, in return for the payment of freight, the use of a ship or part of it for the transportation of goods by sea.

Chattel. Any property other than real estate.

Class rights. Any rights attached to a class of shares, eg, preference shares. Such rights relate to dividend, return of capital and voting rights.

Clearance. (1) A certificate acknowledging a ship's compliance with customs requirements; (2) an indication from a taxing authority that a certain proviso does not apply to a particular transaction.

Collateral. Security that is additional to the main security for a debt. For example, a lender may require as collateral the assignment of an insurance policy in addition to the principal security of a mortgage on the borrower's home.

Collateral contract. A subsidiary contract that induces a person to enter into a main contract.

Collusion. An improper agreement or bargain between parties that one of them should bring proceedings against the other.

Commission. A sum payable to an agent in return for the performance of a particular service.

Compulsory purchase. The enforced purchase of land for public purposes by a statutory authority.

Condition. A major term of a contract, which is regarded as being of the essence of the contract. Breach of a condition is a fundamental breach of contract which entitles the injured party to treat the contract as discharged. Contrast with *warranty*.

Consideration. An act, forbearance or promise by one party to a contract that constitutes the price for which the promise of the other party is bought. Consideration is essential to the validity of any contract other than one made by deed.

Contraband. Goods the import or export of which is forbidden.

Creditor. One to whom a debt is owed.

Debenture. A document that states the terms of a loan, usually to a company, including the date of repayment and the rate of interest.

Debtor. One who owes a debt.

Deed. A written document that must make it clear on its face that it is intended to be a deed and must be validly executed as a deed. It takes effect on delivery. Deeds are often used to transfer land and are enforceable even in the absence of *consideration*.

Deemed. Treated in law as being something. Many documents rely on this concept, eg, by stating that a certain thing is to be deemed to fall within a certain expression or description used in them.

Delegation. The grant of authority to a person to act on behalf of one or more others for agreed purposes.

Delivery. The transfer of possession of property from one legal person to another.

Deposit. (1) A sum paid by one party to a contract to the other party as a guarantee that the first party will carry out the terms of the contract; (2) the placing of title deeds with a mortgagee of land as security for the debt.

Dilapidation. A state of disrepair. The term is usually used in relation to repairs required at the end of a lease or tenancy.

Disposition. The transfer of property by its owner.

Distress. The seizure of goods as security for the performance of an obligation. This occurs (1) between a landlord and tenant when the rent is in arrears or (2) when goods are unlawfully on an occupier's land and are causing or have caused damage. In the second case the occupier may hold onto the goods until compensation is paid for the damage.

Dividend. The payment made by a company to its shareholders out of its distributable profits.

Domicile. The country that a person treats as his or her permanent home and to which that person has the closest legal attachment.

Duress. Pressure, particularly actual or threatened violence put on a person in order to make them act in a particular way. Acts carried out under duress usually have no legal validity.

Emoluments. A person's earnings, including salaries, fees, wages, profits and benefits in kind (eg, company cars).

Encumbrance. A right or interest in property owned by someone other than the owner of the land itself (eg, leases and mortgages).

Expropriation. The taking by the state of private property for public purposes, normally without compensation.

Factor. An agent entrusted with the possession of goods (or documents of title representing goods) for the purposes of sale.

Fiduciary. A person who holds a position of trust or confidence. For example, a fiduciary relationship exists between company directors and their shareholders.

Flotation. A process by which a public company can, by issuing securities (shares or debentures), raise capital from the public, eg, by way of a *prospectus issue* in which the company itself issues a prospectus inviting the public to acquire securities.

Frustration. The termination of a contract caused by an unforeseen event which makes performance of the contract impossible or illegal. It is also referred to as *force majeure*. Frustration brings the contract to an end and automatically discharges the parties from any further obligations in relation to it.

Gaming contract. A contract involving the playing of a game of chance by any number of people for money or money's worth. Gaming contracts are generally void and no action can be brought to enforce them.

Garnishee. A person who has been warned by a court to pay a debt to a third party rather than to his or her creditor.

Goodwill. The advantage arising from the reputation and trade connections of a business.

Guarantee. A secondary agreement in which a person (the *guarantor*) is liable for the debt or default of another (the principal debtor).

Incapacity. Lack of legal competence.

Indemnity. An agreement by one person (X) to pay to another person (Y) sums that are owed, or may become owed, by a third person (Z).

Injunction. An order of the court directing a person to do or refrain from doing a particular thing.

Intention. The state of mind of one who aims to bring about a particular consequence.

Invitation to treat. An invitation to others to make offers, for example, by displaying goods in a shop window. An invitation to treat should be differentiated from an offer.

Jurisdiction. The power of a court to hear and decide on a case before it.

Legal person. A natural person or a juristic person. A juristic person is an entity such as a corporation that is recognised as having legal personality, ie, it is capable of having legal rights and duties. Since a corporation is a legal person, it has the right to sue and be sued in a court of law.

Letter of credit. A document whereby a bank, at the request of a customer, undertakes to pay money to a third party (the beneficiary) on presentation of documents specified in the letter.

Lien. The right of one person to retain possession of goods owned by another until the possessor's claims against the owner have been satisfied.

Maturity. The time at which a bill of exchange becomes due for payment.

Minutes. Records of company business transacted at general meetings, board meetings and meetings of managers.

Misrepresentation. An untrue statement of fact made by one party to the other in the course of negotiating a contract that induces the other party to enter into the contract.

Mistake. A misunderstanding or incorrect belief about a matter of fact or matter of law. Mistakes of fact may render a contract void or voidable.

Mortgage. An interest in property created as a form of security for a loan or payment of a debt and terminated on payment of the loan or debt.

Negligence. Carelessness amounting to the culpable breach of a duty: failure to do something that a reasonable person would do, or doing something that a reasonable person would not do.

Offer. An indication of willingness to do or refrain from doing something that is capable of being converted by acceptance into a legally binding contract.

Ordinary shares. These shares make up the risk capital as they carry no prior rights in relation to dividends or return of nominal capital.

Parol evidence rule. The rule that oral evidence cannot be given to contradict, alter or vary a written document unless there are allegations of fraud or mistake.

Piracy. (1) Any illegal act of violence, imprisonment or robbery committed on a private ship for personal gain or revenge, against another ship, people or property on the high seas; (2) (in marine insurance) one of the risks covered by a marine insurance policy, which extends beyond the criminal offence to include a revolt by the crew or passengers and plundering generally; (3) infringement of copyright.

Pre-emption. The right of first refusal to purchase land in the event that the grantor of the right should decide to sell.

Preference. (1) Where an insolvent debtor favours one particular creditor (for example, by paying one creditor in full when there is no possibility of paying the others); (2) a floating charge created for the benefit of an existing creditor within one year before the commencement of winding-up.

Preference share. These shares carry a right to a fixed percentage dividend (eg, 10% of the nominal value) before ordinary shareholders receive anything. Preference shareholders also have the right to the return of the nominal value of their shares before ordinary shareholders (but after creditors).

Premium. (1) The sum payable, usually annually, by an insured person to the insurer under a contract of insurance; (2) a lump sum that is sometimes paid by a tenant at the time of the grant, assignment or renewal of the lease or tenancy.

Principal. The person on whose behalf an agent acts.

Privity of contract. The relationship that exists between the parties to a contract. In common law, only the parties to a contract can sue or be sued on the contract: the contract cannot confer rights nor impose liabilities on others.

Promoter. A person engaged in the formation or flotation of a company.

Proprietor. One who owns land.

Prospectus. A document inviting the public to invest in shares or debentures issued by a public company.

Proviso. A clause in a statute, deed or other legal document introducing a qualification or condition to some other provision, frequently the one immediately before the proviso.

Proxy. A person (not necessarily a company member) appointed by a company member to attend and vote in his or her place at a company meeting.

Quorum. From Latin, meaning 'of whom', used to indicate the minimum number of persons required to be present to constitute a formal meeting.

Quotation. A listing of a share price on the Stock Exchange.

Rebuttable presumption. A presumption that can be reversed if evidence to the contrary is produced.

Receiver. (1) A person appointed by the court to preserve and protect property that is at risk; (2) a person appointed under the terms of a debenture or by the court to liquidate charged assets and distribute the proceeds to those entitled.

Recklessness. The fact of being aware of the risk of a particular consequence resulting from your actions, but deciding to continue with those actions and take the risk.

Redeemable share. A share issued subject to the condition that it may be bought back by the company.

Reinsurance. Where an insurer which has underwritten liability in an earlier contract insures itself with another insurer against liability for that risk.

Repudiation. An anticipatory breach of contract; ie, where a contracting party's words or actions make it clear that they do not intend to perform the contract in the future.

Rescission. The setting aside of a voidable contract, which is then treated as if it had never existed.

Resolution. A decision reached by a majority of the members at a company meeting.

Restitution. The return of property to the owner or person entitled to possession.

Restraint of trade. A contractual term that limits a person's right to exercise his or her trade or carry on his or her business.

Restrictive covenant. A clause in a contract that restricts a person's right to carry on his or her trade or profession. For example, a contract covering the sale of a business might include a clause seeking to restrict the seller's freedom to set up in competition against the buyer.

Retention of title. A stipulation on a contract of sale that ownership of the goods shall not pass to the buyer until the buyer has paid the seller in full or has discharged all liabilities owing to the seller.

Return. A formal document, such as an annual return or the document giving particulars of shares allotted and to whom.

Rights issue. A method of raising share capital for a company from existing members rather than from the general public. Members are given a right to acquire further shares, usually in proportion to their existing holdings and at a price below the market value of existing shares.

Royalty. A sum payable for the right to use someone else's property for the purpose of gain.

Salvage. The service rendered by a person who saves or helps to save maritime property.

Secured creditor. A person who holds some security, such as a mortgage, for money he or she has lent.

Securities. These include stocks, shares, debentures, bonds or any other rights to receive dividends or interest.

Share premium. The amount the price at which a share was issued exceeds its nominal value.

Share transfer. A document transferring registered shares, ie, shares for which a share certificate has been issued.

Special resolution. A decision reached by a majority of not less than 75% of company members voting in person or by proxy at a general meeting.

Specific performance. A court order to a person to fulfil their obligations under a contract. The remedy is only available in certain cases, generally those in which the payment of damages would not be a sufficient remedy.

Stakeholder. One who holds money as an impartial observer. He or she will part with it only if both parties agree or if ordered by the court.

Statutory instrument. Subordinate legislation made under the authority of a statute.

Subsidiary. A subsidiary company is one which is controlled by a holding company.

Surety. A guarantor.

Tender. An offer to supply goods or services. Normally a tender must be accepted to create a contract.

Title. A person's right of ownership of property.

Undue influence. A doctrine which states that if a person enters into an agreement in circumstances which suggest that he or she has not been allowed to exercise free and deliberate judgement on the matter, the court will set aside the agreement.

Waiver. The act of abandoning or refraining from asserting a legal right, eg, by agreeing to a variation of the original terms of a contract.

Warranty. (1) (In contract law) a term or promise in a contract, breach of which will entitle the innocent party to damages but not to treat the contract as discharged by breach; (2) (in insurance law) a promise by the insured, breach of which will entitle the insurer to treat the contract as discharged by breach.

Winding-up. A procedure by which a company can be dissolved. It may be instigated by members or creditors of the company (voluntary winding-up) or by order of the court (compulsory winding-up).

Written resolution. A resolution signed by all company members and treated as effective even though it is not passed at a properly convened company meeting.